PRAISE FOR
DEADLY ILLUSIONS

**A bizarre true story of Hollywood murder,
cover-up, and lies**

"A MASTERFUL JOB of reconstructing the death of
Paul Bern . . . an excellent portrait."
—Wichita Falls *Times Record*

"RECREATES AN ERA in which movie studios could
cover up a crime by interfering with police investigations." —New York *Daily News*

"A SKILLFULLY PACKAGED INVESTIGATIVE
TALE . . . that lays bare the truth about the 60-year-
old murder of one of MGM's top producers."
—*Rocky Mountain News*

"The book offers glimpses of the personalities and politics that thrived in the glory days of the Depression-era
movie industry." —*Topeka Capital-Journal*

"Marx and Vanderveen unmask many of the mysteries
that have lingered about this case [and] give the city and
the murder the drama it deserves."
—*Boston Sunday Herald*

DEADLY ILLUSIONS

·····

Jean Harlow and the Murder of Paul Bern

---

by
SAMUEL MARX
and
JOYCE VANDERVEEN

A Dell Book

Published by
Dell Publishing
a division of
Bantam Doubleday Dell Publishing Group, Inc.
666 Fifth Avenue
New York, New York 10103

Grateful acknowledgment is made to Macmillan
Publishing Company for permission to reprint an excerpt
from *Off with Their Heads* by Frances Marion.
Copyright © 1972 by Frances Marion.
Reprinted by permission of Macmillan Publishing Company.

ISBN: 0-440-21127-1

Reprinted by arrangement with Random House, Inc.,
New York, New York

Printed in the United States of America

Published simultaneously in Canada

October 1991

10 9 8 7 6 5 4 3 2 1

RAD

"The entire must have a beginning, middle and end."

ARISTOTLE

"A story must have a beginning, middle and end but not necessarily in that order!"

JEAN-LUC GODARD

Foreword

We are especially grateful to our editor, Robert D. Loomis of Random House. He provided us with invaluable guidance in writing the events that were hidden from public view for many decades.

We also wish to acknowledge the help we received from Sandy and Dennis Arcieri of Evergreen Park, Illinois. They supplied important information about the young Jean Harlow.

Our thanks are due to William "Bill" Pettite of Sacramento, who generously shared with us his knowledge of the events surrounding the last days of Dorothy Millette. Thanks also to Meg McSweeney of the American Academy of Dramatic Arts, who found the records of Paul Bern and Dorothy Millette from when they studied for a career in the theater, and to William German, editor of the *San Francisco Chronicle*, who provided us with the writings of Zilfa Estcourt.

Rachelle Blaine went to extraordinary lengths in locating memorabilia and documents pertinent to this story.

In exploring the mystery surrounding Paul Bern's death, many men and women provided us with crucial information: Irene Mayer Selznick, Gilbert Roland, Sydney Guilaroff, Charles Bennett, Dick Sheppard, Dr. Ron Hale, Terry Allen, Adela Rogers St. Johns, author and filmmaker Kevin Brownlow, Fred Nolan, Chuck McCann, Will Pettite, Joe Russell, Auriole Douglas, Marvin Paige, Sally Forrest, Milo Frank, Mrs. Donald Cox, Peggy Klein, Gene Barnes, Ken Dumain, historian and filmmaker James Forsher, Lina Basquette, Marge Champion, Roddy McDowall, Emily Torchia, Milton Holmes, Robert R. Young, Dean Dorn, Terence O'Hara, Shanna Reed, Julian Blodgett, J. J. Cohn, Charles Sachs, Ilse Lahn, Charles Higham, Irv Kupcinet, Kevin Thomas, Mike Kalisky of San Antonio, Texas, Sacramento librarian Tom Tolley, Professor Robert M. Davis of the University of Oklahoma, and Pamela Pfau.

Bob Cushman and Sam Gill provided significant details from the library of the Academy of Motion Picture Arts and Sciences.

We are grateful to Los Angeles County Supervisor Ed Edelman and especially Assistant Deputy June Bachman, who helped us find our way through the maze of county offices.

Special investigator Bob Dambacher, Dorothy Coulter, and the late Bill Gold of the Los Angeles County Coroner's office were especially helpful in providing us with documents from the archives.

We want to acknowledge the help we received from the men and women of the Los Angeles Police Department, the Los Angeles County District Attorney's office, and the offices of Los Angeles City Councilman Joel Wachs, State Assemblyman Tom Bane, and State Senator Alan Robbins.

Also, Jane Thompson, Sacramento deputy public administrator, who found the long lost coroner's inquest into the death of Dorothy Millette.

Contents

Foreword   ix

1 • A Death in the Morning   1
2 • A Man of Breeding   8
3 • The Making of a Star   21
4 • The Creative Team   40
5 • The Phantom Wife   58
6 • A Time of Change   75
7 • Flare-ups   82
8 • Enigma   91
9 • Quest   101
10 • The House on Easton Drive   117
11 • The Fringe   129
12 • A Certain Inquisition   147
13 • The Fixer   171
14 • Cover-ups   181
15 • Masquerade   191
16 • The Morality Clause   209

17 • Suspicions   221
18 • Valley of Retakes   229
19 • Dangerous Games   243
20 • The Butterfly Girl   252
21 • Flight   266
22 • Reunion   275
23 • "Make It Pretty!"   285

Epilogue   294
Postscript   301
Bibliography   305
Index   307

DEADLY
ILLUSIONS

1

·····

A Death in
the Morning

IT WAS MORNING on the sleepy Monday that would end 1932's Labor Day holiday. My wife and I intended to spend lazy hours in our Hollywood apartment, a plan rudely interrupted when I was awakened by a phone call that would haunt me all my life.

The caller was Alfred A. Cohn, a scenario writer with a long list of crime-movie credits. Al had lived in Hollywood longer than anyone I knew and it was a habit with him to keep me informed of interesting goings-on about town.

"Just thought you'd like to know," he said casually. "Your friend Paul Bern has been found dead up at his house. Don't tell anybody where you heard it."

Then he hung up.

•••

While hurrying into my clothes all I told my wife was that I had to go out. "I'll tell you why when I get back."

Marie was as fond of Paul as I was, but until I learned more I didn't want to disturb her. She surely saw how upset I was, but didn't hold me back with questions.

I drove fast through the residential sections of Hollywood and Beverly Hills and into the rustic fringes of Benedict Canyon Drive. I was heading for the house where Paul Bern lived with his bride, the dazzling platinum "blond bombshell" of the movies, Jean Harlow. The dashboard clock on the car showed the time was a little after nine.

• • •

Easton Drive was a poorly defined dirt road that went off to the right of Benedict Canyon in a steep rise. I parked at the foot of it and trudged up the incline to the gate at 9820.

The house that Paul Bern built for himself less than two years earlier was small, almost minuscule by Beverly Hills standards. But even small houses in Beverly Hills had swimming pools and Bern's pool, also small, was set into the lawn in front of the house. The neighborhood was silent with the kind of hush one expects in the presence of death, until a male voice grew audible as I walked toward it.

". . . I found a broken champagne glass here by the pool . . ."

Bern's gardener Clifton Davis, a black man, was describing in a shaky voice what happened earlier that morning when he was about to start his regular landscaping job.

My boss, Irving Thalberg, was listening intently to him, seated on a low stone bench by the pool. He stared at me in surprise as I sat down beside him. The frail thirty-four-year-old Thalberg, who masterminded all production at the Metro-Goldwyn-Mayer studio, was extremely pale, but that wasn't unusual in light of his fragile health.

The gardener continued talking. The broken glass was delicate crystal and he knew it had to be expensive. Thinking it could be repaired he had carried the pieces into the house and washed them in the sink near the dining area.

"They had blood on them and I think he must have cut his hand."

Then he looked down the hall toward the bedroom and saw the body of Paul Bern motionless on the floor. Moving closer, he froze when he saw a second body nearby. As he stared with horror the second body moved: it was John Carmichael, Bern's chauffeur and butler, who had entered the house just before Davis and fainted when he saw Paul's body. Davis said he helped Carmichael get back on his feet.

The gardener shuddered at the ordeal he had just undergone. Bern's corpse was naked, he said, a gaping hole in the side of his head, his brown hair wet and discolored in a puddle of blood. He called it "gruesome."

Meanwhile, I kept looking around, thinking it was odd no others were moving in or about the house.

There was no sign of Jean Harlow, Paul's vivacious

bride, the radiant movie queen who had presided over their wedding reception on this very lawn only two months earlier.

It was an eerie sensation, surveying a serene house and garden while knowing that a few yards away was evidence of horrible violence, my friend's existence wiped out in a flash of light, a crash of sound. What was a dream house was now an oasis of death set apart from the living world around it.

Slavko Vorkapich, a neighbor living on Easton Drive, came through the gate and walked toward us. Vorkapich was a Serb, an excitable fellow, a freelance expert at movie special effects who often worked at MGM. He sat down stunned when told that Paul was dead.

He had heard loud voices during the night, a man and a woman alternately laughing and shouting; sometimes the shouting was angry and ugly.

"She came up the hill in a big limousine with a driver," he said. "She was all in black, wearing a veil, and I never saw her face. The car left but I know there was one over here later. I was asleep but the noise woke me up because it roared like crazy down the hill and turned north. Normally, you never hear any noise on this street and Paul was always very quiet, too, so I just came over now to see if everything's all right."

I looked at Thalberg. I had a good idea who that woman was, but I sensed that he did not.

Thalberg took Vorkapich aside, and they talked together.

Gardener Davis, who stood respectfully silent when

Vorkapich appeared, spoke up again, telling me that Louis B. Mayer had been there before Thalberg. It would have been extraordinary if he had not: Mayer was the colossus of the movie industry, god of the machine that was the MGM studio, an indomitable watchdog over any and all problems besetting that huge film factory. It wasn't at all surprising to learn that he had already come and gone.

When Mayer came to the house, according to the gardener, two other men were with him. "I know one, he's Mr. Hendry from the studio police, he was here when we were getting ready for the wedding reception. I don't know the other one. Anyway, soon as I told them how I found the body they went inside. That's all I saw." He spread his hands helplessly and walked over to pick up his tools.

Vorkapich was leaving too. He waved good-bye.

I had decided not to say what I knew about the veiled woman to Thalberg. Instead, I started toward the door of the house.

"Don't go in there, Sam," Thalberg said, grabbing my arm. "You heard that fellow Davis, it's not a pretty sight. Paul put a bullet through his brain and you won't like what you see, so why torture yourself? There's really nothing you can do anyway."

I hesitated and Thalberg added: "I have to make some phone calls, so why don't you go on home. We've lost a good friend." He patted me on the back, an affectionate gesture—and an abrupt dismissal.

I DROVE SLOWLY BACK to our apartment. The sun was hot, the morning fogs that always hung over Hollywood through summer mornings, much to the despair of film directors and cameramen, were gone. It was going to be a blistering day.

The details of the morning were revolving in my mind. Now I had to tell Marie all about the tragedy. As I feared, she broke into tears.

"I saw Paul every day this past week," I told her. "He never hinted at anything like this. I keep wondering why . . . I feel like crying, too."

"I'm crying for Jean," she said.

• • •

We turned on the radio and an announcer for a News at Noon broadcast reported a Hollywood tragedy in his headline summary. But it was about film stuntman Al Wilson, who had succumbed to injuries sustained at an air show.

No announcement of Paul Bern's death came over the radio that day. The holiday news broadcasts were exclusively concerned with the sporting events that marked the end of summer.

Fresh in my mind was the dinner Marie had prepared in our apartment for Paul and Jean less than a week before.

Jean was playing a very sexy role in *Red Dust* at the

time, and being MGM's hottest new attraction, she was getting the studio's full treatment. Her costar was rugged Clark Gable. It was a very exciting time for Jean and Paul, and all through the meal she glowed happily over her newfound stardom, and he did likewise, sitting contentedly by her side.

There was dessert and coffee and some "shop talk."

As planned, it was an early evening. "My darling wife is due on the set at an ungodly hour," Paul had said.

He had put his sporty camel's hair coat in the hall closet when he arrived, and as they were leaving Marie went to help him on with it and almost dropped it.

"What on earth is in here?" she asked.

"We live in a dark canyon, you know," he said. He reached into the coat pocket and showed a .38-caliber revolver. "I carry this to protect Jean."

A light and charming evening had suddenly taken on a darker side. Now, a week later, it seemed obvious that the gun Paul intended to safeguard their idyll was the one that ended it.

2
. . . . .
A Man
of Breeding

PAUL BERN WAS STANDING in the center of a spacious office, half dressed, when we met for the first time. That was December 1929, in the New York headquarters of Metro-Goldwyn-Mayer on Broadway between Forty-fourth and Forty-fifth streets. He was being fitted for a new suit of clothes: a tailor with a tape measure was calling out his customer's vital dimensions, telling his assistant the jacket was "SB" for single-breasted, the trousers "LD" for left dress, the side on which his genitals hung.

"Forgive me this embarrassment," Bern said, and explained that the studio sent him east so suddenly that he had no time to take along personal belongings.

Louis B. Mayer had waved off the need to carry wardrobe. In his brusque, prodigal way, Mayer told him, "Buy what you want when you get to New York and charge it to the company."

The trip was so hurried, sparked by such necessity,

that he chose the speediest way he could travel that day. Weighing 150 pounds on a post office scale, Bern flew for the price of first-class airmail stamps from California to New York in an open-cockpit biplane. The flimsy propeller-driven carrier with UNITED STATES AIRMAIL painted on its sides whisked him across the continent, making only brief refueling stops on the way. He had an uncomfortable seat on stacks of canvas mailbags, he and the bags tied down with ropes.

This was only a few weeks after the stock market had plunged the world into its worst depression in modern history. But to the movie industry, that historic Wall Street crash couldn't have come at a happier moment.

Picture makers had faced up to the unwelcome truth that the public would no longer accept silent films and wanted all movies to talk. MGM hesitated, with Mayer and Thalberg reluctant to accept the enormous change in their merchandise. Finally, it was obvious that they had remained uncertain too long: their business rivals had moved ahead of them and now they had to catch up.

Ironically, while major industries suffered and businesses went bankrupt, the Depression helped Hollywood's moviemakers recover quickly from those hard times. Talking films were playing to record-breaking audiences. Theater attendance, especially in the afternoons, was high. The market crash filled the world with the unemployed, disheartened, and discouraged men who found that moviegoing was an escape from futile job-hunting, and they lost their problems in the dreams they saw unfolding in the dark.

Silent movie writers had to be replaced by authors who knew how actors should speak and what their characters would say. Dialogue had become an essential commodity.

Creative men and women with a touch for the way people talked lived largely in and around New York's theater district, where forty-four plays were being performed. Bern's trip east was hastened by the knowledge that playwrights were getting to be in short supply, the bulk of them already shipped to Hollywood by Warner Brothers and Paramount. Even smaller independents, Columbia and Samuel Goldwyn had accepted talking films, and had gobbled up a few playwrights.

Bern brought a list, compiled in studio meetings, that included men and women with some sort of connections to the living theater. It was hoped that their experience would help the studio with this difficult element that had revolutionized the business. By the end of his first day in New York he had lined up a dozen of them to come in for interviews, and I was one of them.

The informality of a tailor at work while we talked served to melt away the icy stiffness of a business interview. It helped bring about a swift rapport between us, and I proposed an evening at the theater. I was writing *New York Amusements*, a weekly entertainment guide, and it made "hard tickets" easy to get.

I was also newly wed, so Marie and I invited him to be our guest at the smash musical hit *Show Boat* and suggested he bring a friend. He asked Mary Duncan, an actress who had electrified New York when she portrayed a fiery young drug addict in *The Shanghai Gesture*, but she turned him down. "One doesn't replace Mary easily," he said, and sighed. Sighs often punctuated his conversations. He didn't ask anyone else to *Show Boat*, and came alone.

After the theater the three of us had supper in the MGM suite where he was staying in the Waldorf Hotel Towers. We were dwarfed by the enormity of the apartment, high over the city, one of Manhattan's most elite addresses—the street entrance was separate from the hotel's lobby. He had ordered champagne and caviar for starters. It was life at the top, when much of the population had hit bottom.

"I'm not born to this luxury, my dear," he told Marie, his voice low, apologetic, and charming. He had produced a film, *Hungry Hearts*, picturing a squalid neighborhood like the one where he was born in Germany. Written by Anzia Yezierska, it probed deeply into hardship in a European ghetto, and her words aroused poignant memories in him. He brought the author to California and poured months of his life into the making of the film. "But it didn't turn out well," he sighed. Miss Yezierska disliked him on sight and made no secret of it. "She told people success is my meat and drink, my reason for living." He gestured around the huge living room and asked, "What's wrong with success?"

Then he reminisced about the path he traveled to his current position, one of Irving Thalberg's most important producers. He had freelanced for many years, he said, an itinerant writer and director accepting assignments as they came until he settled down in the big studio in Culver City.

"I had to do some soul searching before I took this job," he said. "Irving doesn't put his name on our films and we who work with him have agreed to that same anonymity. Until I went to MGM I always took screen credit for what I did. It's quite important, you know, and it's practical, too. With credits, your name becomes known, especially in the industry, when you go looking for employment. But there are rewards that go with my job at MGM—I have no regrets if people don't know me or anything about me. That's perfectly all right. I'm one of a half-dozen who are sometimes referred to as Irving's Boys, and I wouldn't trade that for all the screen credit the movies can give me.

"Irving humors my tastes in material," he went on. "I'm not inclined toward violence."

The Broadway theatrical season was awash with gangland melodramas depicting underworld characters, bootleggers, and beer barons waging their private wars. The titles told the stories: *Guns, Gang Wars, Broadway, Chicago, Street Scene, The Racket* . . .

"It's the men and women who write these plays that interest me most," Paul said. "We must keep the language up to date in our films."

Playwrights were introducing theater audiences to a new lingo of the times, depicting fugitives "on the lam," victims "bumped off," being jailed was "taking the rap," suppressing truth was "a cover-up," government agents were "G-men," and district attorneys were "D.A.'s."

Before the evening ended, he said, "I'm recommending to Irving that we put you on as a writer. May I suggest that in the meantime, you consider the kind of stories you'd like to work on? The range of themes is endless." He seemed to reflect for a moment before saying that films dealing with masquerade held special appeal for him. It was the idea behind his own early writing successes.

"I've never known one to fail," he said finally. "I'm sure you know films like *The Cabinet of Doctor Caligari*, for example, *The Unholy Three*, or *The Thief of Bagdad*. They all deal with characters who use deception to hide their true identities. Masquerade is a fascinating theme. Very little in this world is what it seems."

Standing in the apartment doorway saying good night, Bern said he found the evening "memorable."

We were on a first-name basis, it would be Paul and Sam from that evening on. Marie and I left the hotel with a lasting impression of our new friend. He had no resemblance at all to the widely circulated caricatures of movie moguls; loud, blatant, and obscene, men with limited education and vocabularies to match.

"I feel positive Irving will want you to come west," were the words that rang in our ears as we returned to our small West Side apartment. It was a memorable evening for us, too.

IRVING THALBERG and I had known each other back in 1919, when both of us were employed at Universal Pictures in the Mecca Building at 1600 Broadway, New York. It was my very first job, secured by answering a newspaper ad for an office boy in the company's Export department.

Thalberg, a slim dark youth, secretary to the company's president, Carl Laemmle, was sitting at a desk in the office next to me. Working nights as we did, we grabbed cafeteria dinners together and analyzed the movie business with sharp expertise and profound insights—at least that's how our observations seemed to us.

However, we were separated and our personal contacts languished. Laemmle took Thalberg to his studio at Universal City, California. By 1924, Thalberg had achieved a sensational success as the "boy genius" of Universal, then left and became even more famous as the production head of MGM. I left Universal and followed my literary ambitions.

• • •

Soon after the evening with Paul Bern I came face to face with Thalberg on a New York street. He was ready with a writing deal then and there, all businesslike and to the point as we stood on a midtown sidewalk.

"See if you can arrange a leave of absence from *New*

York Amusements. Come out west whenever you like and I'll have an assignment for you. I'll start you at the same salary you're making now, and if all goes well I'll adjust it."

A cynic told Marie, "When those big Hollywood studios want somebody they'll send a private railway car. They didn't even send your husband a pair of roller skates."

"Where's your contract?" asked another. "There isn't any," he was told.

In the spring, we drove our small car to Hollywood.

SEEN FROM OUTSIDE, May 24, 1930, the MGM lot had a cold, forbidding appearance.

Talkies had become the established way of life and the changeover from silent movies gave the old studio a new look. Solid cement stages had replaced glass structures, the windowless buildings loomed up in rows, resembling huge packing cases. In the era of silent movies, doors to the stages opened freely while cameras were rolling, people came and went while filming was going on. But when the silent moviemaking era disappeared, noise had to be controlled, voices and sounds were confined to what the scripts called for. To bar interruptions when scenes were being shot those stage doors were usually locked. Outside, on the studio streets, swinging red lights attached to loud, jangling bells gave further warnings that personnel should not enter. The stages were so soundproof that none of the din directly outside them could penetrate. The climate of openness had vanished and the studio had become a walled city.

• • •

I parked near the auto gate on Washington Boulevard in Culver City and asked a security officer to inform Thalberg I was there.

"You gotta have an appointment," he warned. Reluctantly he made the call and then said with some surprise, "Go on up!"

Thalberg was busy but interrupted his conference to tell me, "One of my department heads has just resigned." He mentioned the name of a man, someone I'd never heard of.

He went on, "I was wondering who would replace him when they told me you were downstairs. I think you can handle it. If you'd arrived yesterday, I'd have given you an assignment and forgotten about you. If you arrived tomorrow, the job would be filled."

That was all he had time to say.

Back at our hotel I told Marie, "Something important has happened but I don't know what it is!"

A Hollywood acquaintance brought me up to date.

"I'll be damned! You're the story editor!"

• • •

Next morning, Paul was my first visitor. "Please call on me any time you have a problem. You will have them, of course. I've had this job and I know."

The story editor's job encompassed the finding of writers and overseeing their assignments. It meant supervising three related departments: Secretarial, Research, and Reading, the last a group of men and women who condensed the flow of story submissions into brief synopses. The most demanding part of "the job" was finding and recommending material for the fifty films a year Thalberg and his associates were trying desperately to produce.

During my first week, I was suddenly confronted by matters of international scope. The twists and turns of the job propelled me constantly into Paul's office for help.

The most pressing problem was the need to rescue *Trader Horn*, a half-completed silent film bogged down since the coming of sound destroyed its value. I was asked to find a writer who could depict life in the African jungle. But that was just one of the studio's headaches. There was also the matter whether to renew the writing contract of British humorist P. G. Wodehouse and how to get someone to translate the newly arrived playscript *Menschen im Hotel* from German into English.

Within a short time all those problems were solved: Cyril Hume wrote the words for *Trader Horn*, P. G. Wodehouse moved to the Riviera, and the German play went on to become the hit *Grand Hotel*. Paul was a big help, and I was back in his office whenever new difficulties arose.

A popular fan magazine, *Photoplay*, had run a piece

about Paul called "A Modern Samaritan" by Jim Tully, a rugged ex-hobo turned author and actor. Paul's secretary, Irene Harrison, showed it to me one day while I was waiting to see her boss.

"Paul Bern has the elegance and the poise and the manner of one with centuries of breeding behind him," Tully wrote. "The best read man in Hollywood . . . a great emotional psychologist . . ." There was more, all praise, all depicting a man of sensitivity with a willingness to make sacrifices for others.

• • •

House parties were all the rage, and Jean Harlow was at one to which Marie and I were asked soon after our arrival. It was hosted by another pair of recently transplanted New Yorkers.

Edgar Allen Woolf was a raucous comedy writer, unashamedly homosexual. Benny Thau, a former vaudeville booker, was as quiet as Woolf was noisy. Thau smiled lamely when Woolf loudly proclaimed, "Benny and I have two things going for us here. He goes for the girls and I go for the boys!"

Jean sat beside her mother on a couch in their parlor. With her shining blond hair and fair complexion, she was a demure standout among the other young actresses, mixing and mingling, buzzing with studio chitchat. *Hell's Angels* had premiered on Hollywood Boulevard earlier that week with Jean in the leading female role, and all the other aspirants to film fame at the party were deferring to her, as if she had graduated from their ranks. But Jean shrugged off the congratulations that a young actress offered her.

"Did you see what they said about me?" she asked. "The airplanes got better notices than I did."

"Now, baby, you're not to worry about it," interjected her mother. "We're going to make it." She patted Jean's hand.

Jean smiled warmly at her mother, settled back, and didn't leave her side the rest of the evening.

● ● ●

At noon one day Paul suggested we drive over to see the home he was building on Easton Drive.

We clambered around the wooden framework that outlined the structure. A single bedroom showed above the living room. The sharp slanting roof was to have a red-tiled turret in the architectural style of middle Europe.

The swimming pool was still a dry hole, he wasn't terribly enthusiastic about it, saying wryly, "It's one of those quaint requisites that southern California architects say no one can live without."

He planned to carve a footpath on the wooded hill rising behind the house and to string lanterns between the trees. There was to be a shelter at the top, a retreat where he could read and "get away from it all."

"You know how I love solitude," he said, with soft accents that at times revealed his German childhood. "This will be my first real home."

Driving back to the studio on Benedict Canyon Drive

we passed the lavish estates of the comedian Harold Lloyd and that of my old boss at Universal Pictures, Carl Laemmle. The two huge mansions stood side by side, symbols of diversified Beverly Hills royalty. In contrast, Paul's house, only a short distance away, seemed very small.

"It's exactly right for me," he said. "When a man isn't married at forty it isn't likely he ever will."

3

·····

The Making
of a Star

THE *SATURDAY EVENING POST* was the mother lode in the studio's unending search for filmable material. The weekly magazine provided high-quality serials and short stories, plus an enormous readership that guaranteed solid attendance when a *Post* story showed up on movie screens. The studio covered every issue as soon as it could get its hands on it.

The first episode of "Red-Headed Woman" by Katharine Brush gave a tantalizing glimpse of Lil Andrews, moving from bed to bad to bed. If Lil continued in that provocative vein, the story of her life would be a "natural" for a movie. It was imperative that the studio find out more about her.

Transcontinental and Western Airline, using twin-motored DC-3 planes, carried passengers to the East Coast in fourteen to sixteen hours, if weather permitted. With Thalberg's approval, I sped east on one of them to learn the rest of Lil's story.

In Philadelphia, the *Post's* editors obligingly gave me two more episodes of this book-length serial, but that was as far as they could go.

I grabbed the first train I could get to take me to Miss Brush in New York. The author was a stylish and engaging lady, herself a vivid redhead like the Lil Andrews she was creating. She lived in a massive new apartment devoid of furniture. She and her husband had been wiped out by the stock market crash before they finished decorating. I suggested MGM could help recoup some of their losses if we knew enough about "Red-Headed Woman" to buy the film rights.

"I have no idea how my story is going to turn out, but I always start this way," she said. "I did that with my last one and it came out just fine."

She was referring to "Young Man of Manhattan," a big Paramount hit film, a glossy society drama that contained special appeal for shopgirls and store clerks, a class of cinema devotees highly cherished by money-minded producers. "Surely the *Post* wouldn't have started to run my new story if the editors didn't believe I could come up with a good ending."

While talking with her about someone adapting her story for the film, I had mentioned F. Scott Fitzgerald as the possible writer. She caught fire at the suggestion. He was her literary idol, and to prove it she showed me some notes she was accumulating for a future autobiography.

" 'I remember when I discovered Mr. F. Scott Fitzgerald,' " she read from the manuscript. " 'And I remember that I wasn't the same again for years. Even my titles improved under his influence, you will be glad to hear. I made no bones whatever about my sedulous aping of the fair-haired boy.' "

I acquired the film rights to "Red-Headed Woman" for MGM after reporting to Thalberg what I had learned and recommending he trust the lady's ability to complete it satisfactorily.

Thalberg assigned the story to Paul and asked him to move as fast as he could. He hoped the movie could be shown while the story in the *Saturday Evening Post* was still fresh in the public's mind.

Paul, too, agreed that F. Scott Fitzgerald should adapt the magazine serial for the screen. Fitzgerald's stories dealt with the beautiful, the wealthy, and damned. An inquiry to his literary agent revealed that he was available and would welcome the assignment. While he was coming from his home in Baltimore, Paul negotiated with Marcel De Sano to direct the film. De Sano's career was languishing, and it was characteristic of Paul to give him a chance to make a comeback. When the director was signed for the film, he was told by Thalberg to keep close tabs on Fitzgerald, whose taste for alcohol was world-renowned.

"I'm on the wagon and I'm going to stay there," volunteered Fitzgerald when he arrived. He was apple-cheeked, handsome as any movie hero, friendly and sober.

Thalberg made only one suggestion to him about Lil Andrews's characterization. She had to be amusing in her eagerness to trap a wealthy husband. "I want audiences to be on her side, to laugh *with* her and not *at* her." Fitzgerald promised to complete a script in six weeks.

With the story progressing each week in the *Saturday Evening Post,* Lil's amorous adventures were being avidly followed by the reading public and casting the sexy, streetwise heroine seemed a simple matter. Actresses, agents of actresses, and the friends of actresses who learned that Paul was supervising the production, besieged him while magazine readers wrote to the studio from all over the country suggesting candidates.

Thalberg had his contract list of stars. "Every woman on the lot knows she's just right for it," he told Paul. Jokingly referring to Marie Dressler, their elderly and popular character actress, he added, "She's the only one I haven't heard from yet."

Joan Crawford told friends she was sure to lose out to Thalberg's wife, Norma Shearer. "I can't beat pillow talk," she lamented, and then spread the thought around in hopes that the complaint would help her own chances.

The New York office maintained two talent scouts who turned their full attention to the search; their night wires to the studio recommended a growing list of candidates from the Broadway stage. Thalberg thought Francine Larrimore and Hope Williams were worth consideration; he sent a copy of the wire containing their names over to Paul, who sent it back to him with the notation, "excellent actresses but not for this."

Paul had found his ideal for the role in Jean Harlow, whom he met early in 1930. Thalberg vetoed her instantly. In his view, the young actress owed her audience recognition to her platinum blond hair and moviegoers would not accept her as a redhead. He had seen big stars fail at the box office when they changed their familiar image.

Paul was deeply wounded by Thalberg's rejection of Jean. But he couldn't deny that she had already flunked her two big chances, playing leading roles in *Hell's Angels* and *Platinum Blonde.* She had also appeared in two films at MGM, minor performances as gangster molls that met with monumental indifference from audiences and critics alike. Thalberg based some of his decision on that account.

Paul maintained that her career had suffered in *Hell's Angels* and *Platinum Blonde* because she was miscast as an English debutante in both films. It wasn't Jean's fault, as he saw it, because directors Howard Hughes and Frank Capra had deliberately attempted unusual casting by making Jean perform against type. He claimed he could see that she had the talent to be a superb comedienne, but it didn't advance his cause—he had little proof. Thalberg saw no point in risking the likely success of *Red-Headed Woman* on a kid "who is already a has-been."

Jean's movie career skidded to a new low. She went east, making personal appearances, flouncing onstage before the feature picture went on—a picture that she wasn't in. She tossed her blond locks and some saucy jokes in the air while showing off her body in a dress that revealed most of what she had to offer. Her name was on the marquees and drew good-sized audiences, mostly males, of course.

Paul wanted her back in Hollywood and asked to make a test of her. Thalberg's curiosity was aroused by Paul's persistence. He was also amused.

"You're behaving like I did when I first met Norma," he said, referring to his movie-star wife. "I knew positively that she could play anything. It's a kind of romantic astigmatism that attacks producers when they fall for an actress."

"Jean'll be a knockout as a redhead," insisted Paul. "My dear Irving, she deserves a chance to fail."

"Not with Louis B. Mayer's money," retorted the production chief, and refused to okay a screen test.

• • •

Six weeks later, Thalberg scheduled a story meeting in his office. Fitzgerald was summoned, along with director De Sano, who had actively worked on the script with him. But before they were due, Paul and I were called in. There was no need to ask why; Fitzgerald had completed his screenplay on time but it lacked the comedy elements that Thalberg expected of it. There wasn't time or inclination to let Fitzgerald rewrite it.

We all knew full well that rejection would demoralize the high-strung author. As a consequence, it was decided that lying was the charitable way to handle it. Thalberg spelled it out. We were to praise Fitzgerald for his work and thank him. When he was back in Baltimore he would be told the truth.

The meeting went as planned: after receiving compliments for his screenplay, Fitzgerald left elated, unaware of the deception played on him.

Marcel De Sano, still slated to direct the film, was then told the screenplay would be entirely rewritten. He had concentrated hard on the rejected script with Fitzgerald and was obviously piqued. The charade we played on Fitzgerald created a cloud of despondency, which hung over the entire group. Selecting another writer went slowly.

Several sophisticated screenwriters were on the studio staff and could be made available. Anita Loos was one of them. The petite, doll-like author had written plays, books, and more movies than she could remember. The title of one of her books, *Gentlemen Prefer Blondes*, had become a catchphrase used throughout the country.

Anita was one of the true standbys of the writing department. When called to Thalberg's office she was sure she could deliver a screenplay in three weeks, and promised to say nothing about it until Fitzgerald had checked out of his hotel and was homeward bound.

"I don't want a word of this to reach him," Thalberg warned us all as the meeting broke up.

• • •

Fitzgerald had expressed a desire to return to the east immediately and, per his "one-picture deal" contract, the studio had to supply his railway ticket. It was going to be delivered to his Hollywood hotel, but instead he reappeared at the studio. He came to pick it up, he said, and to celebrate, to say his good-byes in a truly courteous fashion. There were handshakes for the men he knew and kisses for the women. To those of us who knew how much he wanted to be a successful screenwriter and had deceived him into thinking the way was now open, it was a heartbreaking moment. He was just going out the gate when De Sano caught up with him.

"They've made a fool of you," he told the writer. "Your script is being thrown out and Anita Loos is starting all over."

Fitzgerald never used the ticket in his pocket. He took off on a three-week drunk. Thalberg, in a fury, fired the director. Paul pleaded for him to no avail. Finished in Hollywood and unable to find another assignment, a depressed De Sano said good-bye to Paul and moved to France.

• • •

On a Sunday morning when Anita Loos was close to finishing her rewrite, Paul assembled a production crew on an MGM soundstage. He swore them all to secrecy. They were there to film a scene from the new screenplay as a test for Jean, and the cost of studio equipment and manpower was to be charged to Paul's personal account.

A routine production test didn't usually require that much staff and equipment. Actresses simply posed before the camera in makeup and costumed for the character they might play, but that was all. It could be taken for granted they knew how to say dialogue, so the silent test, cheaper and easier to do, would be shown to the executive staff to determine if the performer was right for the part. But Paul wanted Jean to get the full treatment. She did.

She was looked after by Paul's many friends in the studio, including the heads of the Makeup, Hairdressing, and Wardrobe departments.

He had chosen a standing set resembling an Ohio business firm. Jean and Una Merkel, an MGM actress, were dressed as office workers in conventional attire, although a bit more fashionable than the real thing—in typical MGM fashion, glamour took precedence over reality.

Paul settled himself in a camp chair, facing Jean.

"Lil is in absolute control of this situation, my dear. She is self-assured and completely confident. I want to enjoy watching you—you understand?"

She nodded.

He signaled all was in readiness to Hal Rosson, one of the studio's top cameramen. The lights came on. "Quiet," shouted the sound man. He listened through his earphones, then reported, "up to speed."

Jean stepped into the scene with a flair: she whirled around like a fashion model, showing off her body before speaking her first line. It was, not incidentally, a plug, a not-too-private joke that Anita Loos had inserted in the script the title of her best-known book. "So gentlemen prefer blondes, do they? Well, we'll just see about that!" Jean said.

She had covered her blond hair and gestured to the red wig she was wearing. The black and white photography would convince audiences that she was indeed a red-headed woman.

She danced before Una Merkel, the hem of her skirt flying above her knees as she swayed her hips seductively.

"Can you see through this dress? If you can I'll wear it. I'm on my way to the boss's house with his mail. Maybe I'll get a chance to take dictation."

Merkel registered shocked surprise: "You know the boss is crazy about his wife."

"Don't be dumb. She's out of town and he's a man, isn't he?"

Paul said, "perfect" before he remembered to say "cut!" He was enthralled by Jean. That was evident to all.

• • •

Jean's stepfather, Marino Bello, was waiting outside the stage. It would be equally correct to say he was lurking there. He was exercising his parental prerogative, by dominating the actress's mother, also named Jean. "Mama Jean" was his submissive and obedient wife and "Baby Jean" was her submissive and obedient daughter.

Bello seemed to enjoy a sinister and villainous appearance with his slicked-down black hair and curled-up mustache. Nobody at MGM knew what he actually did for a living, but he claimed talents in many fields, including show business. In Hollywood, he had brushed aside Jean's agent, Arthur Landau, and took over as her personal manager. He welcomed Paul's entrance into their lives because of the promise it held for improving the Bello fortunes. Both men were the same age, but their interest in Jean was the only thing they had in common. Paul had no liking at all for Marino, which was why he had asked him to wait outside the stage while the test was being shot.

• • •

Thalberg's office was being inundated with suggestions of who should play the role. Under Marino's management, Jean went back east to continue her personal appearances while Paul telephoned her almost daily.

Jean was facing an ever-growing array of rivals. Aside from the formidable list of MGM players, Thalberg expressed a surprising preference for Dorothy Mackaill— surprising because she was under contract to Warner Brothers. He was undoubtedly swayed by a photo he was shown, artfully posed by the actress as a sex kitten sitting with a telephone in hand, her legs up on a table and her short skirt far above her bare knees. There were bottles of liquor around her and a bed in the background. She stood at the top of Thalberg's list.

Other possibilities outside the MGM stock company included young movie actresses Helen Twelvetrees, Nydia Westman, Peggy Shannon, Wynne Gibson, and Dixie Lee, wife of crooner Bing Crosby. When MGM's casting head in New York complained on the phone that they were all virtually unknown, Thalberg told them,

"When this picture comes out they won't be unknown anymore!"

The New York office was pitching hard for Broadway ingenues Margaret Perry and Muriel Kirkland, who were winning critical acclaim for their comedic abilities in current plays. Turndowns by the studio simply brought renewed urgings for their reconsideration. Through the month of March 1932 the nightly wires from the New York office also repeated strong recommendations for red-headed musical comedy stars Ethel Merman and Harriette Lake. The latter would become an MGM star in five years when she had changed her name to Ann Sothern.

All were still in contention when Anita Loos's screenplay was stamped FINAL. Paul continued to remind Thalberg that Jean was the perfect choice, but Thalberg wasn't convinced. Paul had refrained from showing Jean's test scene: he was waiting for the perfect moment, but also fearing that his constant pressure could backfire.

Meanwhile, he turned to Marino Bello, knowing how hungry Jean's stepfather was for her to land the part. He reached Bello backstage in a New York theater where Jean was performing and suggested a strategy. Fully agreeing, Bello joined forces with Paul, an odd alliance born of necessity. From April 8 through 12, Bello telegraphed a series of wordy night letters to Thalberg from New York and Chicago, reporting Jean was asking audiences if they would like her to star in *Red-Headed Woman*.

EVERY HOUSE RESPONDS WITH ENTHUSIASTIC AP-
PLAUSE, he repeated in each telegram.

On the day that the casting decision required an answer, Paul showed his test scene. Among those viewing
it in Thalberg's private projection room were director
Jack Conway, who had replaced De Sano, and cameraman Hal Rosson, who had made Jean's test and would
also film the picture. Conway's opinion could be the
decisive vote. All the possibilities were presented to him,
some verbally, some with film clips that were run and
rerun over and over.

In the projection room, arguments in favor of and
against the actresses went on for more than an hour.
Paul was tense and nervous, although it was a convivial
gathering. Finally, Conway declared for Jean and was
seconded by Anita Loos and Hal Rosson. Pretending to
be uncertain, Thalberg mulled it over, reserving his decision with suspenseful timing until he said, slowly, "I
have a feeling that if I don't give her the part I'll lose my
producer—and I don't want to lose my producer so let's
go with Jean Harlow."

Back from her personal appearance tour, Jean was
waiting in Paul's office and he rushed over to tell her,
whereupon she dashed off to tell her mother. Suddenly
alone, he broke the news to his secretary, sitting just
outside his office.

"I could see by the look on her face when she went
out," said Irene Harrison. "And by yours when you
came in!"

• • •

Making a story like "Red-Headed Woman" into a full-length feature film could be a breeze for the professionals engaged in the process at Metro-Goldwyn-Mayer. It was a straight-line plot requiring mostly interiors, conventional offices and bedrooms, settings that stood permanently on one soundstage or another. With newly painted walls and different furniture, they wouldn't reveal how often they had been used in previous films.

The few outdoor scenes called for in the story could be photographed on the back lot, where small town streets abounded. *Red-Headed Woman* was to be made entirely within the studio itself, except for a brief tag that needed a few scenes shot in France. But members of the cast would not have to travel abroad; there would be a double for Jean.

The young star was the only real question mark, in Thalberg's view, the one element that might hamper the smooth-running production machinery. Despite Paul's faith in her, Jean was taking on a starring part that, considering her inexperience in sophisticated comedy, gave the studio staff good reason to keep a close watch on her. But they needn't have worried, as was soon apparent. She registered everything asked of her and brought flair and an endearing personality to the role.

After viewing the first scenes in which Jean appeared, even Thalberg was pleased with her performance. He could also congratulate himself, for he had approved buying her contract from eccentric millionaire Howard Hughes, the producer of *Hell's Angels.*

The final shots of *Red-Headed Woman* would show Lil Andrews at the height of her career, fawned over by a bevy of bearded admirers at Longchamps racetrack outside Paris.

Paul prevailed on Thalberg to let Marcel De Sano, now settled in France, function as second-unit director. It was De Sano who filmed the atmospheric shots around Paris and back-projection scenes that would give the illusion Lil Andrews was in France, routine work used in the film without screen credit.

Throughout the movie, a subtle touch hinting at Lil's amorous adventures was the constant appearance near her of a sly, handsome foreigner who never spoke a word. Casting that role called for an actor whose knowledgeable expression would convey beyond doubt that he was Lil's secret lover.

MGM had brought many Europeans to Hollywood to "dub" their English-speaking talkies. For the French versions these actors would make American stars appear to be speaking French. It made the new films suitable for international showings. Among those actors was Charles Boyer, an attractive young Frenchman with ample ability to project the smug cat-who-ate-the-canary expression that was called for in the role of the lover.

But when he was asked to play that small, silent part Boyer refused.

"I do this dubbing temporarily because times are hard in the French theater," he explained. "In France I am a star. You must understand, Monsieur Thalberg, I would like to oblige you but if my friends see me in this film they are sure to say that poor Boyer is a failure in Hollywood, look at the small part he is reduced to playing. I apologize to you and thank you but no, I cannot do it."

"Mr. Bern and I understand," said Thalberg, "but we're so anxious to have you that if you'll do it, we'll see that the picture is never shown in France. Your friends will never know."

Boyer played the part, the movie was never seen in France.

De Sano had hoped that the work he did on the film would show him to advantage and help him revive his career, but by withholding it from the French market he was unable to make use of it. His depression deepened and shortly afterward, he killed himself.

• • •

A myriad of postproduction departments, functioning with clockwork efficiency, took over the completed footage and readied the movie for its preview.

Red-Headed Woman was seen by its first-time audience the evening of June 2, 1932, in Glendale, a suburb of Los Angeles.

Jean sat in the last row at the preview theater, relishing the final moments of the film, refusing Publicity head Howard Strickling's urging that she let herself be hustled away by his men before the lights came on. When the audience saw her it took all of Strickling's men and the full corps of studio police to get her out to

Paul and the waiting limousine at the curb. Their driver was Harold Allen Garrison, the studio bootblack, known as Slickum, a colorful, versatile favorite with all the studio personnel. The odd jobs he performed were legendary and he liked to talk about them—God had made no provisions for Slickum to keep any secrets to himself.

He related to all who would listen that Jean and Paul rode away from the preview sitting apart in the back seat. Then, suddenly, "They flung themselves into each other's arms and kissed like crazy!"

• • •

Red-Headed Woman was released nationally June 24, 1932. It was such an instant box-office hit that Jean's popularity exploded, her stardom was assured. She and Paul were married less than two weeks later.

Their wedding took place Saturday, July 2, at the Bello home, attended by only a few close friends and relatives. Paul's sister Friederike Marcus, a widow living in California, and brother Henry Bern, of New Rochelle, New York, were among them. It was an unpretentious ceremony, quite unlike the usual display of exhibitionism that accompanied most marriages of Hollywood celebrities. Paul wanted it that way.

Bello, having sent the telegrams to Thalberg, took credit for winning the role of Lil for Jean and guiding her rise to stardom. With the title of personal manager, and assured income for himself, he became insufferably arrogant.

Paul didn't argue over Bello's claims. When Thalberg's assistant Al Lewin expressed his annoyance, Paul said, "Let him have the last word, I've got the last laugh." His wedding gift to Jean was the deed to the dream house on Easton Drive that he loved.

The sober wedding ceremony at the Bello home was followed the next day by festivities that were uncorked, literally, at a garden party on the grounds of Paul's house. Marie and I were among the guests greeted by the radiant bride with hugs and kisses. Paul accepted congratulations and kept repeating that he was the happiest man alive.

All of Irving's Boys were on hand, none more jubilant over Paul's entrance into matrimony than Thalberg. Lifting his glass of champagne, he welcomed Paul into the brotherhood they now shared, producers wedded to stars. He reminded Paul that "when Jean says 'I'll never stop loving you,' you won't know if she means it or is memorizing a line in a script."

His wife, Norma Shearer, interrupted, raising her glass in turn and warned Jean to expect her producer-husband to give every woman a long look because she might be just the type for the movie he has in mind. "And when he should be lying in bed beside you he'll be sitting up somewhere reading a script, or he's in conference, wherever those mysterious conferences are."

Other guests spoke up, toasting the bride and groom with an outpouring of affection that spilled into the evening, the glow of the lanterns overhead lighting the swirling movements of the beautifully gowned women and their spruced-up escorts. It gave the scene the dreamlike aspect of current movies, almost all of them ending with the illusion that marriage is forever.

Marino Bello was prominent among the guests at Paul's house, reminding everyone of his importance. His approval of her marriage seemed genuine enough: not even Paul's associates, who disliked and distrusted him, questioned it. But later, Paul revealed to them that despite Bello's jovial demeanor, while Mama Jean and Baby Jean were exchanging farewell embraces, Bello leaned forward to shake Paul's hand and said, softly but menacingly, "Better take good care of my baby . . ."

4

·····

The Creative Team

THE STORY BROKE on Tuesday, the morning after the body was found; it was reported in headlines around the country. The *Los Angeles Times* proclaimed BERN DEATH MYSTIFIES on its front page. Under it, JEAN HARLOW'S MATE SUICIDE and further down, VARIANCES IN SERVANTS' ACCOUNTS SIFTED.

I was annoyed by the newspaper accounts that tried to sensationalize Paul's suicide. They claimed the police were baffled in their attempts to solve the mystery of filmdom's latest tragedy.

John and Winifred Carmichael, his married housekeepers, said that Bern and his wife parted on the best of terms when she left for a dinner with her parents, Mr. and Mrs. Marino Bello, of 1353 Club View Drive, Beverly Hills. Bern was to go with them but decided at the last moment to send the cook and housekeeper ahead with his wife. According to John Carmichael, when Miss Harlow departed she said to her husband, "Good-bye dear, I'll be seeing you." There was no harsh words or an indication of a quarrel.

Gardener Davis had a different account. He said they had quarreled just before Miss Harlow left.

As for discovering the body, Carmichael reported that he saw the body first, after he pulled up the shades in the bedroom. "Mr. Bern," he said, "was slumped in the closet doorway."

Davis told reporters that Carmichael had fainted and that really it was he who discovered that his master had been shot.

In the Tuesday morning coverage of the *Los Angeles Times* some editorial color was added. "Bern's suicide, according to police, apparently was accomplished after the manner of a death scene in *What Price Hollywood?*, a recent film release depicting the life of Hollywood film celebrities, in which the leading male character, tiring of what was termed 'an artificial life,' stood before a mirror and shot himself."

Some of these accounts didn't always jibe with what I heard at the house Monday morning, nor was there any mention of the visit by the woman in black. I dismissed this as careless reporting.

The Tuesday morning newspapers also declared that a detective had discovered a suicide note on top of a dresser. It was written on a page in an ornate diary, and this is the way it appeared in the press:

> *Dearest Dear,*
> *Unfortunately this is the only way to*
> *make good the frightful wrong I have*

> *done you and to wipe out my abject*
> *humiliation. I Love You.*
>
> > *Paul*
>
> *You understand that last night was only*
> *a comedy.*

The note fixed public attention on Jean. Sightseers gathered outside her mother's home hoping for a glimpse of her, but they only saw doctors and nurses who informed them she had become hysterical and was under sedation. The vagueness of her condition was a stimulus for the curious throng, and the drama increased because nobody was talking.

IT WAS ALL anyone talked about at MGM Tuesday morning, from the crowded commissary counter where men and women breakfasted, to the soundstages where they were preparing to set up scheduled scenes. Those who didn't know the dead man listened to those who did. They exchanged theories and attempted explanations, all wrapped around the word on everyone's lips, *suicide.* But nobody knew why.

At noon, a somber collection of executives drifted into the executive bungalow, a Spanish-style headquarters provided by the company for their relaxation. Usually, they came to eat a gourmet lunch for free and while away an hour or so with a rubber of bridge.

The "regulars" who showed up every day made a special effort to set aside the cares of moviemaking. Talk about production problems was taboo inside the bungalow. The hours from twelve to two were an intermission, normally punctuated with jokes, gossip and good-natured ribbing. This was not a normal day.

A sit-down lunch was served in the large room to the left as one entered. Chairs for Mayer and Thalberg were always held ready for them at either end of the oblong walnut table, with telephones hanging under the table-top within their reach. Howard Strickling and studio manager Eddie Mannix, staunch Mayer's Men, were often in the bungalow at lunchtime but had not shown up yet. Normally they sat side by side with the group called Irving's Boys.

Those men comprised a varied assortment of individuals, all of them fiercely loyal to Thalberg. Silver-haired Harry Rapf was a warm, kindly man. Thalberg wisely assigned him a full quota of tearjerkers to oversee. Bernie Hyman and Larry Weingarten were Thalberg's age, tied closely to him by family connections but competent enough to fend off accusations of nepotism. Hyman was adept at making both sophisticated comedies and adventure films. They benefited from his lively imagination, for he was neither sophisticated nor adventuresome. Weingarten was exclusively involved with slapstick comedies starring acrobatic Buster Keaton and also a series of farcical vehicles for two older and very popular costars, Marie Dressler and Polly Moran.

Hunt Stromberg was an astute, no-nonsense creator whose tastes ranged into all types of story material on which to base the movies he supervised. His tall, loose-limbed body was topped off with a large mop of unruly dark hair. In his early career, he was publicist for Thomas H. Ince, an independent producer-director who met his death after weekending with Charlie Chaplin and publisher William Randolph Hearst on a yacht at sea. It was yet another of the tragedies that befell several Hollywood celebrities throughout the 1920s, mysteries never satisfactorily penetrated. Ince had made no preparations for his demise and his studio operation expired with him: the personnel dispersed through Hollywood and Hunt Stromberg was propelled onto Thalberg's producing staff.

Paul Bern was part of that brotherhood, but there was never a place set for him at the table. It was his custom to lunch off a tray in his office, in the solitude he loved, usually with a book or a script for company.

On the other hand, Thalberg's assistant Albert Lewin always lunched with them. A diminutive five-footer, he was permanently aggressive and belligerent. The former college professor was the resident intellectual at the studio, opinionated and full of scorn for the paths the world was taking. Ready to do battle on almost any given subject, his opinions enlivened the lunchtime conversations in the bungalow.

It was Thalberg's view that those men made for a balanced group and provided him with all the help he needed. He had affection for them all and they returned his feelings with undeniable hero worship.

• • •

Department heads were welcome there if they wished, and on this day I was there, along with art director Cedric Gibbons.

The men in the bungalow were Paul's most intimate associates; he was one of them, his endeavors were similar, and since they all felt they knew him better than anyone else, the shock of his sudden loss hit them harder. It showed on their faces when they came together that day.

Almost all of them had been out of town over the holiday, and had all their information from the newspapers. Mayer and Thalberg could have supplied more, but they were missing from the bungalow when the group convened.

The men who were there knew many kindnesses attached to Paul's past. The help he extended Marcel De Sano was an example of an attempt that failed. But he had given material aid to others, a majority of them women. Harry Rapf recalled how Paul bought a wedding ring for exotic Barbara La Marr when her seventh husband couldn't afford one, and he also foraged through Hollywood late that bridal night to find a bootlegger to supply liquor for the newlyweds.

"Only Paul would do crazy things like that," concluded Rapf.

Producer Weingarten said Paul rescued young starlet Joan Crawford's dream home for her after her fiancé

Michael Cudahy was killed in a car crash. "Paul gave her the money for the down payment," he said.

"Cudahy was a drunk," scoffed Rapf. "He wasn't going to marry Joan anyway. His mother wouldn't let him, she was against it and she was the one with the money. The only thing Cudahy had in common with Joan was that they both loved to dance the Charleston."

"All I know is that Paul saved the house for her," asserted Weingarten. "Typically Paul Bern. A beautiful gesture."

"He was crazy to do it," said Rapf.

I knew firsthand about a *Ziegfeld Follies* girl, Jeanne Williams, who artfully passed herself off as a Russian actress to director Cecil B. DeMille. Paul contacted her after her disguise was exposed and a furious DeMille had her physically removed from his studio. "She was in total despair," I recalled. "She was amazed that Paul wanted nothing in return for the help he offered her."

"Perhaps he wasn't very satisfying in bed," observed Stromberg. "I've heard stories about him."

"All lies," said Lewin.

The argument they might have had was interrupted by the arrival of Thalberg. He was haggard, but managed a slight smile as he took his seat.

"I don't suppose I need to ask what is Topic A," he said, and his relaxed manner sent a wave of relief around the table. Ever present in the minds of Thalberg's close associates was how he would react to tension. Paul's sudden death added an extra dimension to the constant and frenzied wheeling and dealing of picture making at MGM.

•••

I had a special reason for observing him closely. Having sold some pieces to *The New Yorker*, I had called on editor Ralph Ingersoll before going west and proposed writing a profile of Thalberg. The magazine often ran regular articles about celebrities that they called "profiles." Ingersoll liked the idea, and Thalberg did, too, when I told him about it. Consequently, I was noting everything about him that I could, particularly his personal characteristics.

•••

In 1932, thirty-four-year-old Irving Grant Thalberg lived with a cardiac condition that threatened to end his life without warning. That illness put a permanent weight in his chest that wouldn't go away, one that might easily prompt an average man to take it easy. That threat of an early death had the opposite effect on him: if Death was waiting in the wings he would work hard day and night until it reached out for him. As a result, his studio associates worried more about his life expectancy than he did.

He had developed a dry sense of humor, impish, elfin, and at times bitter, and he used it purposely when needed as relief from the stress imposed on him by his position as head of production. His close friends knew that the witticisms he injected into crisis-created conferences were intentional life preservers, a special form of painkiller to remind him he must never chase his blood pressure uphill.

Their apprehensions about his health lessened when it appeared to them he was bearing up well under Paul's death. They nodded knowingly with him when he stated he had just left Louis B. Mayer's office, where the studio's top man was deciding what would be revealed to the world.

"LB is writing the script for the inquest," he said. "He and Strickling are deciding who'll get the starring roles. They don't want Jean to appear, so they're figuring how to ask Marino Bello to be her stand-in." Ironically, he added, "After all, fellows, it's no accident this place is known as Mayer's Valley of Retakes!"

As a filmmaking team, Thalberg and Mayer were incomparable in the movie industry, the younger man as creator, the older as administrator.

Veteran supervisor Harry Rapf had come on the studio lot the first day Mayer and Thalberg began its operation. Leaning as he did toward the making of sob-story-type movies, he was intensely serious in his views on life. "What made Paul do it?" he asked.

Thalberg turned to him with an expression of mock surprise. "Ask LB," he said. "He'll tell you. He's got it all figured out."

His evasion brought forth a chorus of shouts demanding an answer.

"Impotence," he said, finally. "Paul couldn't make it with Jean, he was embarrassed, humiliated, frustrated

. . . so, he had a gun handy and that ended all his worries about it."

"I thought so all the time," said Stromberg. His agreement brought forth some nods of agreement, but not from everyone.

Albert Lewin hooted raucously, then shouted, *"Bullshit!"*

"Watch your language, Allie," Thalberg said mildly.

"Come on, Irving," said Bernie Hyman. "Do you believe that impotence stuff?"

"I know three women, at least, who'll tell you Paul was one hell of a lover!" insisted Lewin.

"So do I," said art director Cedric Gibbons. The precise, immaculate head of the Art department rarely raised his voice but he was becoming excited and reached across me to Thalberg. "Hand me the phone, Irving. I know a lady I can call right now."

Thalberg sat still. "Wait for LB. Hear him out, then you're free to say what you like."

At that moment, Mayer came in with publicity director Howard Strickling and studio manager Eddie Mannix.

Louis Burt Mayer personified raw energy, stocky and muscular, filled with confidence and righteousness. In eight years, he had guided the merger of three companies, Metro, Goldwyn, and Mayer to the top of the film industry. He had risen from his father's junk business to global importance and was often reported in the press to be the highest-paid executive in the United States. He was convinced that his success was a gift that God had personally bestowed upon him.

He combined thoughtfulness for others with instant displays of pugnacity, and his quick mind and his fists were always at the ready. Former adversaries John Gilbert, Charlie Chaplin, and Samuel Goldwyn found out he could use them, too—all had a clear view of his prowess just before landing in prone positions on the floor.

He was king of a domain that went beyond the studio walls, his influence extended around the world. He was sincere in his homey approach to life, far beyond keeping hot chunky chicken soup "like my mother used to make" ready for him at all hours in the commissary and the executive bungalow.

Thalberg and Mayer were independent thinkers: their ideas often clashed and they didn't pull punches when voicing opinions of each other. But while Thalberg kept his emotions in check, Mayer let his explode in pyrotechnic displays, roaring out his views, personifying the lion, literally transforming himself into the symbol of the studio he so dearly loved.

Strickling and Mannix were prominent members of the group known as Mayer's Men. Utterly devoted to his boss, Strickling was Mayer's alter ego, holding a tight rein over the Publicity department, guarding with fanatical zeal the likeness of the studio skipper that he publicized.

Bulldog-jawed Mannix grew up a laborer in the crews that built the amusement park on the top of the New Jersey Palisades. It gave him his muscular physique and profane vocabulary before he climbed to the post of studio manager. He too maintained unswerving loyalty to Mayer.

The mood that the three men met within the bungalow was one of curiosity, but it was tinged with a bit of defiance from Lewin and Gibbons. Mayer, acutely attuned to adversarial reactions, knew it before a word was spoken.

He looked keenly at Thalberg and said, "I'm sure you told them why Paul did what he did." No one spoke.

"You would think," he went on as he turned toward the men, "that if he really loved Jean, that wonderful child who gave him all her trust, he would confide in her before leading her into marriage. I can tell you, no man should keep secrets from his wife, ever. If Paul would have been honest with her, he would have had nothing to be ashamed of and he would be alive today. Am I right, Eddie?"

Mannix nodded vigorously.

"Howard?"

Strickling nodded vigorously.

"You see? He could never be an honest husband to her," Mayer summed up. "I will always hold that against him, although he did the right thing when he picked up the gun. For that, yes, he deserves a place in our hearts."

It was typical Louis B. Mayer. His speech was replete with the emotionalism he was so expert at offering his listeners when occasions demanded.

Al Lewin scowled through it. "If you're telling us that Paul was impotent, Mr. Mayer, I have to disagree."

"I respect Allie, of course," he said to Thalberg. It was a way he had, to talk to another person while delivering a message for the listener. "But there are things that go on in this world that even *he* doesn't know.

"I talked to Dr. Jones, who told me Paul was impotent. Think of a man like that marrying a girl like Jean Harlow! Believe me, the public will understand. She'll be a bigger star than ever!"

He looked around at the doubting faces. The silence bothered him.

Mayer's face reddened, an early warning sign of rising temper. "Irving, you agreed with this." His right arm made a sweeping gesture around the table. "These are your boys, it's your duty to tell them what we learned about Paul. Go ahead, do it." Thalberg hesitated. Mannix gestured to Mayer to stay calm.

Howard Strickling chimed in, "We know for a fact that Paul was impotent. You know about the note he left to Jean about the humiliation it caused him. Dr. Jones is cutting short his vacation in Hawaii, rushing back to testify it's true."

"Ethical doctors don't violate patient confidentiality," said Lewin, his elocution slow and deliberate. "But then, whoever called Doc Jones ethical?"

"What about Jean?" asked Harry Rapf. "What does she say?"

Mayer glared at the questioner, as Mannix spoke up.

"Nothing! To anybody! I just talked to Marino. He'll handle her. He knows the score. He didn't like Paul any more than I did. We both pegged him right, a wishy-washy queer, posing as the little father-confessor. Father, hell! He was a fucking—"

"That's enough, Eddie," snapped Thalberg. "We don't want your opinion of Paul and we won't have his memory smeared!" He looked across at Mayer, at the far end of the table. "We all loved Paul, LB."

Mayer literally leaped from his chair and ran around the table to Thalberg. He was livid.

Mayer-watchers always knew when the old pro was giving a performance. He was assuredly the best actor in a studio of great actors. Tears would rush to his eyes, his voice would quaver, he would slump into the nearest chair, sometimes to his knees. But this was no histrionic affectation—it was the real thing. His fists were clenched, his voice rising to a hoarse scream. He shook off Mannix's restraining hand.

"This is the most terrible moment in the history of our company," he yelled. "If you don't stand by me now you will destroy MGM and yourselves with it. Do you hear me? Am I talking to intelligent men or are you a bunch of fools? Tell them, Irving, they'll listen to you. Tell them in the name of God there is only one answer to all of this and you know it as well as I do. Tell them —*tell them!*"

Mayer made Thalberg the focus of all attention while he stood near. Actual tears were running down his cheeks.

Thalberg looked into the eyes of the men around the table, took a deep breath and said, "Fellows, Paul took his life because of a personal problem he couldn't do anything about. We have to go along with LB, he's doing everything for Jean and for us and we owe him our thanks . . ."

Satisfied, Mayer turned and marched out of the bungalow. Mannix and Strickling jumped up and rushed after him.

Thalberg, pale and unusually flustered, signaled to Lewin and Hyman, "Let's go to work." The room emptied behind them. Portions of minute steaks and broiled chicken were left on their plates. The two white-jacketed waiters assigned to the bungalow emerged from the kitchen and stared at the remnants. They had never seen anything like that before.

FROM THE TIME that the police were notified of Paul's death they tried to question Jean.

A flood of rumors raced through Hollywood that a mysterious veiled woman was seen at the Bern house late Sunday night, and detectives speculated that it could have been Jean Harlow. They wanted a statement that pinned down her whereabouts.

The two detectives who asked to see her were barred from the Bello home by doctors, lawyers, and her parents.

They had to negotiate a deal not to ask her any incriminating questions, agree that their interview would be confined to Paul's possible motive for suicide, and, if she could, she would help them unravel the meaning of the note.

When finally admitted to the house on Tuesday, they found the star close to collapse, visibly shaken and unable to control her tears.

"I can't understand why this terrible thing had to happen," was all that she said. "As for the note left by Paul, I have no idea what it means. This frightful wrong he apparently believed he had done me is all a mystery. I can't imagine what it means."

It was a busy afternoon, busier than usual because Story department matters had piled up over the long weekend and needed attention. Also, the writers who were working for Paul had to be notified that they were on hold until Thalberg reassigned their projects to other producers.

One of my visitors that afternoon was John Lee Mahin, who wrote the scenario of *Red Dust* and was fashioning an original story, "Bombshell," for Jean to film in the future. He was followed almost immediately by Anita Loos, who wanted to know if she should complete the two Harlow stories assigned to her, "Hold Your Man" and "The Girl From Missouri." Both writers were concerned whether Paul's death would affect Jean's career.

"Johnny is only on one, but I'm knocking out two at the same time," Anita said in her little-girl voice and with a silvery laugh declared that she was doubly entitled to know if she was to go on.

I assured her, as I had told Mahin, that the studio

brass showed no intention of abandoning Jean. "Irving and Mr. Mayer are backing her to the limit," I said.

• • •

Story department activity would always wind down in the evening and it even did so on that bizarre Tuesday, September 6. The phones stopped ringing, the secretaries took off, the studio lights that illuminated the walkways came on.

Two years and four months had passed since Thalberg ushered me into the immensely private, immensely elite world of MGM. I was made welcome instantly, and if my appointment to executive status had aroused objections or jealousies I was never aware of it. The studio bosses bared their secrets before me without restraint, clear signs that I was one of them.

Mayer and Strickling were logical men seeking to control an illogical situation. They were going to make it known that Paul's reason for killing himself was impotence and they hoped it would inspire a wave of public sympathy for Jean. The executives had listened to them scream and cajole, and even those of us who didn't believe it were expected to back it up. It was important that we do our best for Jean; there was nothing that any of us could do anymore for Paul.

• • •

That summer, 1932, was impressed in my memory for many reasons—a season of high excitement when

MGM, busily manufacturing magic images, was at its peak of success.

Mobs crowded the studio gates, their eyes fixed on the occupants of every car arriving in the morning, every departing one at night. That summer, the combination of the blockbusting *Tarzan* and the Olympic games in Los Angeles helped increase the usual sightseeing movie fans with sports lovers from around the world. Men, women and children milled around on the grassy lawns to gasp and rush and cheer. Boxer Max Baer and all-around athlete Johnny Mack Brown were favored, but the loudest screams signaled the thrill of seeing Johnny Weissmuller, the swimming star of *Tarzan*.

It was a summer of mounting political activity, too. The elections in November were moving closer, and Louis B. Mayer was deeply involved with the campaign to reelect the president, his friend Herbert Hoover. Famous figures in the field of American politics were among his daily visitors, their egos sadly jolted when peering fans turned away with a loud and impolite "That's nobody!"

When I snapped out the lights in the office and headed home, the fans at the gates were gone. In that quiet and subdued night I couldn't help thinking how sad it was that Paul would be forever remembered by the way he performed in bed with Jean Harlow. That was all the studio thought the world needed to know.

But I knew something about Paul's past that the others didn't know.

5
#####
The Phantom Wife

I DROPPED INTO PAUL'S OFFICE on the Tuesday before that fatal Labor Day holiday. The producer was pacing the floor, obviously in a disturbed frame of mind. He gestured for me to come in and locked the door.

He began to pace again and struck his desk violently with his fist. I sat down, waiting, watching. Finally, Paul calmed down.

"Forgive me, dear Sam. I have a situation on my hands I'm unable to deal with." He stopped as if uncertain that he should go on. He sighed deeply, before starting again . . .

"There's a woman I knew in New York . . . You'll treat this confidentially, please . . ."

Then he launched into a rhapsodic description of Dorothy Millette. "She was an actress . . . breathtaking, enchanting, indescribable . . . the loveliest girl I'd ever seen . . . an ethereal-will-o'-the-wisp.

"We didn't get married. There was no need for it.

We were madly in love. We lived at the Algonquin more than five years and it became a common-law marriage. She was known as Mrs. Bern to the doorman, the elevator operator, at the newsstand.

"One morning," Paul said, "she didn't wake up. I couldn't understand it, I called her name, I shook her. I sent for a doctor. What happened the rest of that day was horrible. She was in a coma and the best medical brains couldn't bring her out of it. Her doctor told me she would never recover.

"I placed her in a sanatorium and came out to California. That was ten years ago." He stopped and sighed forlornly, a long, reflective pause.

"Now," he went on, "she has regained consciousness. As suddenly as she lost it. It's incredible, the way she woke up just like that. To her, these ten years have passed like a single night!"

Paul related that when Dorothy was released from the sanatorium, she moved back to the Algonquin Hotel and wanted him to come to her. He had made a series of excuses, always telling her he was too busy to go east. On the day he told me about Dorothy, she had already come west and was staying at the Plaza Hotel in San Francisco.

"If I don't go and see her by the weekend, she's coming here!"

I asked him if Jean knew about Dorothy and he shook his head.

"I'll tell her when she's more mature."

DOROTHY'S NAME was never mentioned in the executive bungalow, when Paul was branded as impotent. Cedric Gibbons and Al Lewin, who proclaimed their friend's virility, said nothing about the woman who shared his life so many years.

There was a good reason why they didn't. Even his closest associates didn't know about her, they had never heard the name of Dorothy Millette. Paul had guarded his secret successfully.

Now I was sure that Thalberg didn't know about her or he would have realized she was the woman Vorkapich saw Sunday night. She fitted perfectly into what Paul said, "If I don't go and see her by the weekend, she's coming here." But Paul didn't go.

I decided not to divulge what I knew about Dorothy Millette and keep it confidential as Paul had asked. It was possible that nobody else knew.

Nobody, that is, until Wednesday, September 7.

That morning, Paul's brother Henry Bern denied that Dorothy Millette was Paul's wife before anybody said she was.

He revealed it to an astonished group of reporters when the plane flying him to Hollywood stopped to refuel in Kansas City. It came literally out of the blue.

Described by those reporters as a "businessman from New Rochelle, New York," Henry had little of the friendly countenance that radiated from brother Paul. In the flashbulb photographs of Henry that blossomed on newspaper pages around the country he bore little resemblance to Paul's dapper, finely tailored look.

"Paul was never married before he wedded the screen star Jean Harlow," Henry said, "but he lived with a woman once, a long time ago.

"He took care of her just the same as though she were his wife. He had been keeping her in a sanatorium. Miss Harlow knew of it because Paul told her. He concealed nothing but lived openly. Nothing was misrepresented when he married Miss Harlow, I know this."

Henry's disclosure received front page coverage in the Hollywood press, but reporters were unable to confirm if Jean was aware of Dorothy Millette. The young widow remained secluded in her mother's home. Besieged for a statement, attorney Ralph Blum, delegated by Marino Bello as spokesman for Jean, declared she had never heard of Dorothy Millette.

That same day, Louis B. Mayer called in the reporters and told them that Dr. Edward B. Jones, the MGM physician, knew that Paul Bern had a medical problem that caused impotence.

He read them a telegram he received from Dr. Jones, who was vacationing in Honolulu: UNDERSTAND MOTIVE WILL LEAVE AT ONCE TO TESTIFY FOR YOU AND MISS HARLOW IF NECESSARY.

However, a coroner's inquest was scheduled by Los Angeles County Coroner Frank Nance for Thursday morning; obviously Dr. Jones's ship was not going to get him back to Los Angeles in time.

• • •

Henry Bern's plane touched down in Los Angeles and he stepped out to face a cadre of reporters waiting for him. They resembled a small army.

"I want no secrets veiling the matter of my brother's death," he said. "He never had secrets from anyone." He was surprised that his listeners were so skeptical. Henry promised to look into the entire tragedy and make an important statement "soon enough!"

Howard Strickling moved quickly to take Henry in tow in order to prevent him from making further provocative headlines, especially since the impotence motive that MGM was promoting was now being eclipsed by Henry's disclosures. Strickling believed that if it weren't for Henry Bern's revelation about Dorothy Millette, Paul's death would have been a quickly forgotten story.

Immediately after he spoke out, Henry's statement that Paul "took care of her just the same as though she were his wife" touched off an intensive search for the woman newspapers around the country were describing as "Bern's Other Wife" and "Bern's Phantom Wife." There was no way now that Strickling could stop that from spreading.

In Colorado Springs, insurance salesman George C. Clarken revealed he had sold a life policy to Paul payable "to a woman he married ten years before and never divorced."

In New York, attorney Henry Uttal stated that back

in August 1920, he drew up a will in which Paul left most of his wealth to "my wife, Dorothy Millette."

"She was a blonde," Uttal declared. "Not the platinum blond type of Jean Harlow. They came to my house often and I knew her as his wife. There was never any suspicion in my mind that they might not be married."

The attorney added that he had received a letter from Paul a week after his marriage to Jean. In it, the producer spoke of his happiness at finding the perfect wife.

"I had no idea what had become of his first wife," the lawyer went on, "but in view of his marriage to Miss Harlow I assumed that she was dead."

Los Angeles detectives issued an urgent request that informants come forward and answer these questions: "Who is this mysterious Dorothy Millette? Where is she now? Was she actually the wife of Paul Bern and is she alive now and divorced from the film man?"

No relatives, friends, or acquaintances appeared. Paul had told me in confidence about his affair with Dorothy Millette, it was a private matter, so I continued to keep secret what I knew.

• • •

The coroner's inquest was to be held at the Price-Daniel funeral parlor in West Los Angeles, where Paul's body still lay.

Studio attorney Mendel Silberberg told the press, "We can see no reason for conducting an inquest in view of the fact that the police and everyone else is satisfied that Bern took his own life. There is no mystery about the matter; nothing further to be investigated."

"Nevertheless," declared coroner Nance, "I have ordered the inquest to do away with any thoughts that anyone is trying to conceal anything in this case, any idle gossip, therefore there will be an inquest as planned."

There were high expectations that Jean would be the star of the proceedings, but Dr. Robert Kennicott sent a letter explaining that "Miss Harlow suffered a severe nervous collapse and her appearance could gravely endanger her life." She was excused.

So was Henry Bern. He was supposedly too exhausted from his trip. When he failed to show up, the coroner proceeded with the inquest without him. Bello, Thalberg, and Paul's servants testified and satisfied everyone.

The official verdict was "death by gunshot wound of the head, self-inflicted by the deceased with suicidal intent. Motive undetermined."

A CROWD OF TWO THOUSAND curious sightseers stood outside the Grace Chapel where the funeral took place Friday, September 9, in the Los Angeles suburb of Inglewood. Services were conducted by Rabbi Edgar Magnin behind a floral display estimated to cost $25,000, some of it piled around the coffin and some out onto the lawn. "The greatest in Hollywood history," said the undertaker.

Film star Conrad Nagel offered a eulogy, describing Paul "as naive as a child, never bowing to insincerity, a creative artist living in motion pictures where one lives a dozen characters." Among Nagel's listeners, Jean Harlow wept softly and Paul's sister Friederike Marcus screamed loudly. Later, Mrs. Marcus gave this printed statement to the press:

PAUL'S SISTER SPEAKS

The dearest soul on earth is laid to rest today. He did not want to rest yet. He wanted to live. Life had everything for him to enjoy to the utmost capacity. He loved his work and his surroundings. He had faced many big problems in his life. Many big heartaches but he always faced the music. About twenty years ago he fell in love with a girl by the name of Dorothy Millette. He was never married to her but he lived with her for several years. Then she became sick and was admitted to a sanatorium.

Paul was heartbroken. The man went around like a shadow. He mourned like he mourned for a dead one. He did not take his life. He would not think of putting her in a cheap sanatorium, although he could not afford to keep her in such an expensive place.

He struggled hard. He fought to give her all possible comfort and supported her since. He told me long ago that his love for her was gone, but his sympathy remained. It was a terrible blow to him but he stood up.

His idea of happiness was to make someone else happy. The Metro-Goldwyn-Mayer Studio was his home. He was extremely happy in it. Then along came Jean.

He thought he was the luckiest man on earth to find all that he wanted. It was a short dream because two months later he took his own life.

Why did he do it? What drove him to it? What does it mean? "Last night was only a comedy," he wrote in his last note. We were not there to see it. Why don't the ones who know tell us about it? Aren't we entitled to know?

He was more to me than a brother. He told me many of his secrets, and told me many times how he spent his life in the company of young girls, living with many of them in Hollywood, and enjoying life to the greatest extent.

I think he was a good man and if he found life unbearable now, then let him rest and sleep as he deserves to sleep. A big soul, a big heart and a big character have been laid to rest.

JEAN HAD REMAINED out of sight until the funeral, while fan magazines and movie feature writers pondered her future. They questioned if she could survive the burning glare of sensational publicity, which they themselves were subjecting her to.

Some movie magazine writers claimed to have quotes from her about Paul's physical disabilities, but there was no truth to them. She had promised the studio she would never ever discuss it and she never did.

Mayer and Thalberg were convinced that, in a short

time, Jean's natural appeal to audiences would surmount the stigma attached to her by her precipitate widowhood.

Production of *Red Dust*, in which Jean was costarring with Clark Gable, was temporarily shut down in deference to her mourning.

A huge quantity of letters and telegrams expressing sympathy for Jean piled up at the studio, helping to reinforce the company's faith in her continuing career. She had landed among its great young women stars: with Norma Shearer, Joan Crawford and Greta Garbo, she had become a priceless asset to be protected at any cost.

It was MGM's custom to shelter all aspects of the lives of its stars. It stemmed from Louis B. Mayer's reverence for them—he was, if anything, a bigger fan than anyone who mobbed the players at the gates.

He was always on the lookout for that elusive something he called "star quality." He recognized the potentials, he said, by a gleam in a performer's eyes, face, or personality. He compared himself to a horse trainer knowing a thoroughbred: he trusted his intuition that he saw "winner" written all over them.

The records do indeed show how much better he was at discovering a star than Thalberg, who was best at selecting the parts they should play and maintaining them in their exalted places.

But Mayer's discoveries needed Thalberg's talent to keep their names shining on theater marquees. Their complementary abilities were the real foundation of their success: they accepted each other's differences and gloried in their talents that brought them money and fame.

When Jean joined MGM's constellation of luminaries, trained men and women went into action, as they had with others, their mission being to maximize her winning ways and minimize her liabilities. All her public appearances came under their professional scrutiny. Although designers would give consideration to her personal tastes, the clothes she wore carefully matched the image the studio had chosen for her.

All telephone calls to Jean at the studio were screened and her mail was opened. Obscene letters—and Jean got plenty of them—were instantly trashed. A studio secretary was assigned to her, one who could imitate her handwriting, "personally" answer legitimate fan mail and autograph her photos, duties that, in Jean's case, had heretofore been handled by her mother.

All the contract stars were constantly admonished that these studio's rules were in their own best interest and it would be wise to obey them. They were not to drink in public. Unmarried players were asked to accept studio-chosen escorts for public appearances and the studio sought to break up any alliance with characters considered unwholesome. It was an unending war to avoid scandal.

It was pointed out to Jean that her well-being would now be sheltered by unlimited money and power, she was secure against hostile forces whenever they appeared.

At the time Paul died—and Jean's newly acquired stardom was largely due to Paul—no one knew better than Mayer that her films would bring millions of dollars into the company. Any investment that had to be made, any actions that had to be taken on her behalf were worth it. Jean was the youngest, prettiest, and most ravishing of all those glittering luminaries. Not even Mayer could see the limits of her future career; she might soar into the stratosphere, that was a possibility he *could* see.

Consistent with his belief that the men and women who toiled at MGM were his children, Jean had become a precious new daughter. He was willing to overlook her previous sins because, in effect, she was born again when MGM took over her contract from Howard Hughes. The studio even increased her paycheck over the amount that Hughes was paying her. That was consistent with their desire to make their stars happy, prevent them from complaining that they were being exploited.

Mayer wasn't happy with her marriage to Paul—visions of her in sexual intercourse with a man twice her age could tarnish the fantasies of her fans, but the sexy comedy roles Thalberg would give her would overcome that. The way was all mapped out for her, with no foreseeable obstacles.

• • •

After the police showed up at Paul's house the morning he was found shot, Thalberg's wife, Norma Shearer, came over to drive her husband home. "Irving was a wreck," she told me years later, when we talked about what had happened that day. "I was anxious to get him to rest but he insisted that he had to talk to Jean. He was lost in thought all the way there.

"I parked near the Bello house by the golf course and I saw Mama Jean show him out on a little balcony. I could see through some wooden slats of the balcony railing, he was pacing back and forth and then, finally, Baby Jean came out. She was wearing fluffy feathery lingerie over a long nightgown. They stood facing each other and he was saying something, then she slumped but he caught her and helped her back into the house.

"I thought Irving had been chosen to break the news to Jean that Paul was dead because her mother had given her sedatives and she slept all that morning.

"But when Irving came back to the car, he was looking kind of strange. He slumped down in the seat next to me and then I found out that he had gone there to tell her that the studio had everything under control. 'She claims she doesn't understand what I mean,' was all he said. Then he burst into tears. It was a terrible, terrible day!"

• • •

Although Henry Bern did not appear at the inquest, later that day he managed to talk to the press again about Dorothy and revealed that about two months earlier he had taken her to the train in New York to go to San Francisco. She was staying there at the Plaza Hotel.

Henry's statement was electrifying and from that moment, reporters began searching for her like a pack of hunting dogs. Close behind them were the MGM studio police and Strickling's publicity men. They learned Dorothy was away from her room in the hotel through the Labor Day weekend; then she returned and checked out without leaving a forwarding address.

She had last been seen by hotel employees the day after Paul's body was found.

"I believe poor Dorothy is dead," said Henry Bern, with tears streaming from his eyes.

• • •

While reporters were searching for Dorothy in the San Francisco area, the Los Angeles press attempted to trace Paul's movements during the final days of his life. The hunt was spiced by a tip from a bellhop who saw and recognized the producer going into one of the Ambassador Hotel cottages Saturday evening with an unknown man and woman. Armed with that information, the newshounds took off in full cry. Unable to identify the couple, they blasted away with sinister conjectures that the couple must have been involved with the events leading to his death.

When the search for that man and woman was at its height, I received an urgent call to come to Thalberg's office. Producer Bernard Hyman was curled up on a couch, a picture of abject misery.

"Meet the mystery man," Thalberg said to me, putting a grim twist of humor into his greeting. "I better tell you the whole story."

He explained that Hyman had become enamored of

Barbara Barondess, a young actress, recently arrived from Broadway. He made a dinner date with her, hoping it would progress to a more intimate Saturday night encounter. But where? Hyman had asked Paul, the studio's executive sophisticate, for help.

"The Ambassador Hotel," Paul had advised.

Hyman, married and nervous, knew that the hotel's lush, romantic Coconut Grove was the most popular gathering spot in town, the "in" place where one went to be seen. Being seen was just what he did not want. The very idea frightened him.

"You don't need to go near the main part of the hotel," Paul had told him. "Phone ahead and reserve one of the bungalows. Ask the room clerk to leave one unlocked for you and charge it to your account."

But Hyman was still uneasy. "Come with us," he had pleaded with Paul. "Have a drink and then you can make an excuse and leave."

Always willing to help a friend in distress, Paul did exactly that. He was right, Hyman was not recognized, but ironically, Paul was. It was the last time he was seen in public.

When Hyman confessed to Thalberg that it was he whom the newspapers were looking for, Thalberg made a personal call to the publishers of the Los Angeles newspapers, the *Times* and *Examiner*, and persuaded them to call off their search because the identity of the "unknown couple" was of no consequence.

He also called Barbara Barondess to tell her she mustn't talk about the incident. But the young actress had already leaked to New York *Daily News* columnist Sidney Skolsky that she was the girl and MGM producer Bernie Hyman was the man they were looking for.

Thalberg knew that Skolsky and I were friends from the time we prowled the Broadway theatrical scene together.

Irving asked me if I could persuade Sidney to kill the story. I hustled back to my office and phoned him. Unlike other Hollywood gossip columnists on the order of Walter Winchell and Louella Parsons, who would have given their right eye for that kind of item, Sidney wasn't interested in what went on behind bedroom doors. Even though he had a hot and exclusive scoop, one that would have made a juicy yarn for readers of his tabloid *Daily News* column, he spiked it. He never put it out and nobody knew; the mystery couple dropped right out of the news.

Finally Dr. Jones arrived by boat from Honolulu and declared, "Bern's suicide was due to an acute melancholia and nervous strain which developed into a mania. His case was entirely mental. He was in good physical condition when I left for Honolulu."

He would have nothing further to say until he conferred with Mr. L. B. Mayer, which he did—and after that conference he still had nothing further to say. While he had been sailing home the public's attention had shifted to Dorothy Millette, who was still missing. It was no longer necessary to speak of Paul's impotence.

● ● ●

It had been a rough week for Henry. The disclosures he promised fizzled out, although he did say, "Certain complications which have come to my attention make it impossible for me to give out a statement. Please don't ask me what these complications are. Let's just say that when they have been straightened out I will tell all."

MGM had let him use Paul's office during this trying time, and while Dorothy was still among the missing, I went over to pay my respects. But Henry had left town —he was gone, vanished suddenly. He rode into Hollywood like an avenging hero in a western thriller and disappeared like a star whose role had landed on the cutting-room floor.

• • •

On September 14, a decomposed body was found in the Sacramento River. The remains were that of a woman five-foot-three in height. A few wisps of titian-colored hair, when shown to the personnel of the Plaza Hotel, helped to identify Dorothy Millette. Henry Bern's prediction that Dorothy was dead proved to be all too true.

Nobody claimed the body, no one showed up to throw new light on who she really was; in death she was as remote as she had been in life, and as each new day turned the world's attention to other things, Paul and his phantom wife faded into history.

6
·····
A Time of Change

I HAD MY HANDS FULL, literally, in those days.

Story department readers at the studio in Culver City and the offices in New York and London were covering an average of four hundred books, plays, short stories, and news features every week, everything that might be considered a possibility for a movie. They digested twenty thousand pieces of material a year and forwarded them to my attention. The only way I could diminish the stack of reports on the desk was to engage in a non-stop reading marathon.

There was little chance to mourn Paul, although a fleeting thought about him sometimes flashed through my mind, especially when a story I was reading dealt with characters torn by a hopeless love. I was convinced that Paul was caught in that sort of situation and I theorized that he was unable to find his way out of his predicament.

Two months after Paul died, Franklin D. Roosevelt

unseated Louis B. Mayer's friend Herbert Hoover as president of the United States. Mayer's devotion to Hoover's Republican party was so strong that the changeover to Roosevelt's Democratic administration caused him to curtail his political activities. He went back to fulltime devotion to studio operation—a very timely decision because one month after that, Thalberg sustained a severe heart attack and needed time to recover. He sailed to Europe for a rest and some medical attention.

Mayer took command. He engaged in valiant efforts to maintain the glory and hold his empire together. He asked David Selznick, a highly regarded film creator and the husband of his daughter Irene, to join his staff. Selznick agreed on condition that he receive a producer credit on the titles of his films; since this was not done at MGM, his demand had to be put to Thalberg.

Thalberg cabled from Europe that he had no objections to producer credits and advised "his boys" that they, too, were free to put their names on the screen. For the first time, MGM productions showed who made its movies, all except Thalberg's, for he still rejected screen credit when he returned six months later to resume filmmaking for his own new unit.

He had become an independent producer on the MGM lot but fumed at his inability to use the studio's great stars, many of whom he had developed. Selznick and other newly added producers had already cast them in stories developed in his absence. But with the passing of time, he got the actors back, making a string of successful films that included *Mutiny on the Bounty* with Clark Gable's Fletcher Christian opposing Charles Laughton as Captain Bligh, *A Night at the Opera* with the Marx Brothers, Helen Hayes in *What Every Woman Knows*, Norma Shearer in *The Barretts of Wimpole Street* and *Romeo and Juliet*, Greta Garbo in *Camille*, and Jean Harlow romping joyfully with Gable and Wallace Beery in *China Seas*.

During the Labor Day holiday, 1936, four years after Paul Bern died, Irving Thalberg fell ill and passed away —the dreaded moment that everyone knew would come. His last film, *The Good Earth*, Pearl Buck's epic of China, was still incomplete when he died. A tribute to Thalberg was offered on it, the only screen credit he ever had. He was thirty-seven years old.

After Paul died, studio life had never seemed quite the same to me, and with Thalberg's passing I felt a strong need to assert myself. I no longer felt bound to sidetrack my writing aspirations.

That long-deferred desire to emulate some of the very people I had been hiring was news to Louis B. Mayer. He was not impressed.

"Why do you want to be a writer?" he asked. "You're a boss of writers. I'll make you a producer and you can be an even bigger boss of writers." To Mayer, being boss was everything.

I segued into producing, tutored by Lucien Hubbard, a versatile individual who had come and gone and come back again many times to the studio since 1927, sometimes writing, sometimes directing or producing. He had returned in 1937 as the head of a B-picture unit, making low-budget films. Hubbard was affectionately called "the keeper of the bees" when I became his associate. I made two forgettable little films and the third, *A Family Affair*, was still in the editing process on a day that Mayer requested my immediate presence.

It wasn't due to my making a couple of unsuccessful movies—I don't suppose they even entered his mind. It was because of *Gone With the Wind*.

When the still unpublished book was first submitted to MGM, a detailed synopsis was circulated to all the producers on the lot. I, of course, was one of them. We were asked to read it and return our opinions on a detachable memorandum to Edwin Knopf, my successor in the Story department. Based on those producer comments, MGM rejected *Gone With the Wind*.

After only a short time at MGM, David Selznick formed an independent company and bought the film rights to *Gone With the Wind*. After he acquired it, the book became a great best-seller and Mayer, miffed that it got away—perhaps more so because it was his own son-in-law who had corralled it—wanted to know how it happened that MGM missed out on it. He called Knopf to bring him his producers' comments about the book. What he read caused him to send for me.

He was standing by his oversized cream-colored desk when I entered his office. He had my memorandum (which I had forgotten) in his hand, all the others were in a pile on the desk in front of him. He was wearing reading glasses, and it was evident from the way his hand was shaking that he was fighting to keep his emotions intact.

He said, "Listen carefully, Marx," and then read: " 'This has all the elements anyone needs to make a great movie. Too bad it's out of my reach in a B-unit, but the studio should buy it immediately!' "

He put it down on the desk, then picked up all the others and flung them on the floor. This was drama in the making. His voice started low but climbed to a roar.

"Why didn't you come to me? Why should you care if it was out of your reach or what it would cost? Don't you realize that if you had come to me to buy that book for you, you would be the biggest man in the motion picture industry today?"

I stood there, numb and speechless. He made it seem like I was the one who had done something wrong, but I knew that if I had asked for *Gone With the Wind* it was more than likely he would have said, "You're getting too big for your britches, stick to the B-movies you're supposed to make."

A few days later I was told that the Lucien Hubbard unit was being disbanded and Mr. Mayer wanted me to resume my old job as head of the Story department. I talked it over with Marie and we agreed it was a backward step. Now, I was a producer.

A Family Affair was yet to be previewed when I left the studio and joined the staff of Samuel Goldwyn. A smiling, beguiling Goldwyn was very understanding of my desire to write. He said, "You found fifty stories every year for my friend Thalberg. I only make four a year, so in a month you'll be producing for me and writing, too."

His mathematics seemed adequate, but he failed to take into account that he couldn't make up his mind which four stories he wanted, so he turned down everything submitted to him. Story editing had become my full-time job again. I was part of a small, unhappy group toiling under an unreasonable entrepreneur who was convinced that everyone taking a salary from him was robbing him. Life on the other side of town, at MGM, didn't seem so bad after all. My little film *A Family Affair* had caught on in a big way and was to be continued with further adventures as the Hardy Family. I had jumped ship too soon.

JEAN HARLOW died on June 7, 1937, while I was working for Goldwyn. Her death at twenty-six at the height of her career was a devastating shock. Mama Jean was a Christian Scientist devoted to the tenets of that faith and she denied medical treatment for her daughter until it was too late. When doctors finally saw her they claimed that newly discovered sulphur drugs could have saved the young star's life. They attributed her passing to a massive infection but its cause was never documented, only rumored that it might have started from such disparate origins as a neglected toothache or a botched abortion.

I still maintained an interest in the details of Paul

Bern's death even after these five years but Jean and I never discussed it. Adela Rogers St. Johns, a hardworking Hollywood journalist, trumpeted that she had been given the only interview with Jean after Paul's death.

It appeared in *Liberty* magazine, headlined JEAN HARLOW TELLS THE INSIDE STORY ABOUT HER HUSBAND'S SUICIDE. A careful reading produced little more from Jean than the known facts and that she loved him. She simply kept repeating, "Isn't this too terrible! But I mustn't talk about it—I can't—I can't." Miss Rogers quoted Mrs. Bello as saying, "Do you know Jean never told even me of the circumstances of her marriage? She has the most beautiful, loyal nature." As Miss Rogers was leaving the house, Jean's mother said to her, "There is something I *wish* I could tell you. But I cannot—now or ever." And true to that statement, no one ever found out what she meant.

Along with Paul and Dorothy, Jean, too, left unexplained the details that she knew. There could no longer be any intimate information from any of the three principals in the Bern triangle.

There were only rumors that continued to flare up through the coming decades.

7

·····

Flare-ups

AFTER A PERIOD of desperation with Goldwyn I circulated through the executive corridors of Harry Cohn's Columbia studio. It was a relief to escape Goldwyn. Cohn was moderately amusing, unreasonably argumentative, and utterly erratic. While the films of Goldwyn and Cohn gave evidence that both men possessed a flair for showmanship, Mayer and Thalberg were towering giants alongside them.

On an afternoon in August 1939, Cohn sent me to Saratoga, New York, to see the play *Gaslight*. Theatrical productions were performed only at night in Saratoga, because the days of that month were reserved exclusively for the city's racetrack. I was absorbed in the intricacies of the racing form when a man came over and stood next to me. It was Louis B. Mayer and he asked, "When are you coming home?"

Mayer was in Saratoga to buy thoroughbred race horses for himself, which he did, and the film rights to

Gaslight for the studio, which he also did, outbidding Columbia. In 1940, in response to his invitation, I went back to MGM. It was like returning to the old hometown: you walk familiar streets and the people are comfortable to be with, but you must adjust to changes made in your absence.

In the three years I was away, the old front office building, that busy beehive of production activity, once occupied by Irving and his boys, had become headquarters for Howard Strickling's Publicity department.

An enlarged group of producers were now housed in the four-story Thalberg Building, newly built, a huge white edifice, quite majestic in appearance, even awesome. It gave substance to the once flimsy industry.

The Thalberg Building was just outside the studio wall. Paul Bern, had he lived, would surely have had his office there, but the old-timers were thinning out. Harry Rapf was still prominent; with his lengthy producing experience, he now headed the unit in which I was placed. There was no further talk of returning to the Story department, nor, for that matter, was there any talk of writing. I was given a ground-floor corner office in the building; my windows looked out on a busy undertaker's establishment next door. The individuals housed in my side of the Thalberg Building were known rather unflatteringly as "The Dead-End Kids." I had become a full-fledged producer without trying.

Louis B. Mayer had a large suite on the third floor. There were six projection rooms in the basement; a gymnasium and a chiropractor were set up on the fourth floor, where the doctor did a brisk business cracking the necks and vertebrae of the stars and the big and small monarchs who kept developing muscular pains from success.

Also on that floor, an executive dining room functioned exactly the way the old one did. The food was the same, it was free for all who were invited there—but the intimate feeling of the Thalberg days was gone, the room crowded up at noon with a large staff of assorted functionaries, successors to Mayer's Men, now called "The College of Cardinals."

The bungalow that once housed the dining room had become a school for the studio's underage actors and actresses. Mickey Rooney, still playing Andy Hardy in continuing spinoffs of *A Family Affair*, was an occasional pupil, as were Elizabeth Taylor and Roddy McDowall, stars in *Lassie Come-Home*, the best of the movies I made in those early 1940s. Our friendships that began then would continue unbroken from that time, when the moments crawled but the years flew by.

I was still there in the 1950s, when ambitious Dore Schary took away the power of Louis B. Mayer. Mayer was still hanging on to some semblance of his earlier importance, but the executives in the company's New York office chose to favor Schary. Mayer's control of the studio was slipping away.

The problems and the changing character of MGM were affecting me personally, so I went abroad to wander through the metropolitan areas of Europe—and I fell in love with London and Paris. It would always be the cities that would attract me, I had a fondness for pavement underfoot.

Hamburg, Germany, where I spent a few days, reminded me that Paul was born in Wandsbek, a suburb of that city. It was a part of the general information I had learned about him when I read the old *Photoplay* magazine piece by Jim Tully.

I was always curious about Tully's opening statement, one that I thought was truly extraordinary: "He was one of a weird brood of eighteen children."

Only brother Henry and sister Friederike were at Paul's funeral, both of them highly visible. If Tully's count was authentic, where were the others? What had become of fifteen brothers and sisters? What better way to check that out than in the town where he was born?

But, as a stranger in that war-ravaged city of Hamburg and not knowing the language, finding the records of a Jewish family named Bern—one that moved to America long before the holocaust of World War II—proved to be a verbal struggle. In fact, Paul's family had moved away before World War I. The German authorities might have tried to help me if I proved a blood relationship, but I couldn't, my curiosity wasn't enough to move them; against such handicaps, my search for papers went nowhere.

I went back home with thoughts of writing, but an offer arrived from Universal Pictures, and in 1955 I rejoined the company I was with when I first met Thalberg.

Universal was in disarray, its two top administrators,

convivial and extremely uncreative Eddie Muhl and Jim Pratt, were in awe of ace producer Aaron Rosenberg, a former University of Southern California football star. Rosenberg called all the signals, he assigned two productions to me in which I had little interest. Marie and I were raising two young sons, and the alibi I gave my friends for again postponing the speculative way of an author's life was the corruption imposed on us by a weekly paycheck. We settled back into life in Beverly Hills.

Universal had numerous players under contract, most of them very young, almost all of them bearing names designed to set them apart from such familiar stars at other studios as Clark, Cary, and Gary. The juveniles on Universal's roster included Rock, Rory, Race, and Rip, the ingenues Mara, Mamie, Lisa, Shelley, and Piper.

When I met Joyce van der Veen at the Universal studio, a beautiful young ballerina who had been signed to an acting contract, I naturally thought that she, too, had been christened by the company's imaginative Publicity department, where most of those names originated. But Joyce van der Veen was her real name, she did not see any point in changing it but agreed to put it all together as Vanderveen. In time, Joyce would figure strongly in the search to unravel the mystery surrounding Paul Bern.

• • •

After-dark socializing among Hollywood executives always revolved within the circle of one's daytime associates. But there was very little camaraderie at Universal. Gone were the lively and glamorous nights, the previews and parties at MGM, the gambling in Sunset Strip casinos with associates of Goldwyn and Columbia. Consequently, Marie and I did little mixing with the workers at Universal.

We spent many evenings walking through the residential sections of Beverly Hills. Often we stopped at the post office for the mail in box 44, the address I used during my European sojourn. Occasionally we ran into acquaintances—the post office was a meeting place where one exchanged news and gossip. One evening a woman talent agent declared she thought box number 44 so attractive that she wanted me to will it to her. I kept it.

During those walks it was impossible for us to ignore the blue lights that glowed in the windows of the houses we passed: it appeared that everybody who might be at the movies was at home watching television.

Lucille Ball and her husband Desi Arnaz had formed Desilu Productions, and their cavortings in *I Love Lucy* kept most of America glued to their sets every Monday night. Television was becoming too intrusive to be ignored, and I accepted an invitation from Desilu to enter the world of electronic entertainment.

For two years as their executive producer I studied the incredible economics that ruled the making of TV shows. Advertising agencies dictated what could and could not be done. The medium was presenting a form of glitzy costume jewelry and it dazzled the country.

Involvement in television in those pioneer times, especially with Desilu's successful series like *I Love Lucy* and *December Bride*, gave me an aura of knowing more than I really did.

It may have seemed that way to Joseph Vogel, the new head of MGM. Vogel had become the top executive in the company after the New York office got rid of Dore Schary. With television in mind, Vogel said to me, "You're just the man I've been looking for!"

Metro-Goldwyn-Mayer had been turning out full-length feature films for thirty years and was poorly equipped for the making of small-screen entertainment. Neither Louis B. Mayer nor Dore Schary had shown any liking for that form of production, and their attitude was shared by most of the studio's employees. Vogel felt differently: he knew nothing at all about it but considered television a necessary adjunct to the big studio.

I took the job as executive producer of the Television Division, and discovered that pushing MGM into that new medium was like trying to get an elephant out of the starting gate at Santa Anita racetrack. It seemed as if every move wedged it tighter into its stall.

When a pilot for *The Thin Man* was finally sold, it created an entirely new problem. Actor Peter Lawford had assumed the male lead and, by virtue of being the brother-in-law of the president of the United States, John F. Kennedy, Lawford believed that he, too, was a commander-in-chief. I endured that situation for two years and then, besieged with offers from other companies, I accepted one from Associated British Television in London, a highly regulated equivalent of the big American networks.

In America, a tyrannical advertiser could raise hell with programming, but in England, licensing regulations imposed by a government-appointed bureaucrat could destroy a company. Producing acceptable programs was an ongoing battle around the world. All television companies were struggling with the anguish of their pioneer existence.

I was in the middle of that in England, in 1960, when Ben Hecht wrote a column in America for *Esquire* magazine proclaiming that Paul Bern was murdered back in 1932. Hecht stated that director Henry Hathaway knew all about it; the Los Angeles authorities checked this out, but they dropped the investigation when Hathaway could reveal nothing new.

I, too, dismissed Hecht's assertion. It was contrary to my own ideas, but the incident was indicative of how stories about Paul's death continued to hold the public's fascination.

Four years later, when I was back in Hollywood, I looked at a book called *Harlow* that had just appeared. Author Irving Shulman wrote Jean's life story using material chiefly provided by her agent, Arthur Landau. The book is filled with scandalous and vicious innuendoes. It falsifies many incidents, portraying Jean, her mother, and especially Paul as such freaky people that I was utterly enraged.

He portrayed Paul as a nonentity and wondered how he could get himself someone like Harlow. The book claims that Jean Harlow married a "cruel, insane, sex pervert."

Anita Loos, Adela Rogers St. Johns, and other friends of Jean called me to a meeting, intending to do something about it, something "to show we mean business," Anita said, "like publicly denouncing it."

But Howard Strickling, whose public relations expertise was expected to spearhead our protest, said, "You may as well face it, you can't stop the book, you'll just be calling attention to it. All you'll do is sell more copies." Consequently we took no action.

The book *Harlow* continued to circulate. It reports in detail that Bern brutally beat Jean on their wedding night, her body bruised and bleeding. This account is the source of the legend that has persisted through the years. Typically, careless researchers, gloating over its raw allegations, made use of the incorrect items about Jean and Paul from that time on.

8
·····
Enigma

EARLY IN THE 1970S, I finally said to Marie, *"Nobody is going to stop me from writing."* I had written a few screenplays in my odd hours, which were performed by such capable players as Edward G. Robinson, Robert Taylor, and others; but fifty years in the world of movies and television had interfered with my true goal, book writing.

The notes I had gathered for a profile of Irving Thalberg, combined with newer observations of Louis B. Mayer at close range, provided the contents of *Mayer and Thalberg: The Make-Believe Saints*, which Random House published in 1974.

It was accomplished at last, I had written my first book! But sadly, Marie wasn't there to share it: she died suddenly during the writing. I dedicated the book to her, writing of the loss I sustained, "Her years were not enough."

The death of Paul Bern, such a dramatic interlude in

my early years at the MGM studio, comprises an entire chapter in my reflections—a chapter called "The Suicide of Paul Bern," in which I speculated on why Paul Bern killed himself.

Many readers who were not around when it happened had to be brought up to date, so I described the marriage of Jean Harlow and her adoring groom: the momentous drama that began to unfold beneath the surface of laughter, romance, and glamour. The reasons for his suicide, less than three months after the wedding, had remained a mystery.

The press was in a frenzy: all kinds of theories were presented by reporters who delved into every nuance that they were able to find in the life of a man who so violently removed himself from the living.

I tried to make sense of what I knew at the time and I included the suicide note as it was reported in the early editions of the newspapers—the puzzling words "frightful wrong" and "last night was only a comedy." Henry Bern's revelation of Dorothy Millette, known at New York's Algonquin Hotel as Mrs. Paul Bern, seemed to be the key: I reasoned that his relationship with her, his common-law wife, was the "frightful wrong" Paul supposedly did to Jean.

It is likely there would have been no others in Paul's life, certainly no Jean Harlow, had not Dorothy Millette been stricken with an illness that caused amnesia. She was confined to a Connecticut sanatorium where a succession of doctors diagnosed her as incurable. Bern had agreed to take care of her as long as she lived, and he moved to Hollywood, where he tried to leave the nightmare behind.

Suddenly, in the summer of 1932, Dorothy Millette's mind cleared: the years she had spent in the sanatorium seemed to her like a single night. She was told Paul was in California, married to Jean Harlow, of whom she had never heard. Dorothy Millette believed Paul was *her* husband.

She left the sanatorium and waited for him to come see her. It put him in a desperate predicament; he wrote her that he was too busy to come east, until she became angry and said she would come west to California. Then he asked her to go to San Francisco, where he promised to see her. However, he kept putting that off too, until she told him she was on her way to see him in Los Angeles. When Bern found out, he deliberately quarreled with Jean, who behaved as predictably as a conventional-minded bride—she went home to Mother. Bern the writer had staged "last night's comedy" in a truly bravura performance.

The argument the neighbors heard by the swimming pool was followed by the departure of the veiled woman: Dorothy had refused to understand Paul's situation. He knew that if she brought a charge of bigamy, it would finish Jean's career. The broken glass by the edge of the pool was a silent witness to the way Bern clenched his fist when he decided what he had to do.

After Bern's death, Dorothy boarded the *Delta King* and threw herself into the swirling muddy waters of the Sacramento River.

• • •

I finished Bern's story with a blast at the studio-inspired reports of impotency. Instead, I presented his suicide as the ultimate gesture of a chivalric gentleman torn by the fear that his bigamous action, committed when he thought Dorothy Millette was past caring, would bring disgrace to the two women he loved.

And my account of the tragedy found a place among the many legends of Hollywood.

IN THE BELIEF that Hollywood was eager to put flesh on skeletons in its closets, the editors in charge of television's *Entertainment Tonight* focused on the suicide of Paul Bern in the autumn of 1986. The story of the producer's death was a part of movie history. Mention of it was sure to cause someone to say, "Oh yes, he's the guy who killed himself because he was impotent!"

An acquaintance, Wayne Warga, previously employed by the "Calendar" section of the *Los Angeles Times*, was helping write the show. He called and asked me if I wanted to air my view of the tragedy.

Although fifty-four years had passed, I remembered perfectly the event, especially the day in the executive bungalow when Louis B. Mayer had so dramatically rammed the motive—"Impotence!"—down his executives' throats. I agreed to appear, and we set a time to tape an interview during the next week.

At a Sunday night screening for members of the Motion Picture Academy, I saw Joyce Vanderveen, my friend from Universal, in the audience. She had the classic look of a ballerina, a slender figure topped by dark hair pulled sharply into a tight bun—she could have stepped daintily out of any Degas painting. In her native Holland, Joyce was a famous dancer. She went to Paris and joined the renowned Grand Ballet du Marquis de Cuevas and performed with that company all over the world. After coming to Hollywood, Joyce combined her career in the dance world with film acting, and while under contract at Universal, she met Louis Blaine, the studio's director of foreign publicity, and married him. Their marriage lasted a quarter of a century.

When we met at the Academy, Joyce was agonizing over her husband's death and I was still getting over the loss of Marie. After the screening, we sat down in a café to catch up with the years since we had last seen each other.

We spoke of Marie and Louis Blaine, then changed to a less painful subject. The *Entertainment Tonight* interview concerning Jean Harlow and Paul Bern was due to be taped on Wednesday. I sketched out a few points I intended to make, to fight the innuendoes against Paul's reputation and stress his gallantry.

Joyce listened intently.

"You're a good audience," I told her.

"I know very little about it. This is the first time I've heard any details. There are things about it that strike me as very odd."

"Really? I always thought it quite clear. A suicide by a gallant man caught between two loves. The other woman was in a coma for ten years and then came back in his life. I plan to tell what I know about her on that TV show. Do you want a preview?"

"Go ahead," she said and ordered another cup of coffee.

JOYCE CAME ALONG with me that afternoon of September 24, 1986, when I was interviewed for *Entertainment Tonight* at the Paramount studio in Hollywood. It was conducted by an assistant producer who remained outside camera range while she persistently asked questions far afield from what I planned to say. Nevertheless, I managed to maneuver my answers back on track at times, and we covered a great deal of ground during the hour the camera focused on me.

But the Paul Bern segment that I taped bore little resemblance to what was shown when *Entertainment Tonight* aired November 3. Joyce and I watched it together.

Actress Rue McClanahan appeared as guest host. It looked like she was interviewing me on the show, but I never met her.

"We walk a tightrope in Hollywood," she said, "with our private lives on one side and your public perceptions of us on the other." Over a scene of Harlow in *Hell's Angels*, she introduced "Jean Harlow, that great platinum blonde of the 1930s, sexy, alluring, the perfect screen star."

Television shows based on reality generally provide their audiences with someone who seems to have all the facts about a subject and can talk earnestly about them. *Entertainment Tonight* faithfully followed that format but came up with Laurie Jacobson, who was not around when it happened. The author of *Hollywood Heartbreak,* a collection of plaintive vignettes of the past, spoke with great authority about Paul.

"He was about the only man in Hollywood who had never made a pass at Jean, and that was his biggest attraction for her. On their wedding night he had a big surprise for her, he revealed to her that he was impotent and that he truly did believe in her screen image, that her sex-goddess magic could cure him. They had a terrible fight during which he beat Jean brutally and savagely."

Hearing Jacobson's accusations over the air, I asked Joyce, "Where was this lady, under the bed?"

Author Bob Thomas, another guest on the show, contradicted Miss Jacobson and said, "I can't imagine Bern would strike her. There was no evidence that she was bruised or hurt. It's again pure speculation on some dreamer's part."

The show supplied some balance with brief clips of actors Ralph Bellamy and Lew Ayres, both of whom knew Jean and had a high regard for her.

My long interview was cut down to two appearances, ten seconds for one and fifteen seconds for the other.

Over a photo of Dorothy Millette, McClanahan reported, "Paul Bern had a common-law wife who had been institutionalized for ten years with incurable amnesia. But shortly after Bern's marriage to Harlow, Dorothy Millette arrived on her husband's doorstep while Jean was away."

I came on and commented about Dorothy's reappearance in Paul's life. "That put Paul into a terrible situation," I said. "He had love affairs with two women he was seriously in love with, and could be branded a bigamist."

Miss Jacobson came on again and said, "He saw no other way out. Instead, he wrote a cryptic suicide note, took off all his clothes, stood in front of Jean's full-length mirror and put a bullet through his head."

Over a shot of Louis B. Mayer, McClanahan said, "According to some, a cover-up was engineered by MGM mogul, Louis B. Mayer."

That was the cue for my second appearance: "The story of impotence, which was so well regarded, was a fabrication. Now, I was present when Mr. Mayer decided that that was the way that the studio should explain Paul Bern's suicide. Jean might be guiltless, of course, if she had a husband who was impotent."

I had told the interviewer that if impotence became an acceptable motive for suicide it could wipe out a large part of the male population—but the public never heard it. Everything else I said landed on the proverbial cutting-room floor. Rue McClanahan wound up the show: "Harlow recovered. She completed the movie she started, but within five years she, too, was dead. Complications from beatings by Bern? That account seems to follow everything else that had been reported. Or fabricated by the studio?"

• • •

"I'm disappointed," I told Joyce after watching the telecast. "All these terrible stories Miss Jacobson told about Paul are based on the words she could have read in Shulman's biography of Harlow, the sensationalism that keeps being repeated. Impotency is what people remember about Paul. We keep hearing that truth is stranger than fiction, but in this case fiction has outlived truth."

"You still feel deeply about your friend, that's obvious," she sympathized. "Even after all these years."

"He was a very unique person."

"I know. From what you've told me, he had a wonderful reputation, a big income, and he was married to Jean Harlow . . ."

"Of course, suicide was against his own best interests; but Paul was the most gallant and compassionate man I ever met. I know it's hard to believe anyone would go that far, but he did it for the good of Jean and Dorothy."

"Are you sure, Sam? I don't accept your idea that suicide is an act of gallantry. It's more complicated than that, it can grow out of anger or depression. The people left behind are most affected. For a man who had a great need to help people, how could he overlook the agony his suicide would bring to those who loved him?"

I admitted I had no answer for that.

"And there's something else, Sam. As far as Dorothy Millette is concerned . . . You still believe she spent ten years in a coma?"

"Paul said she did and I believe him, yes."

"I'm a dancer, Sam. I know what happens to muscles when you don't use them. If she was bedridden—my God! Ten years! —*in no way* could she wake up and go out in the world just like that!"

"I don't believe Paul would lie to me."

"Aren't you hanging on to an old-fashioned theory about gallantry that was more believable in the past?"

"Look, Joyce, when I went to the house that morning, my friend was lying there dead with his own gun in his hand. He left a suicide note for Jean! He's dead, that's it, he's dead, he took his own life and it's over, he did it!"

"Very well," Joyce said mildly. "But what if he didn't do it? Why would a man who had everything kill himself?"

9

· · · · ·

Quest

ALL I HAVE RECORDED so far I knew well, because I was there when most of it happened. I was *sure* I knew the real reason for Paul's suicide, but Joyce's question and the certainty of her instinct unsettled everything I had believed about my friend's death.

I was bothered because I'd had fifty-odd years to think about it, and I wasn't exactly enchanted at the possibility that I'd been wrong all this time. But Joyce had a let's-find-out dare in her eyes, and I was remembering Paul's line: "Things are seldom what they seem."

I heard myself agree to look back with an open mind —but at the same time, I had a feeling I was going to hate doing it.

· · ·

Irving Thalberg had a rule, "The end of a story should be what the beginning is about."

To find out more about Paul, Jean, and Dorothy Millette meant going back to their beginnings . . .

• • •

He was not named Paul Bern when he was born. The future film producer, whose birthday was December 3, 1889, was Paul Levy, the son of Henrietta Hirsh and Julius Levy.

He was nine years old when the family came to the United States from Wandsbek, Germany. They lived for a time in Newark, New Jersey, then moved to 3781 Third Avenue in New York City—so poor they used packing boxes for furniture. Paul was one of a "weird brood of eighteen children," but they were not all his brothers and sisters; they came from Julius Levy's desire to look after the poor and homeless children in the ghetto. The sacrifices that Paul saw his father make inspired him to help many, including strangers.

Paul attended a two-year course in acting at the American Academy of Dramatic Arts and Empire Theatre Dramatic School. That prestigious institution was the first school founded in America for the purpose of giving a complete course for the stage. Students were warned, "The Academy does not pretend to do the impossible—to teach all the art of Edwin Booth in two short years. Our work is both educative and practical; it cultivates imagination and intelligence and it furnishes theatrical knowledge and experience. With its reputation and special advantages it would be easy to fill its classes with crowds of mistaken enthusiasts and present long lists of graduates, with most of them failures on the stage. It is our policy to admit only those who are in earnest in the choice of their life-work and have such qualifications as may be developed with a fair chance of success."

When Paul Levy auditioned, September 13, 1909, at the age of nineteen, the tuition for his junior year cost eight dollars. The senior course, he was informed, could amount to anywhere from fifteen to thirty dollars.

His audition report and acceptance as a student was signed by academy president Franklin Haven Sargent, who was in charge of classic drama. In his report, Sargent made an assessment of Paul's type for future casting agents, noting he is "very dramatic and expressive, but handicapped by size and appearance." He further noted, "of fair proportions and in good physical condition, a German Hebrew with a good voice and memory, no previous dramatic training and only amateur stage experience." Paul was very good at reciting Shylock's speeches from *The Merchant of Venice,* but with a German accent.

Paul Levy decided he needed a new stage name, more suitable for an actor than the one he had. He settled on Bern, and his brother Henry and sister Friederike changed their names, too. He had difficulty selecting a first name, choosing Philip for a time. Then he called himself Edward Paul Bern in seven shows he played in, staged by the academy for private and public viewings, beginning with *The Teeth of the Gift Horse* on the evening of November 18, 1910. In other plays, he portrayed a versatile mix of American and English characters; when the curtain fell on *Friends of Youth* on February 23, 1911, at the Empire Theatre, he had lost most of his German accent, become an American citizen and settled on the name Paul Bern.

• • •

Two weeks later Harlean Carpenter was born in Kansas City, Missouri. Her birthday was March 3, 1911. Her mother's maiden name had been Jean Harlow until she married Montclair Carpenter, a dentist.

• • •

Among Paul Bern's thirty-two fellow students in the senior class, Paul was hailed as a bright, ambitious fellow with a droll and whimsical sense of humor. That was how he appeared, too, to Mrs. L. Melett, as Dorothy signed her name when she entered the junior class of the academy's April 1911 term.

She was auditioned for the academy by Charles Jehlinger, whose jet-black mustache and hair parted down the middle gave him a fearsome appearance. A stern, forbidding taskmaster, the legendary Jehlinger's tenure as director of instruction continued for fifty years.

When Paul told me about Dorothy, he described her as "breathtaking, enchanting, indescribable . . . the loveliest girl I'd ever seen . . . an ethereal will-o'-the-wisp."

Jehlinger, however, assessed her in his report, "in good physical condition but stout and heavy. Her voice is light, her memory is fair, as is her pronunciation and dramatic instinct." She had no previous training or stage experience, but he marked Dorothy's "imagination" as "good."

"She gave an intelligent reading," Jehlinger noted. "But her spontaneity is weak, her versatility too self-conscious."

Dorothy portrayed some Shakespearean heroines in class, but her affair with Paul began then and she never graduated from the Academy of Dramatic Arts. She left without completing her junior year and secured a job with Paul in Frank Craven and John Cromwell's comedy *Too Many Cooks*. The show ran a full year on Broadway and toured Canada and New England. After the show closed, Paul began acting, stage managing, and directing various plays on Broadway, but there was no job for Dorothy in New York. Her yearnings for acting laurels would be long and frustrating.

IN CONTRAST, Harlean Carpenter never took a drama lesson in her life. She was to win superstardom with her platinum blond hair, her captivating smile, a brash show of her body, and by the sheer force of her personality.

Harlean enjoyed a comfortable upbringing, attending private schools. From 1916 to 1921 she was a pupil at Miss Barstow's School in Kansas City. Harlean was a very pretty, blond child.

Her mother was blond, too, and pretty also when she was young, but she was heavier than her daughter would ever be. Both had restless natures, but in general were extremely easygoing. And there was a close bond that tied them together all their lives. Even when they turned to and away from men, daughter and mother always remained within a consoling arm's length of each other.

Jean Carpenter divorced Harlean's father in 1921 and secured sole custody of their ten-year-old daughter. It seemed to the little girl that her father had dropped out of her life. Mother and daughter then left Kansas City and went to California. Determined that Harlean continue her good education, her mother enrolled her in the highly respected Hollywood School for Girls. One of Harlean's favorite schoolbooks, which she saved from those classroom days, was *Ten Boys from History* by Kate Dickinson Sweetser. Harlean was growing up fast.

Louis B. Mayer's daughter Irene was Harlean's classmate at that Hollywood school, and in her autobiography *A Private View*, Irene remembered, "Little Miss Harlean Carpenter was unforgettable. There had been something spectacular about her even in her school uniform, which was seductive only on her. No middy blouse but hers was cut so low and, despite admonitions, her hips swayed under the ankle-length pleated skirt. She had been one of the school's few boarders and on Friday afternoon we would huddle behind the shrubbery at the entrance to watch a big foreign car drive up, in which was hidden a veiled woman. A mysterious dark gentleman would emerge and usher Harlean into the car and off to places undisclosed. The rumors were that it was her mother with a lover of unknown origin. After a few years she dropped out of school without notice."

• • •

In 1920, while living with Dorothy Millette at the Algonquin Hotel, Paul had taken a writing assignment from the Samuel Goldwyn Company, which was then making films in New York City. It paid him more in a few weeks than he ever made in all his activities in the theater. From that time on Paul concentrated on a movie career.

Dorothy, still struggling to achieve her acting ambitions, became ill in 1921. Paul arranged for her long-term care in the Blythewood Sanitarium in Greenwich, Connecticut. He saw to it that Dorothy got the best medical attention available and he pledged to continue her support.

In 1922 he went west, but freelance writing turned out to be a far from secure career in Hollywood. He moved from studio to studio.

Despite difficult times, he gave evidence that he retained the sense of whimsy that others had noted in him. In a letter to business manager H. E. Edington of the Goldwyn Company, he wrote:

My dear Harry,
The unfeeling Tax Department of the State of
New York insists on my paying a tax to that noble

> *Commonwealth for the year 1920. Unfortunately,*
> *the money which the Goldwyn Company paid me*
> *that year was so little that the distance of two years*
> *has caused the amount to disappear entirely from*
> *my mind. I must, therefore, ask your good offices to*
> *let me know how little I received that year so that I*
> *can make my proper report.*
>
> *Thank you very much for an early answer.*
> *Best regards, sincerely,*
>
> *Paul Bern*

In January 1923, while working at Universal Studio, Paul needed more information about how much he earned the previous year from the Goldwyn Company and told Edington, "Please be sure and do not include in this the bonus I received for helping to launch *What Ho!—The Cook!* upon an unsuspecting and defenseless world."

Paul's career began its upward curve. That year he received a solo screen credit for the original story and scenario of *The Marriage Circle.* It was directed by German-born Ernst Lubitsch, a creator of sharp, sophisticated comedies.

Then Paul turned from writing to directing, guiding five silent films for Paramount during 1924 and 1925 with casts that included Pola Negri, Jetta Goudal, and Leatrice Joy. As a director, with the task of interpreting the characters from the written word, he became known for always attempting to mold the actresses into more sexy images than they had ever portrayed. He was enamored of them all, as they were of him and Hollywood gossip writers often linked their names romantically.

In 1925 Jean Carpenter took her daughter back to Kansas City where they lived with her father, Sam "Skipp" Harlow, a wealthy real estate broker. Fourteen-year-old Harlean adored him. From September to December, her mother placed her in the school of the Sisters of Notre Dame de Scion. In January 1926 she transferred Harlean to Miss Bigelow's School, where Harlean stayed until summer vacation; then she deposited her daughter in a girl's camp.

While spending much of her own time in Chicago with powerful members of the underworld, who were very prominent in that city, Jean Carpenter saw to it that her daughter was brought up among the children of the advantaged. At the end of the summer she moved to Chicago and Harlean was sent to another fine school, Ferry Hall, in Lake Forest, Illinois.

She was boarding at that private school when she met her first love and lost her heart to the young scion of a wealthy family, Charles F. McGrew II.

Mama, in the meantime, had became enamored of Marino Bello, a rainbow-chaser with no practical talents for supporting a wife—a fact that did not deter him from persuading her to be his bride. On January 10, 1927, forty-three-year-old Marino Bello of Highland Park, County of Lake, State of Illinois, and thirty-six-year-old Mrs. Jean Carpenter of Waukegan, County of Lake, State of Illinois, were married.

That same year, the very young Harlean Carpenter embarked on her first matrimonial adventure, running away from Ferry Hall in September to marry McGrew. She was only sixteen, but claimed she was nineteen to secure a wedding license. Her well-developed body offered no doubt to a justice of the peace that she was indeed an adult young woman. The extra years that she tacked on was really just a small misrepresentation but forever confused archivists in the MGM studio Publicity department, who could never be sure how young she was. When unhappy Mama Jean discovered that her runaway baby's union was legal, she sent out conventional wedding announcements.

• • •

In November 1926 Paul had become a production supervisor at the Pathé studio. He quit directing but found time to write a scenario, "The Beloved Rogue," based on the life of swashbuckling François Villon. John Barrymore portrayed the poet and patriot who played the fool in order to save his life. It was one of Paul's favorite characters in literature.

At Pathé, Paul supervised six forgettable movies over the next two years, befitting the general standards of the company at that time. His acquaintance with Cecil B. DeMille began then, and he met Irving Thalberg of MGM.

Thalberg gave Paul a $20,000 contract to write and

direct a dramatic feature for MGM called "Paris," which was to star serious actress Corinne Griffith. While Paul was writing the script, the production head changed his mind and decided the story was better fitted to comedy. Paul's objections to the change had no effect on Thalberg, who told him lightly but very frankly, "I make people do films my way so they'll never know if their way would be better!"

Paul was paid $7,500 not to write or direct "Paris," and Corinne Griffith was also bought off. Joan Crawford, a young Broadway chorus girl with a long-term MGM contract stepped in as star, while light-hearted Britisher Edmund Goulding was assigned to direct. There was irony in this situation: only two years later, Paul produced the blockbuster film *Grand Hotel* and selected Joan Crawford as one of its stars and Edmund Goulding as its director.

Paul had joined Irving Thalberg's staff at MGM, to help wherever needed to keep the production wheels rolling. (This was during the important transition period when the industry went from silent films to talkies.) During the last half of 1928, he found stories and helped to make films without getting screen credit, starting with *Beau Broadway*, a domestic comedy that teamed Lew Cody and Aileen Pringle—successful forerunners of the studio's legendary Powell and Loy of *Thin Man* fame.

Also in 1928, Paul suggested to Thalberg that Greta Garbo be featured in Eugene O'Neill's *Anna Christie* as her first talking film. It was a matter of enormous concern to the studio boss because of the Swedish star's accent. For all anybody knew then, that foreign accent might tear her popularity in shreds. The studio held off its decision to let Garbo talk but went ahead with it in 1929, and Paul supervised the making of *Anna Christie*. Garbo held her place in the MGM galaxy—her popularity remained as great as before, and Paul settled into the role of a supervisor, which was the way the studio designated its producers. He had landed in the position he was to occupy the rest of his life.

• • •

Harlean and her husband Charles McGrew were living on North Linden Drive, Beverly Hills, in a little Spanish-style bungalow he had bought. But their marriage was not working. In 1928 Harlean left him, moving into an apartment with her mother and, of course, Marino. It was then that she launched her movie career.

Harlean needed a professional name but didn't care for McGrew. She didn't like Carpenter either, feeling that her real father had abandoned her. She accepted Marino Bello as her stepfather but that was all, she wanted no part of the name Bello.

Deeply attached to her mother, Jean, as well as Grandfather Harlow, she divested herself of Harlean Carpenter and took her mother's maiden name, Jean Harlow. Because there were now two Jeans, they became Mama Jean and Baby Jean so people would know which was which.

The newly named Jean Harlow secured a couple of

now-you-see-her, now-you-don't appearances in the slap-stick comedies of Laurel and Hardy and also in Charlie Chaplin's silent film *City Lights*. Ernst Lubitsch gave her some visibility in *The Love Parade,* and she succeeded in getting her name in screen credits for the first time when she danced the Charleston in *The Saturday Night Kid* at Paramount.

Her first important break came when Howard Hughes, having filmed a silent version of *Hell's Angels,* a story about American fliers during World War I, decided to do it over as a talkie. He had to replace his leading lady, Greta Nissen, in the role of an English society girl because her strong Scandinavian accent was wrong for the talking version. Hughes chose Jean Harlow and gave her a long-term contract. He devoted the rest of 1928 to refilming *Hell's Angels.*

He continued editing that film right through 1929 and early 1930 while Jean was continually loaned out to other studios. She played a second lead behind Loretta Young in Capra's *Platinum Blonde,* and while the film's title was pointedly in her favor and remained a life-long symbol, her performance left much to be desired.

In 1930 Jean's husband Charles McGrew asked for and won an annulment. The relationship with his wife was over. Among his complaints he alleged that Jean had posed in the nude for a photographer. However, he made a generous settlement, giving her the house on Linden Drive, a car, and monthly alimony of $375.

• • •

MGM's casting director Fred Datig brought Jean to Paul's office. Datig was a tall man with light brown hair, always strictly business. He handled casting at Universal when Thalberg was at that studio and had followed him to MGM.

Screenwriter Gene Markey had whipped up a liberal adaptation of *Sappho,* transforming the poetess of the ancient classic into an artist's model. The movie, called *Inspiration,* was to star Greta Garbo and had received an okay from Thalberg. Paul, its supervisor, was selecting supporting players.

"Paul Bern was always thoughtful of an actor's feelings," recalled Datig. "He knew who Jean was when we came in, so all I told him was that her salary was $250 a week. We were going to walk out right away, though, because we both saw at once that he didn't think Jean was right for the part."

But Paul didn't want her to leave.

"Is it all right, Fred, if we spend a little time discussing this charming lady's career?"

Before Datig could answer, Jean said, "Sure!"

"You see, Miss Harlow, you do not fit the type that I need. I simply cannot picture you as a demi-monde in the Paris Latin Quarter."

"What's a demi-monde?"

"Oh, let's say a kind of prostitute."

"I could do that. Easy."

"Well, it's not acting it, my dear. It's your American look. Besides being so American, you are very much of today. You should never be in a period story. It will take more than acting, more than makeup, hairdos, costumes —and even then you won't look like a European."

"I'm playing an English lady in *Hell's Angels*, Mr. Bern, and that sure is a period picture. It's back in the World War."

Paul smiled.

Datig was certain that their relationship began in the office that day. Paul walked Jean out to her parked car, and before she drove away she suddenly invited him to escort her to the premiere of *Hell's Angels*.

On the evening of May 27, 1930, the picture had its world premiere with unusual fanfare at Grauman's Chinese Theatre on Hollywood Boulevard. This was the week that Marie and I had arrived in California and we received an invitation from MGM to attend. As the film unfolded, Jean provided some memorable moments.

"I want to be free," declaimed the Kansas City girl, striving to speak with a British accent in her role as royal-blooded Lady Helen. "I want to be gay and have fun! Life's short and I want to live while I'm alive!"

In another scene of *Hell's Angels* Jean arrives at her home with American air force officer Ben Lyon and drops her evening wrap to expose a flimsy décolleté gown—especially revealing because Jean never wore a bra or underwear.

"Would you be shocked if I put on something more comfortable?" she asked. The question failed to shock her escort but created pandemonium in the audience, rocking the theater with derisive laughter.

In that embarrassing moment, Al Lewin saw Paul

take Jean's hand in a sympathetic gesture. Lewin groaned and as I was sitting next to him, he pointed them out to me. "Good old Paul is at it again, he's found someone else to make over and fall in love with."

• • •

Jean's career sputtered along uncertainly even after *Hell's Angels* opened. Howard Hughes showed no interest. He still loaned her out, and she appeared in a half-dozen vehicles and made personal appearances before Hughes sold her contract to MGM.

In the summer of 1932 *Red-Headed Woman* changed everything. By then, Paul had perceived Jean's worth as a comedienne and made her a star.

The beginning of the story was clear but the mystery of the ending still lay ahead.

10

· · · · ·

The House on Easton Drive

JOYCE VANDERVEEN and I drove up Benedict Canyon Road and turned at the hill leading to Paul's house on Easton Drive. The place Paul loved stood there in splendid loneliness after he built it. But now it is away from the street view, hidden behind other homes which have sprouted around it.

I was thinking of that pleasant day when Paul brought me to see his future home with its little frame rooms and unfinished swimming pool, all of it unoccupied except by his dreams. Later, there was that joyous wedding reception when Paul and Jean were embracing a future that promised wonderful times to come.

But those happy memories were eclipsed by my thoughts of the morning after he died. I couldn't dispel my recollections of that day when I came here knowing Paul's life was finished.

● ● ●

We had set up an appointment with the owner of Paul Bern's estate, dermatologist Dr. Ron Hale. He bought that residence at a probate sale after it passed through several hands. He was restoring the house and grounds as accurately as possible to the way it was when Paul lived there. Working on it in his spare time, he had a project likely to take many years.

• • •

The entrance into the estate was one of many alterations made since Paul's time. The path to the front door had been only halfway up Easton Drive then, but that had been altered. The way into the grounds was changed to the top of the hill. A high metal gate, securely locked, confined entry to all except those allowed in by Dr. Hale.

A small home near the old entrance used to be a three-car garage with servants' quarters. Gardener Clifton Davis lived there, as well as houseman John Carmichael and his wife, Winifred. She prepared the food in those quarters and her husband would carry it up the hill to the house, because Paul never included a kitchen in the plans for his home. He had a sink and facilities to make coffee, but he didn't want food cooking near his living room.

On the grounds of the estate, stonework paths wandered aimlessly on, set off here and there by low stone walls. There were trees and natural growth everywhere. The path that led from the old entrance to the swimming pool was gone; the empty pool was in bad shape, the earth around it had given way because of a large mudslide. The area where Paul and Jean held their wedding reception was also gone, another victim of the mudslide—a typical California disaster. The lush green was now brown dust, the pool swamplike.

Seeing the grounds in this condition after so many years gave me an eerie and unpleasant feeling. I looked at the stone bench by the pool where I sat with Thalberg, where the gardener first told of finding the body. To me it had acquired a wretched, disenchanting appearance.

The style of the house was a cross between English Tudor and Bavarian miniature fairy tale-type castle. Paul could have been inspired by a hunting lodge in the Alps.

On entering the front door one crossed a little hallway and a few steps down to the left was the living room, cozy under its high-beamed ceiling. In the woodwork by the fireplace were hand-carved heads that represented the four winds. Two large bookcases were built into the wall; Paul could turn one aside to reveal a small bar and behind the bar he had a secret panel leading to a good-sized wine cellar. Those were prohibition times, remember.

A spiral staircase just inside the entrance led to the attic. It was so steep that one had to hold on to the wall while climbing it. Partway up was a small wooden door. That led to the turret, which was originally red tiled, as Paul wanted it. Dr. Hale changed it to copper fish-scale.

Former owners, those who lived there, painted the entire interior of the house in colors suited to their individual tastes, and most of the beautiful woodwork, ceilings, and balustrades were painted white. Plasterwork between the wooden beams had been covered with red-flocked wallpaper.

From the hallway a small staircase with a balustrade led to the dining room—on the same level as the bedroom.

When he went to wash the bloodied glass, the gardener, looking from the dining room into the bedroom that fateful morning, saw Paul, his head and upper body protruding out of the closet.

It became suddenly clear to us, as we stood there, that even the crash of a gunshot would be stifled here. The closet was at the back of the house and crowded against the mountain, which provided an imposing barrier to the spread of sound. The profusion of clothes hanging there must have further muffled the sound of the gun.

• • •

Jean let Paul know that she was less than enchanted, living in such an isolated canyon. Their house became an unending cause of friction between the newlyweds. She didn't share his love for solitude or his yearning for privacy, outgrowths of the years he spent in small family-packed tenements.

Stuck in the countryside away from people didn't suit Jean's love of fun and action, it didn't fit the glittering background in which she felt comfortable. Any time either one brought the subject up, it was sure to provoke arguments.

Dr. Hale said he had been told that Jean Harlow sometimes climbed into the turret "to pout." She really did not want to live there.

In a bizarre twist to a house haunted by tragedy, it was rented for a period of two years by Jay Sebring, a Hollywood hairstylist. At that time, Paul's house was owned by screen actress Sally Forrest and her husband, Milo Frank, a writer-producer.

"Jay was a real oddball," Frank told us. "He was slow paying his gardener and they had some bitter fights. He was always behind with the rent, too. He kept making alterations to the house, but we didn't object because his lease gave him an option to buy."

The "death closet" had been enlarged into another bedroom, but Sebring had used it as a gymnasium.

"I called him after we heard that he had painted the bedroom black and the gym purple," Frank told us. "He did that without asking if it was okay. Sebring suggested that my wife, Sally, and I have lunch with him the next day to talk it over and he would bring film actress Sharon Tate along. We thought he was going ahead with his option to buy the property."

That night, Sebring went to see Sharon Tate at her home. The next morning the Franks read that both of them were murdered there, victims of the infamous Charles Manson killing spree.

• • •

Paul had transferred his ownership in the house to Jean as a gift on their wedding day. It was hers when he died. Everything else of his was filed away in the Hall of Records in the heart of the city.

SOME PERVERSE GENIUS has seen to it that Los Angeles's one-way streets always go the wrong way, all parking areas display signs that read as if engraved, LOT FILLED. WAITING PROHIBITED BY LAW.

Joyce and I edged our car into a space at the Music Center, several blocks from the county archives where we wanted to go, then began a search for the rooms that housed the county archives.

222 North Hill Street seemed like an easy address to find. Men and women, businesslike in appearance, swinging briefcases and looking like they knew exactly where they were, pointed vaguely across streets, muttered some undistinguishable directions and strode on. We blundered into several wrong buildings before locating a door, half hidden behind a bushy pathway.

Finally, we were there.

Records of past court cases were stacked up from floor to ceiling as far as one could see, and finding Paul Bern's probate documents appeared hopeless. But luck was on our side, the Bern papers had been microfilmed, and within minutes we were looking at my friend's financial portrait.

The Paul Bern probate had been opened September 28, 1932, and wasn't closed until five years later.

• • •

Paul had designated his wife Jean Harlow Bern to be executrix of his estate. She was inheriting little more than a headache: despite his $75,000-a-year MGM contract, the total value of his assets at the time of his death was $24,571. One of his most valuable possessions was his Cord touring car, which was sold to a secondhand car dealer for $450.

The government wanted $9,450 for income taxes. That claim was allowed. A. S. Bernson claimed he had a mortgage on the Easton Drive home and wanted the $19,000 he said was still owed him. That claim was disallowed.

Jean's doctor, Robert Kennicott, asked for fifty-five dollars for writing a note to excuse Jean Harlow from appearing at the inquest—he was performing a professional service. MGM's doctor Edward Brant Jones asked sixty dollars for advising Mayer that Paul was impotent. Both were paid.

Then we came across an item that astounded us.

Four days before his death Paul applied for an $85,000 life insurance policy, with Jean as beneficiary. He submitted to a physical examination, which he passed. He was certified by the doctor as having "no medical deficiencies."

When his death was ruled a suicide, the policy was negated. It robbed Jean Harlow of funds that might have paid off the debt-ridden estate. The assessed value of "the life insurance policy that never was" was recorded as: Nothing.

"I'm puzzled," I said to Joyce. "Paul took out life insurance while surely knowing that suicide would invalidate it."

"Yes," said Joyce. "And he did it while knowing that Dorothy was coming. Suicide couldn't have been on his mind."

• • •

We noticed a string of demands from MGM.

"The Accounting department certainly didn't show any emotion or sentiment over Paul," I mourned.

The estate was charged by the studio for hiring cars, also the costs for the guards who held back the sightseers at the Bello residence as well as those at Paul's home. Their food and drink was all on the deceased.

The items were often small but they went on page after page. All the MGM charges in the probate were allowed and paid to the company; combined, they took a healthy chunk out of the assets.

Joyce was writing the names of individuals mentioned in the probate.

"Paul loaned a thousand dollars to agent Frank Orsatti," she said.

"I should think Orsatti would have loaned it to him. He was a rich bootlegger and then became a richer agent with the help of Louis B. Mayer."

"Orsatti paid half of it back," Joyce said.

"It sounds like a business deal . . . But we can't ask Frank about it, he's dead."

"Paul borrowed a thousand dollars from producer B. P. Fineman."

"Bernie Fineman is dead, too."

Harold Grieve demanded and was paid one thousand dollars from the estate for decorating Paul's home. Grieve was a highly acclaimed set decorator and costume designer in the motion picture industry.

"Grieve is still alive," I said. "We'll try to find him."

"Look at this," Joyce said. "Someone used a studio limousine to go to San Francisco on the night Paul was killed. The bill was turned in by the Transportation department a week after Paul died. It was for ninety-six dollars and the estate paid it because the car had been ordered by Paul. There's no mention who used it, no explanation for it, but the charge was allowed. Maybe we can find out more about it."

I made a quick note. There might still be people in the studio Transportation department who could find out about it.

"Here's a man named Dean Dorn who got another limousine for the day of the funeral," said Joyce.

"He was in Strickling's Publicity department. What was it for?"

Joyce checked the item. MGM charged the Bern estate for a company limousine "to transport Mr. Dorn to Inglewood for the ceremony and elsewhere."

"Dean's still around," I said. "He may be one of the few left who's still available."

We found Harold Grieve first. His residence turned out to be just a block away from me. I called him saying I wanted to ask him about his recollection of Paul Bern. He said, "Never heard of him."

I reminded Grieve that he had collected one thousand dollars for decorating Paul's house in 1932 and also that Paul, when at Pathé, had directed his wife Jetta Goudal.

Before her marriage to Grieve, Jetta had a well-publicized love affair with Paul. It hadn't occurred to me that Grieve might not want to recall the man involved in that sixty-year-old romance.

He repeated that he had never heard of Paul and hung up.

• • •

Dean Dorn resided in the splendid Balboa Bay Club, about sixty miles south of Los Angeles, where the Pacific meets many rich retirees.

"The car picked me up early," said Dorn, a large man, when we met. "And when I got to Inglewood, Howard Strickling sat me down near the coffin with instructions to never take my eyes off it. He told me to accompany the body to the crematory after the ceremonies and stay with it until the cremation had taken place. I did exactly that. Howard never explained why he wanted me to do it—I thought maybe it was because Bern was a prominent producer and married to Jean Harlow and perhaps his body might be snatched and held for ransom. Y'know, there were wild rumors floating around Hollywood that maybe Paul had been murdered, that he had several bullet wounds, or that because he was impotent he had taken a razor and mutilated himself. I heard a lot of weird stuff like that. To this day I still don't know why Howard was so insistent that I not let the body out of my sight until it was reduced to ashes. He never talked much about what he knew."

We sat there silent for a time.

"You know," Dorn said, "there was a lot going on about that whole Bern incident that I never understood."

"Me either," I said.

• • •

On New Year's Day, 1988, Joyce and I were invited to a party at the home of David Bradley, a collector of Hollywood memorabilia. We didn't feel like going until he said, "I'm going to have a lot of old-timers and I need someone to pick up Harold Grieve, he doesn't drive. He lives near you—you know who he is, the widower of Jetta Goudal."

We saw a second chance to get Grieve to recall what he knew of Paul Bern and told Bradley that Joyce and I would bring him to the party.

Grieve turned out to be very lost at the party and couldn't wait to get out. "I'll buy you dinner if you take me home," he said, adding, "I have nothing in common with these people."

Ignoring our interests in the array of attractive restaurants that we drove past, Grieve insisted on dinner at

Dupar's, an old-fashioned coffee shop inside the Farmer's Market, not far from his home.

After we arrived, I tried to engage him in conversation about Paul Bern. But he was totally preoccupied with the food and what it would cost, directing his conversation solely toward our waitress.

Joyce mentioned that Jetta was born in Holland, as she was. Momentarily interested, he recalled that Jetta had told him that she was probably French. His attempt to keep Jetta's mystique intact was typical of the era when actresses, their husbands and their press agents sought to maintain their mystery.

We had to turn our attention in other directions. We had tried to find new answers but we were left only with new questions. People and places were disappearing under the pressure of passing years—there was no time to waste.

11
· · · · ·
The Fringe

I HAD COME TO HOLLYWOOD with a fierce desire to write and it was ironic to be unable to do so, while toiling in the center of an organization that depended on writers for its existence.

All I could do was observe the characters around me, who mirrored hope, achievement, or despair in their every move. I jotted down the names and incidents that attracted me, and they were everywhere one looked at MGM then.

There were tragedies occurring with frightening regularity.

Ann Cunningham was a quiet, pretty girl married to Douglas Shearer, head of the studio's Sound department and brother of Thalberg's wife, Norma Shearer. I knew Ann as a competent analyst in the Reading department, which was under my supervision. She left it temporarily to work on the screenplay and production of *Sequoia*, one of the rare, beautiful documentary-type films that MGM occasionally produced.

After returning to the Reading department, Ann departed the studio one noon, drove a few miles to the beach, tossed some coins on the counter of a shooting gallery, picked up a gun and blew her brains out. I never found the reason for it.

Another strange tragedy concerned George Hill, an important director who had an office next to mine. He was a towering giant, a former cinematographer who had been steered to film directing by his wife, scenarist Frances Marion. He directed two of MGM's most successful productions, *The Big House* and *Min and Bill,* both written by Frances Marion, who sat near him on the sets even as she was divorcing him. It was no secret around the studio that George Hill completed most afternoons in a high state of intoxication.

One evening Hill walked out of his office, ripped the paper nameplate off the door, crumpled it and tossed it away. He said good-bye tenderly to Bill, the waiter who adored him and had just brought him a cup of hot coffee. He drove to his beach home and put a bullet through his head.

I carefully noted down what I knew of both these unexpected tragedies. Some day when the turmoil of studio life slowed down I might try to find the answers.

Hollywood tragedies, I was learning, also fascinated my new friend, director King Vidor. Our friendship began with the dramatic events surrounding F. Scott Fitzgerald's efforts to script "Red-Headed Woman." At that time Vidor suggested I meet the author in his suite at the Roosevelt Hotel in Hollywood before he started his work on the screenplay. That evening, Fitzgerald decided we must celebrate our get-together and could do it with just one drink. That drink rendered him incapable of socializing. What was supposed to be a cozy dinner never took place: Vidor and I dined without Fitzgerald, but the director and I remained close friends from that time on.

In 1922, long before he immersed himself in Fitzgerald's problems, Vidor had become enthralled by the failure of the authorities to solve the mystery surrounding the murder of director William Desmond Taylor. The careers of two famous young actresses, Mabel Normand and Mary Miles Minter, were destroyed when the stories of their sexual exploits with Taylor surfaced after his murder. His beloved friend Mabel Normand, the star of fabulous slapstick comedies, tumbled into a pathetic slide from life into alcoholism and then death.

Vidor was forever haunted by what happened to her and sought the solution entirely for the actress's sake. Knowing I was curious, he kept me up to date as it unfolded.

I was fascinated by the odd collection of men and women who were tied to that long-unsolved tragedy. All were drawn to it for vague reasons, which seemed mysterious to Vidor. The varied mix included gangsters, socialites, servants, film stars—even their mothers.

In the Bern case, I had thought for many years that I had the answer, but Joyce's questions caused me to reevaluate it. Many odd people floated on the fringes of that case, too. Among them was Jean's stepfather.

It was going to take Marino Bello five years to realize his luck, but he had struck gold when he married Mama Jean. Until then, the forty-three-year-old adventurer had engaged in fruitless searches for fame and fortune, chasing lost gold mines and sunken treasures with other people's money.

Baby Jean was already in Hollywood, finding a place for herself in the world of films. Bello also pictured himself becoming a movie star and he brought his wife to Hollywood. He showed up at studio gates to be discovered, but when that didn't happen he accepted work as an extra. Gilbert Roland, a star at that time, recalled seeing him in mob scenes. But otherwise Bello wasn't noticed, and soon had to give up his dream of screen glory.

Jean's stepfather then discovered a new career, a thriving industry that was developing in Hollywood—insiders called it the "husband business." While Bello wasn't married to a star, he was husband to a lady whose delectable teenage daughter, like a fine savings bond, might pay splendid dividends when she matured.

The husband business became the pinnacle achievement of Bello's spotty life. He settled comfortably into it and moved in to guard, guide and, he hoped, improve every angle of his good fortune. He became her personal manager, a title considered a notch above talent agent. Peering into his future, he was hopeful that his flair for salesmanship would pay off.

Bello's problem was his inability to get MGM's top executives to take him seriously; they knew too many like him, untalented nuisances they privately wrote off as clowns, tolerated only because they slept with an important asset of the company. Screenwriter Frances Marion described Bello in her autobiography *Off with Their Heads!* as "Jean's philandering stepfather [who] slyly pointed out her assets to men who were in a position to further her career."

Bello used his "Personal Manager" pass to drive on the lot, and he showed up before ten o'clock on many mornings, ostentatiously parking his car just outside Jean's dressing room. He had a shave in the barber shop, read the trade papers and fan magazines, fraternized with Slickum at the shoeshine stand, spent noontime hours in the commissary with the casting directors, and worked hard at spreading his charm among the executive secretaries. Most of the day he sought to capture the attention of producers and directors, the primary targets of his efforts to promote Jean and her career.

Studio executives frowned on Bello; he was no longer needed after Jean's contract was signed. His efforts to handle additional name-clients ran afoul of Louis B. Mayer, who had no use for him and didn't mind letting him know it.

One of Bello's misguided attempts to grab other clients involved the heavyweight boxer Max Baer. Fight manager Ancil Hoffman brought him to MGM. The studio contemplated a story of the ring to be called "The Prizefighter and the Lady." While Hoffman dickered terms with Mayer, screenwriter John Lee Mahin gave the fighter a tour of the lot and introduced him to Jean.

Jean liked Baer. It didn't matter in the least to her when she learned he had a jail record. The young boxer had killed a man in a San Francisco prize ring. Hoffman, then a saloonkeeper, had rescued him from his incarceration and began to guide Max Baer's life.

Baer went bananas over Jean and Hoffman couldn't pry his personable pugilist from her side. Then, while Hoffman was working out the final business arrangements for the movie with Louis B. Mayer, Marino Bello proposed to Baer that he get rid of Hoffman, claiming that he could get him more fights and a larger percentage of the gate than Hoffman delivered.

Bello promised to book the boxer on big-time Vaudeville circuits between fights, and for coast-to-coast personal appearances he could costar with Jean. It was too tempting for Baer to ignore and he went to Hoffman.

"Hey, Ancil, I got a great offer!"

Hoffman did not take lightly to the news that Bello wanted to push him out. He called Louis B. Mayer.

"May I punch him in the mouth?"

"I'll pay you to do it!" replied Mayer.

"The Prizefighter and the Lady" still needed months of preparation, so Hoffman took Baer away, putting Jean as well as Bello out of his reach.

Bello had a lifetime of rejections behind him and one more was of little consequence—but his determination to be an important agent never flagged. He hoped to forge some sort of friendship with Mayer and Mannix but even Clark Gable, making a pitch on Bello's behalf, couldn't shake their open hostility of the urbane hustler.

•••

By the time the Bellos settled down in Hollywood, a battalion of sharp theatrical agents had invaded the studios from the East and waged a fierce war to win representation of the big names.

Myron Selznick was one of them: he ran a studio for his father, Lewis J. Selznick at Fort Lee, New Jersey. That movie-producing company went broke. Billboards proclaiming SELZNICK PICTURES CREATE HAPPY HOURS continued to stand on Broadway long after the company was declared insolvent. Myron blamed its demise on unfair rivals, including Louis B. Mayer, so he went to Hollywood, determined to make Hollywood's tycoons pay for what they had done to his father. He took to wearing a black suit and a wide-brimmed black velvet fedora, Chicago gangster-style, unrelentingly forcing the studios to pay higher and higher salaries to the actors and actresses he represented. That became a matter of deep concern to Mayer and one that the MGM chief bitterly resented.

Bello took Jean to Selznick and asked for a partnership in the new agency, expecting that delivering his stepdaughter as a client was all he needed. But Selznick ticked off Jean as a "nobody" and turned Bello down. Like the other important ten-percenters who were setting up shop in those days, Myron Selznick saw no point in fighting for a struggling fledgling like Jean Harlow; he preferred to leave her to some small agent, one who would knock himself out to build her into a star. Then, if it happened, Selznick was sure he could take her over with a simple promise of superior guidance leading to the big money. It was the new law of the Hollywood jungle.

As a sidelight, Myron's brother David Oliver Selznick also went to California in the aftermath of their father's failure, but without the dark malice of his older sibling. A reluctant Mayer was persuaded to give the newcomer his first employment, but it didn't work out and soon David left MGM. He pursued a producing career and rose to preeminence in and out of several studios. He became a close friend of Thalberg and Paul Bern—and, to Mayer's consternation, his daughter Irene fell in love with David and married him.

The marriage brought about a reconciliation between David O. Selznick and Mayer; ultimately they conceived a guarded admiration for each other.

• • •

In July 1932, when Paul married Jean, Irene was the bridesmaid and David was an important member of the wedding party.

On that day, Bello briefly enjoyed a kindred feeling of alliance with the studio moguls because both he and they disapproved of the union. Mayer thought Paul was too old for Jean and tarnished her girlish image; Mannix spoke out against Paul when told of the impending mar-

Harlean Carpenter was an adorable little girl who would grow up to be MGM's blond bombshell Jean Harlow.

(American Academy of Dramatic Arts)

(Marvin Paige Collection)

(Marvin Paige Collection)

Paul Bern was a drama student at the American Academy of Dramatic Arts in 1911 when he met the mysterious Dorothy Millette.

Paul Bern was obsessed
with creating sexy im-
ages when he directed
his films: top, Pola
Negri; above, Jetta
Goudal pictured here
with actor Maurice B.
Flynn; and right,
Leatrice Joy.

Jean Harlow made one of her now-you-see-her, now-you-don't appearances as an extra only partly visible on extreme left in *New York Nights*, a 1929 film starring Norma Talmadge and Gilbert Roland in their first talking picture.

Paul Bern escorted Jean Harlow to the Hollywood premiere of *Grand Hotel*. MGM producers did not get screen credits at that time, and the film does not show that Bern produced this winner of the Academy Award for Best Picture.

Author Katharine Brush wrote, "Jean was a gilded babe,
the kind the boys always hailed as 'Hello, Gorgeous!' "

Irving Thalberg thought sensuous
Dorothy Mackaill, above, was perfect
for *Red-Headed Woman*, but Paul Bern
fell in love with Jean Harlow and got
her the part that made her a star. She
is shown here looking up at actress
Una Merkel.

Paul saw Jean as an innocent young girl, despite her pose of the sophisticated sex symbol, and he never revealed his secret past. "I'll tell her," he said, "when she's more mature."

Studio gossips were disapproving of the difference in their ages, but Jean and Paul were visibly happy on the day they became engaged.

The police and the coroner converge on the Bern house on Labor Day, after Paul's body was found. His wife, Jean Harlow, was not there.

Housekeeper Winifred Carmichael found a wet yellow bathing suit on the grounds of the Bern house. Her husband, John Carmichael, found Paul Bern's body and fainted.

Jean Harlow, Paul Bern, and their families posed for this wedding photo. Henry Bern would later reveal that his brother Paul had another wife. *From left to right:* Mrs. Frederick Roberson, Jean Bello, Mrs. Henry Bern, Friederike Marcus, Henry Bern, Paul Bern, Frederick Roberson, Jean Harlow, Donald Roberson, and Marino Bello.

Marino Bello and writer Willis Goldbeck escort a distraught Jean Harlow to her husband's funeral.

"The greatest floral display in Hollywood history," said the under-taker when Paul Bern's funeral took place at Grace Chapel.

Both Louis B. Mayer and Irving Thalberg, who were at the Bern house hours before the police came, kept close watch on what was testified at the coroner's inquest. On the far left is attorney Ralph Blum, and on the far right is studio business manager M. E. Greenwood.

Jean Harlow being welcomed back to work by Clark Gable.

Only the studio executives knew how deeply Los Angeles District Attorney Buron Fitts was involved in the mysteries of the Bern case.

(Courtesy Hendry Family)

Studio police chief Whitey Hendry, seen here with the MGM lion, knew what happened at the Bern house long before the police arrived.

Dorothy Millette left San Francisco on the *Delta King*, but she was not on board when the ship arrived in Sacramento the next morning. The *Delta King* is seen here in the early 1930s passing Walnut Grove, the site where Dorothy disappeared.

riage, saying, "What Jean needs is a good cocksman and Paul ain't it!"

That proclamation grew out of his belief that he knew sexy details about Jean. Eddie Mannix always had a friendly relationship with the underworld. It began when he was working in New Jersey and he never lost touch with it.

Mannix had heard through those connections that when Marino Bello was in New York with Jean Harlow on a personal appearance tour, he had presented his well-developed stepdaughter to Abner "Longie" Zwillman, a rising young hoodlum in Meyer Lansky's mob. Longie had a fondness for young girls and Bello expected in return he would get a piece of Manhattan in which to operate in the illegal liquor business. A Lansky franchise was sure to propel Bello on his way to riches at last. He dreamed of owning a truly first-class speakeasy, perhaps right on Fifth Avenue: it would be the most elegant watering hole in the city, catering to society's best.

Zwillman's crush on Jean was important to the deal because the tough hoodlum could guarantee Bello's protection against politicians, cops and even federal agents who might muscle in on his profits. The role of saloon boniface might have fitted Bello very well, and if it happened it might have changed forever the life and career of Jean Harlow. But before Bello's dream materialized, Longie reportedly gave some gangster friends gold lockets, each containing a strand of Jean's blond pubic hair.

Bello almost lost his wife when she found out about

the lockets. Mama Jean demanded that Bello stay away from the mob and he give up all thought of running an empire inside the cozy Lansky family. The episode moved mother and daughter ever closer to each other, while awakening Baby Jean to the perils of Bello's manipulations.

The affair was related to Mannix by a prominent Los Angeles gangster, Eddie Nealis, during a Sunday morning golf match.

"I never laid a hand on her," Nealis told his pal Mannix. He claimed he had heard of Jean's activities from Zwillman. Nealis always found movie stars a headache, saying, "Give me a waitress any time."

Mannix regaled his associates at lunch in the executive bungalow with the story. He also briefed Louis B. Mayer about Jean's ties to Zwillman, and because Mayer saw the matter as Bello's doing, it helped widen the distance between the two men. Mayer came to the conclusion that Jean was "a slut"; Nealis, when told Mayer's comment, called him "a purist" and said, "I hate that whole breed of bastards."

Fraternizing with a gangster helped Jean grow up fast. Moreover, her early willingness to go along with Bello's schemes inflamed the sexual desires of her stepfather who wanted her to belong to him. He left suggestive notes for her that she found in her bed at night. She revealed this to studio acquaintances but kept quiet about it at home.

"It would only hurt Mama," she said. "I can handle

him—I've had plenty of experience with jerks. I just laugh in his face."

• • •

Myron Selznick's agency became the most prosperous in Hollywood, and Jean Harlow proved to be a gorgeous example of the overlooked. When *Red-Headed Woman* transformed Jean into a superstar, it was too late for Myron Selznick, who would then have been happy to take her on. She had signed with Arthur Landau, who was extremely enthusiastic about her, though his agency was small and lacked clout with the major studios. And Paul Bern, not Marino Bello, had become the most important man in Jean's life.

From the time Jean was given the leading role in *Red-Headed Woman* and every day after the shooting was over, she would rush to Paul's office, where he would jump up from his desk and welcome her. Then she would curl up in a large leather chair beside him and sit there, subdued and fascinated, absorbed in the philosophy and banter of the friends whose custom it was to gather there before heading home.

Jean told me then that Paul always put her at ease and she felt thoroughly comfortable when she was with him—a development that did not escape the notice of his secretary, Irene Harrison.

Jean flattered Paul's friends with her open admiration of their bright minds and literary talents. It stimulated them, leading Albert Lewin to describe their antics as those of "adolescent kids opening their pants buttons to impress the new girl on the block." In reality, Jean had turned Paul's soirees into meetings of a fan club.

Willis Goldbeck, one of Paul's closest friends, had come to the studio from Rex Ingram's staff: Yale educated, handsome, erudite, cultured, he was utterly fascinating to women and, in turn, he was utterly fascinated by them—if they were beautiful. His screenwriting credits included the film *Mare Nostrum*, over which Ingram had created such a flap. Goldbeck's devotion to Jean was immediate.

Tall, ungainly Henry Hathaway, long brown hair drooping down his forehead, was another of Jean's admirers. He had given up his job as Paul's assistant, intent on becoming a film director. At this time he was considering an offer to make a western at Paramount, but he was delaying his decision in hopes of getting a drama of human relations, which had more fascination for him. Stolid, rarely joining in their give-and-take, Hathaway was as inarticulate as Carey Wilson was loquacious.

Carey Wilson always sought center stage, wherever he was. Carried away by a dissertation on the joys of authorship, he suggested to Jean that she should try her hand at writing a book. "Every woman has a book in her," he proclaimed. "And you can quote me!"

Jean was intrigued by the idea, revealing a story that was forming in her mind: "It's about a married couple, a love story. I'll do it if you fellows will help me."

Bello, too, was enthusiastic. Dedicated to capitalizing on every facet of Jean's popularity, he rushed into negotiations for a publishing deal for the novel. *Today Is*

Tonight was snapped up, its title created by the budding authoress before any other words of her book were written.

"There's more to me than the body they see up on the screen," Jean told me, thrilled by the idea of becoming a writer. Eventually she wrote her novel with the help of the very industrious Carey Wilson.

Today Is Tonight opened with a chapter that skirted close to genteel pornography, depicting its young heroine lying naked in bed, silk nightie at her feet, reflecting on the pleasures of the agile sex romp she had enjoyed with her husband before he left for work.

"It's fun to be alive and in love with your own husband," thought the book's heroine, Judy Lansdowne. "She flicked away the corner of the yellow sheet which had fluttered across her face. It was a satin sheet, the color of a pale young begonia bud. She was quiet. It was nine-fifteen of a lovely September morning . . ."

The book went downhill from there, pure soap opera all the way. It ended, though, with a curiously prophetic paragraph: "Romance and madness have their place in this world and in ourselves. But this can't last forever, not in anyone's life!"

Marino Bello moved in to guard his stepdaughter's royalties. He demanded that every copy of her book be stamped with a number before distribution to bookstores and that he, as her representative, have access at all times to its sales records. Both requests were unprecedented, but the annoyed publisher agreed to them.

Embarrassed, I bought the film rights for MGM so

that no other studio could exploit Jean. No efforts were made to film it, nor did the publisher promote it. Unfazed, Jean shrugged off the failure. It wasn't even a tiny bump in the road along her path to the top.

• • •

During the two months that Jean and Paul were married, the only agent who maintained a friendly attitude toward Bello was Frank Orsatti. He was amiable, loyal, and the dumbest of the entire group of Mayer's Men.

Orsatti was everybody's friend, but his greatest love was reserved for Louis B. Mayer, to whom he felt he owed his life. As a bootlegger, Orsatti was the prime supplier of booze to Eddie Mannix, who had introduced him to Mayer in 1931. The country's opposition to the Prohibition Act was so intense that repeal was only a matter of time. "You're in a dying business," Mayer told the surprised Orsatti. "Get out while the getting is good."

"Chee!" exclaimed Orsatti, who still retained his Italian accent after forty years in America, "where'll I go?"

"Be an agent," said Mayer. He pointed to Myron Selznick's successful break-in to an occupation for which previous experience was unnecessary. "Don't you realize," he asked, "that every ten years the agents pocket one full year's income of the talented people who work here in my studio? And that's going to get bigger, as salaries move up."

Orsatti's favorite exclamation was "Chee!" and he used it often as Mayer pressed him to switch careers, promising he would throw profitable deals in his path. The upshot of that meeting was the creation of a formidable rival to the big new agencies in town, as well as a court jester, a gofer, and a permanent bodyguard for Mayer. Good-natured Frank Orsatti was always near his mentor's side, available day and night for whatever he was asked to do.

Orsatti also filled an important social need for the studio head, whose love for nightlife was on the rise. Private clubs on Sunset Boulevard provided Mayer with an enjoyable way to stay up late. His energy was such that neither his wife nor his MGM colleagues could keep up with him. Mayer was so important that almost any top industry figure would be happy to go along with him on his nightly parties. Indeed, many called to indicate their willingness to join him; instead, he assembled a small coterie of respectful sycophants to keep him company, and that included Orsatti.

In explaining his preference he said, "A night out with Joe Schenck or Harry Cohn and I won't sleep worrying that I had let them walk away with my studio. The beauty of a night out with Orsatti is that my mind runs a mile ahead of his, I know what he wants from me long before he does. I go home and sleep like a baby."

Orsatti was the comic relief that eased Mayer's daily pressures. "When I ask Frank to run an errand for me he doesn't try to find out why—and even if I told him he wouldn't understand it."

"Always use Orsatti," Mayer once said to me. The MGM Story department had recommended filming the life of Broadway showman Flo Ziegfeld, whose annual production of *Follies* glorified the theater with beautiful girls. The rights were owned by Universal, but that studio was wavering after a year's effort to go forward with a production. Negotiating to buy it from Universal would normally be my duty as MGM's story editor. Producer Hunt Stromberg was eager to make it.

Mayer never went over an executive's head, so he called me in to talk. "If you make the deal for MGM, Sam," explained Mayer, who was a master at the art of gentle persuasion, "the price will go sky high. I suggest you let Frank take it on, he can drop in at Universal, make some dumb remark about seeing if he can sell it for them and get it for us at a reasonable price. Do you agree?"

"Yeah, boss," broke in Orsatti, nodding so briskly that the gray-felt chapeau he always wore, night and day, indoors and out, nearly fell off his head. "I'm doing it just like that."

MGM's production of *The Great Ziegfeld* won the Academy Award as best picture of the year.

THE PAUL BERN PROBATE, with its ephemeral collection of invoices, claims, and counterclaims, had resurrected many names and faces of people who hadn't initially seemed important or even relevant to the mystery of Bern's death. But the first attempts that Joyce and I made to track down some of the fringe characters seemed of no avail. Still, the official story made little sense, so we began to pursue the marginal people, the exploiters, and the hangers-on, in hope of finding some clue.

It was important for us to know what part Marino Bello had played in the tragedy of Paul Bern. Joyce and I would have liked to talk it over with Frank Orsatti—he might have known the answers—but he, too, had died. We met with his brother Victor, who had been Frank's assistant at the Orsatti Agency.

Victor warmed up to the subject. "A lot of people thought Frank a kind of dope. He once told me it was good for his business to let them think so, which proves right there he wasn't so dopey after all.

"You know how close Frank was to Mr. Mayer. If he thought he would impress the boss by jumping off the Brooklyn Bridge he would have done it."

Mayer needed to get a message to Bello to appear at the inquest and what he must testify while there. Acting under instructions from Mayer, Frank Orsatti took Marino aside as if he had a great original idea for him.

Bello had spent the Labor Day holiday at a Mojave Desert retreat with Clark Gable and a pair of charming females, engaged in the kind of weekend commonly publicized by Hollywood's gossip columnists as "dove hunting." They did shoot off a few bullets at some passing birds, and while they were there, Paul Bern died. Any admission by Bello of his actual whereabouts would bring "the King's" name into prominence in the Bern inquest.

Marino had to invent a different alibi—without Gable—and protect Jean at all costs. Of course, it meant Marino would have to commit perjury about his whereabouts over the weekend, but that didn't matter a damn to Marino. He told Orsatti he'd be glad to do it and thanked him for suggesting it.

But Victor knew Marino was smart enough to know that Orsatti was acting on behalf of MGM. "So okay, he knew the score but he was willing to play his part, even though he couldn't claim that some bigshot at MGM asked him to do it."

Taking the stand as the first witness at the inquest into Paul Bern's death was a moment of triumph for Bello. He had quit aspiring to be an actor, but his appearance at the inquest gave him a fleeting moment of glory. It shows in the newspaper shots of him—arrogant and confident.

12

·····

A Certain
Inquisition

WELL, SAM, we've come to the right place."

"How do you know?"

Joyce indicated a large black hearse that was backing into the parking space alongside her car.

One of our several differences of opinion was the question who was the best driver. I considered Joyce an impossible passenger—every time I was driving and approached a traffic light she pushed her foot down hard against an imaginary brake.

Going to the Los Angeles County coroner's office I willingly let her drive. I was not looking forward to the details of my friend's death. I slumped in my seat while casting an unhappy look at the hearse being parked right by my side of the car.

"This is your production, Joyce," I said as we got out.

Joyce had negotiated our visit with Dorothy Coulter, the chief of documents. She was able to dredge out of storage the public transcript of the coroner's inquest, which occurred at the Price-Daniel Mortuary on September 8, 1932. They had not been microfilmed.

The yellowed papers were ready for us and we carried them to a desk in a small private room where we began to study: IN THE MATTER OF THE INQUISITION UPON THE BODY OF PAUL BERN—DECEASED.

As Joyce turned her attention to the pages before us, the list of subpoenaed witnesses jolted me to an upright position.

"This is incredible. I had forgotten who was called, but now I'm amazed at who *wasn't*. Look at who testified and just think of who didn't. I knew that Jean was apparently too ill to appear, but I don't see Henry Bern's name on the list either. He could have told them about Dorothy Millette.

"And what about Louis B. Mayer? He was photographed by the newspapers that day, he sat there through the inquest—but he wasn't called to testify."

"Ah, but remember," said Joyce, "this is not supposed to be a police investigation. It's a hearing—a formality to establish the cause of Paul's death."

Marino Bello, we knew, was the first witness. After he stated his name and address, coroner Frank A. Nance asked his profession. He replied that it was "Mining." Then Nance asked, "Mr. Bello, have you seen the remains of the deceased in the adjoining room here?"

Bello answered, "Yes, sir."

Q: What was the date of his death, so far as you know?

A: I don't know the date. It was Sunday or Monday.

Q: You are not sure of the day or time?

A: No.

Q: You were not present at the time of his death?

A: No.

Q: When did you learn of his death?

A: About nine o'clock Monday evening. It was a holiday, Monday was a holiday.

Q: How did you learn of his death?

A: When I arrived—I was late coming in—and I telephoned to tell my wife that the reason I am late is because the motorboat stalled in the middle of the channel . . .

Bello went on to state that he rushed home after Mrs. Bello told him Paul was dead. He didn't know the name of Paul's servant who had notified his wife.

Q: When you got home did you learn from Mrs. Bello what time she was notified of the death, how long she had known it, in other words, before you got home?

A: No.

Q: You did not see his body until today?

A: The first time.

Q: Do you know the cause of his death?

A: Suicide.

The balance of Marino's testimony was also routine. He stated that he was Jean Harlow's stepfather and that her marriage was a happy one. There were a few minor inaccuracies; for instance, he testified that, as far as he understood, Paul had been a producer at MGM for six-teen years. He was adding ten years to Paul's employ-ment.

I knew Marino Bello was lying about where he was that weekend, but that was unimportant in this case. Bello was called to take the heat off his wife and step-daughter. He had absolutely nothing important to say and he did it well.

• • •

John Herman Carmichael identified himself as Bern's chauffeur and butler. He first spoke of what he remem-bered happening on Sunday afternoon, the last complete day that Bern was alive.

> Well, about a quarter of five I heard Mr. Bern in the bathroom and I knew he was awake at that time. He had been sleeping most of the day. I went and told him there had been a number of telephone calls and while I was in there he told me to go out and tell his driver to go home and that was the last time I seen him and later in the eve-ning Mrs. Bern came in, having finished her work at the studio.

Q: About what time was that?

A: That was between seven and eight.

Q: She hadn't been home during the day?

A: No, sir.

Carmichael testified that one hour later, he drove Jean to Mrs. Bello's house, where he and his wife were to prepare the dinner.

Q: Was anything said between Mrs. Bern and Mr. Bern, the deceased?

A: I just heard Mrs. Bern say "In case you don't come over, good night, dear."

Q: Then it was your impression there was some doubt as to whether he would come over to the Bello house?

A: Well, I didn't hear Mr. Bern say anything, only, "Well, I will be seeing you, dear."

According to his testimony, he and his wife maintained a home of their own in West Hollywood, and they went there after serving dinner at the Bello home. He further stated that they did not go back to the Bern house that night.

Q: When did you go back to the Bern house again?

A: I should say it was about eleven-thirty Monday morning.

"That's wrong, Joyce," I said, pointing to the document. "What's he talking about? He was there much earlier."

Nance then asked, "What did you do when you got there?"

A: Well, we stopped down at the little house—we live a little way from the main house. We stopped there to change clothes and my wife went up ahead of me approximately two minutes as she usually does, you know, to put on and make coffee and my wife stayed in the kitchen and when I came in I went on through the house and found Mr. Bern.

Q: What did you observe about him as you saw him laying there?

A: Well, it was quite pitiful. He was laying in a puddle of blood.

Q: What did you do when you saw him there?

A: Well, I run back to the door and I called Davis, the gardener. I wanted someone to see him. You know, I was quite nervous and have been ever since.

I looked over at Joyce. "He doesn't mention at all that he had fainted, as the gardener told Thalberg and me that morning at the pool. He doesn't say anything about the body being partly in the closet."

Q: Was there any evidence that anything in the room was disturbed before you got there?

A: The room was kind of upset after him having been in bed. Mr. Bern would read quite a bit and books laying on the bed and nothing more than that.

Q: What did you do besides calling the gardener?

A: I told my wife to call Mrs. Bello, Mrs. Bern's mother.

Q: How soon was it before anyone came?

A: I believe it was approximately an hour.

Q: Then who came?

A: Mr. Selznick and Mr. Thalberg, I believe, were the first. I am not sure.

Q: You showed them the room and the body of Mr. Bern?

A: Yes sir.

Q: Did you hear them put in a call for the police?

A: Yes sir.

Q: Immediately?

A: Wasn't but a very few minutes.

Q: Didn't hear them call the coroner, did you?

A: I would not be positive. Mr. Thalberg called quite a few numbers and I was quite nervous and I was going back and forth to the kitchen and various things. I couldn't say who all he called or how many times he called.

Q: I was wondering if there was any unnecessary delay in the police being called. The records show they were not called until about two-fifteen and that you discovered the body about eleven-forty-five. Do you know any reason for that delay?

A: No sir, I do not.

At that point, the questions turned to Bern's state of mind.

Q: Did he express any unhappiness or dissatisfaction over anything at all or do you know of any reason for his taking his own life?

A: No sir, none whatever.

Q: Was he happy and cheerful and good-natured disposition?

A: Seemed to be, yes sir.

Q: Did you notice any nervousness on his part at times?

A: No sir, I never noticed any nervousness other than some times when he would ask for some little thing to be done. He is a man who likes everything just so.

Q: Did he ever discuss suicide in your presence?

A: No sir.

Q: Never mentioned it?

A: No sir.

Q: Did you know he had two guns?

A: Yes sir.

Q: Was he in the habit of carrying a gun?

A: Yes sir.

Q: Did he ever tell you why he carried his gun?

A: No sir, he never mentioned the gun to me at all.

Q: Do you know of any reason why he should take his life?

A: No sir, I do not.

Q: From your observation, the domestic relations seemed to be happy?

A: Seemed to be very happy.

Q: Never heard any quarreling?

A: No sir.

CORONER: Any questions?

JUROR: Ever see him take any of these tablets?

A: No sir, I never did, but I never was in his room before he would wake up in the morning. He was a fellow who liked things to be quiet when he was sleeping, and we would never go in before he came out in the morning.

CORONER: Was it his habit to sleep a good deal during the daytime or work at night?

A: Not ordinarily. He would get up around eight-thirty to nine o'clock.

Q: Do you know why he remained in bed last Sunday?

A: No sir.

Q: Didn't complain of illness, did he?

A: No sir, he didn't.

Q: As far as you know, he was only resting.

A: Yes sir.

CORONER: That is all. You are excused.

Carmichael's wife, Winifred, was the next witness called.

Q: Mrs. Carmichael, you were at the Bern residence at the time your husband has stated in his testimony when he discovered Mr. Bern's body?

A: I was.

Q: Do you know of any reason why Mr. Bern should take his life?

A: None.

Q: Did you ever know that he was ever unhappy or melancholy?

A: Mr. Bern was a very reserved sort of man and apparently didn't express his feeling to any of us. We were around him very little and I had no opportunity to observe him.

CORONER: Any further questions?

MR. WAYNE JORDAN [deputy district attorney]: No questions.

Irving Grant Thalberg was duly sworn and he stated that he was well acquainted with the deceased. "I received a telephone message from Mrs. Mayer that Paul Bern had committed suicide. She didn't know the details."

Q: Did she tell you who had notified her?

A: She said—I believe she said—I was so stunned at the moment I could not give you much detail but my impression is that she said Mrs. Bello.

Q: And you went out to the Bern house?

A: I asked her to call Mr. Selznick, who lived next door to me, and the two of us went out there together.

Q: About what time did you get out there?

A: I would say some time around one o'clock.

On reading that, I stared at Joyce.

"I saw Irving there at about nine-thirty," I reminded her. "That was some three and a half hours before one o'clock. I never saw any sign of David Selznick there. He could have been in the house or maybe he was gone. But I did not see him."

Thalberg said he had called the police.

Q: Do you know how long it was after you arrived at the house the police were called?

A: I would say within a few minutes.

Q: There was no unnecessary delay?

A: I hadn't even been upstairs before—

Before Thalberg could complete his answer, the coroner answered for him.

Q: That is, you hadn't even been upstairs to see the body before you called the police. Who did you call?

A: I tried to get Chief of Police Steckel and I was held up on the line several times. They finally told me he wasn't in, and they asked me to talk to the chief of detectives. I spoke to him and told him where I was and what I knew had happened and asked him to please send someone right up and do it as quickly and quietly as possible and he said he would.

Q: So you didn't lose any time in calling the officers, Mr. Thalberg. You are well acquainted with Mr. Bern and knew him a long time?

A: Yes sir.

Q: And also knew his wife and their domestic relations?

A: Yes.

Q: Did you know of any reason why he should take his life?

A: Well, that is not up for me to say. I don't know of any—

Q: Was he working under severe strain at times, at any rate?

A: Yes, he was.

Q: Did you notice that he had been nervous at times?

A: Yes, he had been nervous at times and he would get better.

Q: Did you know that he had been in the habit of taking a great deal of medicine?

A: Not that I know of.

Q: Did he ever discuss the suicide problem with you as a scientific fact or in any way?

A: Yes he did.

Q: Did he ever mention that he might do that some time?

A: Yes he did.

Q: Do you know anything about his family history? Did he ever mention that some of them had ever taken their lives?

A: He might have.

Q: Did he ever state to you that he might do that himself?

A: In a philosophical way, as I take it, not in a direct way.

Thalberg was wording this rather cleverly, I thought. His testimony had a separate meaning for me: it was not that suicide was in Paul's mind, but that they discussed suicide because it was common to stories under consideration. Irving and Paul must have talked about it a hundred times, how to show it on the screen and make it palatable, especially during a period when we were leaning toward movies with happy endings. But there was a suicide in *Grand Hotel*, in *Anna Karenina*, and of course in *Romeo and Juliet*. Irving wanted to make a movie of that classic for years although the tragic suicides at the end made it "dubious box office." That kind of talk went on all the time.

The questioning of Thalberg's knowledge of Bern continued.

Q: So far as the domestic relations between Mr. Bern and his wife are concerned, do you know of anything in that that would constitute a reason for him wanting to take his life?

A: I don't know of anything directly. I have heard of lots of things but I don't know of anything.

The jury had no questions for Thalberg.

• • •

Martin Greenwood, MGM's long-established business manager, appeared next.

I remember him as tall, white-haired, and with a kind of forbidding look. He looked like an aged Gary Cooper. You wouldn't want to argue with him. It was reported around the studio, and I'm sure it was true, that he killed a man once when he was a gun-toting sheriff back in Arizona.

He testified that he was at Bern's house when the police arrived. Greenwood quickly acknowledged that he was uncertain what time he got there. He said, "It was probably about half past two, something like that."

Q: How long have you known him?

A: Approximately twelve years.

Q: He was with the Metro-Goldwyn-Mayer studio all that time?

A: No, I think he has been with us about six years.

Q: Also know his wife?

A: Yes.

Q: Have you visited in their home?

A: No, never.

Greenwood admitted that he had no knowledge of anything relating to Paul Bern's suicide. "As I look back now, I can't recall a single time when we talked in that manner."

Q: Do you know of anything that would cause him to take his own life?

A: No, I don't. I was the most surprised person in the world in knowing that he had done so. I only knew the good side of him.

Q: In suicide there should be a motive as well as in homicide. We would like to know the truth as to what prompted this act. Was he ill at any time? Or nervous?

A: Of course he has been nervous. We all get nervous in the picture business. But it is not always so. I don't think I ever saw him melancholy in my life.

Q: That is all, Mr. Greenwood. You are excused.

• • •

Clifton Earl Davis was the next man in the witness's chair. After being sworn in, he said he was working around the swimming pool at about eleven-thirty that morning and Carmichael summoned him.

Q: Did Carmichael come outside and call you?

A: He did.

Q: Did you enter the house?

A: I did.

Q: Go up to the room where Mr. Bern was?

A: I did.

Q: And you saw him lying there?

A: I did.

Davis did not mention that John Carmichael fainted after he found Bern's body and made no reference to carrying a broken glass inside. He failed to report my appearance at the house, or that of Mayer or Whitey Hendry. He completely changed his early story.

He identified the photos of Bern lying dead.

"Ever hear him say anything about suicide?" Nance asked.

A: No, absolutely not.

Q: Had you known of any domestic inharmony there at all?

A: No.

Q: Any unpleasantness between he and his wife?

A: No.

Q: Do you know of any reason whatsoever why he might take his life?

A: None whatsoever.

CORONER: All right, that is all. You are excused.

• • •

The next witness was Harold Allen Garrison, the delightful Slickum, MGM's resident bootblack and storyteller.

Q: What is your business or occupation?

A: I have a shoeshine stand out at the studio and as a rule I work extra for Mr. Bern.

Q: As chauffeur?

A: At nights, yes sir.

Q: When did you learn of his death?

A: Oh, it was about five o'clock Monday evening.

Q: You were not there when the officers arrived?

A: No, I was out at the park picnicking.

Q: Driving with Mr. Bern, has he ever mentioned the matter of suicide to you?

A: Quite often. He said his mother had and his father—I think his grandmother or grandfather —and it run in his family, but he hoped he would never have to do it.

Q: Say he might have to do it?

A: He said, every now and then he said "Life is hard" and would clasp his arms and slide down in the car like this [indicating] and I would slap him on the shoulder and say "Don't feel like that" and he said "Slickum, would you ever commit suicide?" and I said "No, never in the world, why should I? You don't need anything, only money and I can get plenty of that from you and Mr. Thalberg."

Q: He frequently mentioned suicide?

A: Every now and then. Well, I don't think it has been within the last two or three weeks. He might have within the last two or three weeks, just slightly.

Q: Did he ever give any reason why he might commit suicide?

A: No. I said "I don't see why you would talk like

that. You are happy and have everything you
could wish for in life."

Q: You drove for them quite often?

A: Yes.

Q: Nothing like inharmony?

A: Just hugging and kissing all the time, just make
me mad.

Q: There never was any quarrel?

A: Never.

Q: Saturday night, did you take Mr. and Mrs. Bern
somewhere?

A: I took him. We left the studio and went to the
Ambassador Hotel. We arrived there five
minutes past seven and he gave me a dollar for
my dinner and said, "I will be down about eight-
thirty, not before, so you will have plenty of
time, anything you want to do."

Q: How did he seem to feel that night?

A: Well, he was very happy at times.

Q: How did he indicate that? Did he joke with
you?

A: Yes, he joked with me and then he would go
along. He was kind of worried because his wife
had to work, and there was a big party going on
and he really wanted to go to it.

Q: Where was this party?

A: Fredric March's home—he mentioned it two or
three times and when we were going along the
canyon up the road, he said "My, Slickum, I
hate to miss that," and I said "Why don't you

come on and go?" and he said "No, I would not
go without my darling wife."

Q: That was your understanding, that he didn't go
to the party because of his wife?

A: Yes sir.

Q: Would you say he was upset or unhappy or at
least a little unhappy?

A: No. He was a deep thinker and if you haven't
got anything to talk with him that is interesting,
don't talk, and if you have, it is all right.

Q: When you left him that night was he happy and
cheerful?

A: Just as usual.

Q: Was he alone?

A: Yes. Had to go about seventy-five stairs to his
house and I would take the car home and I
would watch there through the trees until he got
in the house and then toot the horn and go
home.

Q: He frequently stayed in the house alone?

A: Oh, yes, before they married. I don't know what
they did after they married.

JUROR: Did Mr. Bern ever tell you why he carried
that gun?

A: I used to ask him why he carried it and he said
if anybody tried to rob him he would cripple
them up but would not kill them, but if anybody
tried to overpower him or anybody that he liked,
he would kill them.

Slickum could not identify the pills in Paul's bedroom and was excused.

• • •

Blanche Williams had been Jean Harlow's personal maid for almost two years. She said she knew of no reason why Mr. Bern might want to take his life, she saw very little of him but Mrs. Bern was very happy with him.

• • •

Next, Coroner Nance called out, "Is Mr. Bern, the brother of the deceased here?"

No response.

"I understand he arrived late last night from New York and was very tired but that he told the officer he would be here."

No response.

"Is Mrs. Paul Bern here?"

No response.

"I understand she is not. I have here a letter, which I haven't looked at yet. I presume it is relative to her. I have a letter from Robert Helm Kennicott, which I will read to the jury.

" 'My dear Mr. Nance, Miss Jean Harlow has been under my care since Monday, September 5th, 1932, and has been suffering a severe nervous collapse. Her appearance before the coroner's jury would severely endanger her life. Sincerely yours, Robert Helm Kennicott.'

"Under the circumstances, we can't have her here. I am very sorry she is not here to assist us."

• • •

Detective Lieutenant Joseph Whitehead of the Los Angeles City Division stated that he arrived at the house at two-thirty in the afternoon, fifteen minutes after the call was received from Mr. Thalberg.

He describes the deceased as holding a .38-caliber Colt revolver, number 572972, firmly clasped in the right hand under the right side of the body. One shell was discharged, five bullets were still in the chamber.

Q: Were there any fingerprints on this gun?

A: On the side they were very faint, too faint to take a picture of, due to the fact there was oil on the gun.

Q: When you arrived there it appeared that no one had disturbed the position of the body or anything else about the room?

A: No, it didn't.

Q: Did it appear there had been any scuffle or anything of that sort in the room?

A: No sir.

Q: What is your conclusion as to whether or not this gunshot was homicidally or suicidally inflicted?

A: It was my conclusion it was suicide.

Q: I show you this book. Is that what you found there?

A: Yes sir.

Joyce and I assumed that detective Whitehead was being shown the diary.

Q: Where did you find it?

A: That was on the table in the bedroom.

Q: Laying open just as that is?

A: Laying open just as it is here.

Whitehead testified that he found no other writing of any kind in the house.

Reading through these pages in the transcript we were surprised that there was no mention at all of the suicide note that the detective had supposedly found in the diary. Instead, the inquest veered onto another subject.

"Isn't it customary," Whitehead was asked by one of the jurors, "when one commits suicide that the gun falls by the side and does not stay in the hand?"

The detective replied, "Not necessarily, no."

Before being excused, Whitehead declared that he first heard of Paul Bern's death when the Central Police Office relayed the call to him at approximately two-fifteen.

"There's an additional mystery here for me," I told Joyce. "Al Cohn called me early that morning and he knew Paul was dead. I always assumed he heard it through the Los Angeles police wire that he had in his house. Al had a close relationship then with the city's top brass and when he was writing crime stories he was always the first to know the details of a death in Los Angeles. But with Al long gone, I see no way to find out now how he knew that Paul was dead so early in the morning."

• • •

The next witness was Detective Lieutenant F. Condaffer of the Los Angeles Police Department. His testimony dealt with numerous bottles of pills found in the house. They were aspirin, quinine, "probably there would be a quart of pills all put together."

JUROR: Did you find in any of these tablets any of them that were labeled narcotics?

A: None of them labeled narcotics.

Joyce concentrated on the testimony of the last witness, Dr. Frank R. Webb, the assistant autopsy surgeon of the coroner's office. I had no desire to get immersed in his gory details about my friend.

At one point, Joyce called my attention to a statement by Dr. Webb that was confusing. "A gunshot wound entered his right temple, two inches in front of his right ear. It went through the skull and brain, exiting on the right side of the head, two inches above the attached border of the left ear."

"This doesn't make sense, Sam. It says the bullet went in on the right side and came out on the right side. Of course the bullet had to come out on the left side. It looks like a typographical error."

Dr. Webb concluded that the powder burns and the seared brain and shattered skull bones indicated a close proximity of the barrel of the gun at the time of the explosion.

Deputy District Attorney Wayne Jordan said, "I understand in your testimony, Doctor, you believe that the wound that caused the death was self-inflicted?"

A: It was of that type that you see in such cases.

Q: Find any deformities?

A: Only as stated, slightly underdeveloped.

Q: What was that?

A: Sexual organs showed slight underdevelopment— I would correct that. I would not say underdevelopment. I would say undersized. They were developed normally but undersized.

Q: In your opinion this could be a cause for this nervousness or melancholia?

A: No, I would not hardly think that would cause the nervousness or melancholia. It was not to the extreme to suggest that.

Q: Were they of such a character from your examination to indicate impotency?

A: No sir.

MR. JORDAN: That is all.

• • •

The coroner's jury was then asked to determine whether the death of the deceased, Paul Bern, was suicidal, homicidal, accidental or natural. The jury retired to arrive at a verdict.

The evidence presented to them permitted only one answer.

"Gunshot wound of head, self-inflicted by the deceased with suicidal intent at the home of the deceased,

9820 Easton Drive, West Los Angeles, California, motive undetermined."

• • •

I found much of this testimony very disturbing. When I got to Paul's house around half past nine, the gardener said Mr. Mayer had already come and gone. Hendry had been there too, but neither man was ever mentioned at the inquest. Nobody mentioned Dorothy Millette being there the previous night, or that Howard Strickling was there earlier that morning. The witnesses backed up Carmichael's testimony that he found the body at eleven-forty-five in the morning.

I was still downhearted about Paul's death when I went to the executive bungalow that noontime after Labor Day. I thought Irving was very lighthearted when he said, "LB is writing the script for the inquest." I saw now that what we've been doing is looking at a Louis B. Mayer production.

They actually were up at Paul Bern's house six or seven hours before the cops rolled in. If it was a simple suicide, what did the studio executives do all that time? They did something we didn't know about, they were covering up something.

In Howard Strickling they had the kind of man who could handle that.

13

·····

The Fixer

HE WAS KNOWN as "The Fixer" to every cop who prowled the late beat in Hollywood, the gamblers and drug pushers in business on Sunset Boulevard, and the madames who operated the brothels near the county line. They usually saw him in the early hours of the day when fixing was needed.

Howard Strickling was the son of a Presbyterian minister, deeply offended when someone suggested that he knew where the bodies were laid and by whom and when. He didn't deny it, however, because it was true.

In all his years as head of MGM's Publicity department Strickling was a press agent second, a suppress agent first. Mild, meek and unassuming, he held down the lid on sin: his was the voice that muted the scandals and quieted the gossip nobody was supposed to hear. It was "business as usual" with him to defuse the rumors of domestic mayhem between married stars, fix drunk-driving raps that piled up against studio workers every weekend, handle the tempers that snapped when newspaper photographers caught personnel in places where they were never supposed to be. Covering up came easily to Howard Strickling.

A prissy upbringing as a child in New England had made for an easy transfer to the highly conservative village of Gardena in Orange County, southern California. After his family moved there, he attended Gardena Agricultural High School with every intention of taking a job on a ranch after his graduation. At the school, he contributed articles that led to his editorship of *The Lark,* the weekly publication of his English class. Newspaper work also attracted him, he stood uncertainly on the brink of manhood, torn between choosing that or ranching, when a meeting with film director Rex Ingram sidetracked both careers and introduced him to the bizarre characters populating the new and colorful world of the movies.

Handsome Ingram, an Irishman full of rebellion and hot tempers, angry and uncompromising throughout his life, was the Metro Company's leading director, tied to a long-term contract. He brought Rudolph Valentino to prominence in *The Four Horsemen of the Apocalypse* and he starred Mexican-born Ramon Novarro in *Scaramouche,* followed by another success, *The Prisoner of Zenda.* Ingram was making outstanding films but couldn't get along with anyone who dared to give orders. Any move to interfere with his personal control of his films brought violent tantrums. It was war without end.

To maintain peace at Metro's Hollywood studio, the

company's mild-mannered president Marcus Loew allowed Ingram to take his entire unit abroad and make his pictures at Nice on the French Riviera. The director took Howard Strickling along.

In 1924, Loew bought the Goldwyn Studio in Culver City and Louis B. Mayer began to oversee all its productions. That was when the name Metro-Goldwyn-Mayer was created.

What Ingram didn't know at that time, and neither did Strickling, was that Mayer and Thalberg had devised a game plan for their operation. They would run a producer's studio and maintain rigid supervision over all film directors.

The fiercely independent thirty-two-year-old Ingram ran head-on into the even fiercer forty-year-old Mayer. Their first confrontation came about even before the three-company merger was finalized. Ingram had demanded from Mayer that he be made the director of the already announced epic *Ben-Hur* and he did not expect to be refused. But Mayer did refuse and Ingram never forgave him.

Those were difficult times for Strickling, because Ingram's animosity toward Louis B. Mayer was carried to extraordinary lengths. Strickling traveled back and forth between Nice and Culver City, trying to justify film-maker Ingram's insubordination to Mayer.

The next crisis occurred when *Mare Nostrum*, Ingram's first movie that he had readied for showing under the new deal, opened at the Criterion Theatre in New York with "Metro-Goldwyn-Mayer presents" on its main title. Ingram was affronted when Strickling reported to him by telephone from the New York theater that the title included Mayer's name. Because his contract was with the Metro Company, the director threatened instant legal moves to stop the film's exhibition. He further insulted Mayer by offering to allow the name of Goldwyn to be used, but not that of Mayer. Strickling was unable to dissuade Ingram from his determination, so quite amazingly, he settled the altercation with a heart-to-heart talk with Mayer. He actually persuaded the new studio head to take his name off the film, and *Mare Nostrum* appeared with "Metro-Goldwyn presents."

Mayer was impressed by Strickling's diplomacy. After Rex Ingram's Metro contract expired, Strickling became available and Mayer immediately offered him the top spot in the Metro-Goldwyn-Mayer studio Publicity department. Their affection for each other was strong and lasting, and Strickling allied himself beside his new boss for the remainder of his career.

He became a foremost figure in Mayer's Men, and knew all there was to know about the powerful executive. Throughout the years that MGM reigned so importantly in the movie industry, Howard handled public relations for Mayer and his studio with discretion. He believed in eloquent silences and that was usually all that anyone heard from him.

• • •

In an early hour of 1932's Labor Day, Strickling had to determine how Paul Bern's death would be presented to the press. It was imperative that the tragedy not cause harm to Jean Harlow—and if carried out successfully it might even enhance her career. Strickling's aim was to release publicity that would create sympathy for her.

That delicate maneuver utilized a very important element: over the years, it was labeled "the suicide note."

There was a report that while Mr. Mayer was in the producer's bedroom, he had found Paul's diary with a suicide note in it. Mayer took it away, but a little later he revealed the diary to Strickling, who convinced him to take it back and put it where he found it.

Detective Joseph Whitehead testified at the September 8 inquest that he found the diary on the dresser in Paul's bedroom. The Coroner's Register stated that "one Diary containing note" was delivered to police officer Whitehead for Jean's attorney Mendel Silberberg on September 15, 1932. The diary has never been seen again.

• • •

A retyped version of the note, which was not entirely accurate, was released to the press on the heels of disclosures that Paul was impotent. We had a photocopy of the original note. *Movie Mirror* magazine had printed it in its September 6, 1932, issue.

The cryptic text did not address Jean by name. It began "Dearest Dear," which was Paul Bern's custom-

Dearest Dear,

unfortunately this is the only way to make good the frightful wrong I have done you and to wipe out my abject humiliation, I Love you.

Paul

You understand that last night was only a comedy

ary salutation to the women he knew. It was on a cropped piece of paper that carried no date.

Those who believed the impotence theory saw the note as Paul's way to end the embarrassment caused by his frustration. I looked on the note as an apology to Jean because of Dorothy Millette's reemergence in his life. But while we were investigating, another possible answer came unexpectedly.

We were acquainted with Charles Higham, an Australian-born writer of biographies who resides on a Hollywood hillside. He heard we were delving into the matter of Jean Harlow and Paul Bern, and he called us to say he had information that could be helpful.

Higham has achieved a sort of fame with a series of word portraits, many of his books containing enough sensationalism to infuriate friends of the people he writes about. He had branded Errol Flynn as a Nazi sympathizer and Cary Grant as a homosexual, and was hard at work on a biography of the Duchess of Windsor. We made an appointment to meet him in a Hollywood restaurant, where he related one of the surprises of his life.

"In 1970 I lived in a humble apartment, coming back to Hollywood after working for *The New York Times*. A year or so later, Howard Strickling called me from Chino, where he had retired and was raising Hereford cattle. He wanted to talk and it amazed me. I was a struggling writer and he had been a real bigshot at MGM. He arrived in the middle of the afternoon, elegantly dressed, starched collar, although he was living on a ranch . . .

"He had a steel-trap face, that's the only way I can describe it. He explained that he was old, had information he wanted to get off his chest. He said that what he was about to tell me could not be published until after his death. He wouldn't allow me to take notes or use a tape recorder."

Strickling called the note attributed to Paul a fraud, Higham told us. Strickling and Mayer went to Bern's house that morning, and it was Louis B. Mayer's idea to create something that would look like a suicide note. He wanted to remove any chance that Jean Harlow could be suspected of a crime.

"That's what Howard came to tell me. I assumed from what he said that Mayer wrote the note . . ."

"Why would Strickling tell this to you?" I asked.

Charles set down his cup of tea. "I was terribly unimportant. It seemed to me he was toying with the idea of writing his life story and wanted someone he could dictate it to. Someone, I think, who wouldn't ask him too many questions. I never heard from him again."

He shrugged. "Strickling's gone now, of course . . ."

• • •

Strickling's confession to Charles Higham was difficult to ignore. It seemed as if MGM's retired publicity man was clearing his conscience of a secret that had burdened him for many years.

Higham's disclosure made us give the note a closer inspection.

"Look at this, Sam, the first word is misspelled," Joyce pointed out. "Unfortunately" is spelled "Unfortuately."

As many times as I had looked at that note, I never saw that before and I don't recall that anybody else had questioned that error.

She went on: "Look at the quotation mark in the last line: You understand that last night was—and there's a quote mark—'only a comedy—it seems as if it is the start of a quotation that wasn't completed. There's no close-quote. It may be that the note was cropped, in which case we'll never know if there was more to the sentence."

"Maybe that's why there's never been a real explanation of what that last sentence meant," I said. "If Paul wrote it . . ."

We went searching for more extended examples of his handwriting. But my letters from Paul are all typed, only his signature is handwritten. MGM's archives has letters and contracts, but all of them are typed.

Over the years, Paul's style of writing his name had changed from neatness to playful abandon and flourishes. Joyce thought that the signature on the note didn't match those on my letters.

We looked with new suspicions at the note and decided to investigate the possibility of forgery.

FORGET IT, you're amateurs."

Charles Sachs, a world-renowned handwriting authority, looked up with what writers describe as "ill-concealed amusement." The big, bewhiskered, and outspoken expert handed back the copy of the note and a letter we had given him signed Paul Bern and said, "The same man wrote both of these. I tell you, this is Paul Bern's handwriting."

Sachs also had a logical comment about the postscript in the note, "You understand that last night was 'only a comedy." He said, "It would never have been put in by a forger! It points to Jean Harlow being in the house.

Why would Louis B. Mayer attract attention to her if she wasn't there? She was over with her mother. That's what I've always heard."

We had to agree with him.

Joyce asked, "But what about the misspelling—"

Sachs stopped her in midsentence. "Erudite people—people like Paul Bern—often have sloppy handwriting. That's probably why he typed his letters."

Joyce was taken aback by his curtness. Annoyed, she said, "Look at it again. See if you can tell us what makes it a suicide note?"

Sachs folded his arms, stared at her a moment and then snapped, "I didn't say it was a suicide note! I just said Bern wrote it!"

14

· · · · ·

Cover-ups

WHENEVER LOUIS B. MAYER frowned on what appeared to him as censurable goings-on at the MGM studio, it had a ripple effect through the people close to him. When the studio boss opposed certain activities, there were men who followed his lead.

Eddie Mannix was one the boss could count on. Casting himself as a house detective, Mannix paid close attention to the love affair between Jean Harlow and Paul Bern.

There was a funny side to that, because Mannix was a top-level woman chaser himself.

His first wife, Bernice, played around like he did, she spent a lot of her time in the company of other men, and let their friends know she wouldn't quit that game until her husband did.

Al Wertheimer operated the Dunes, a gambling house in the desert, a few miles south of Palm Springs. He was driving Bernice back to her hotel after the

Dunes closed one night—it was actually by the dawn's early light—when his car went off the road. It plunged into the sand and rolled over. The accident crippled him for life and killed Bernice Mannix. Her death hit the executives of MGM hard, as incidents like that always did: they were in the business of creating magic, the films with happy endings were still the vogue, and death rarely figured in their thinking. When it occurred so suddenly, as was also the case with Paul Bern, the pall it cast over them was tangible. On days like that, the magic stopped.

Mannix mourned Bernice only briefly and was soon enjoying the company of other women. He never made a pass at Jean Harlow; on the screen, Jean superbly portrayed the hard-boiled characters he was drawn to, but offscreen she wasn't his type at all.

Broadway showgirl Imogene Wilson, a notorious two-fisted drinker, was the kind of girl he liked. That was until she registered a complaint with the Culver City Police Department, charging Mannix with beating her. The next thing she knew she received a visit from a detective who said he had evidence that she was dealing in narcotics. The information, which was true, had come from Mannix. The detective offered to drop the narcotics matter if she left town.

Imogene Wilson, who used the name Mary Nolan in the two movies she had appeared in at MGM, thought it wise to withdraw her complaint and return to Broadway. Mannix put a studio car at her disposal to take her to the railroad station—the chauffeur was one of

Whitey Hendry's men, making sure she caught the train.

At this point, a brassy Broadway showgirl, Toni Lanier, once renowned in Broadway revues as "the girl with the million-dollar legs," moved in with him and in time became Mrs. Mannix.

With men, Mannix preferred the company of bon-vivant talent agents, bootleggers and bookmakers, to whom he gave unlimited freedom to roam the studio lot. Most of them made a point of dropping into his office in the late afternoons. There was booze for everybody in the portable bar that he opened to all comers. Frank Orsatti, before and after his career as a bootlegger, saw to it that Mannix always had plenty of liquid refreshments on hand.

In the fall, choice tickets for football games, particularly those played by the popular University of Southern California team, could be had in his office. Agents contrived ways of getting hold of seats on the fifty-yard line and brought them to Mannix to curry his favor. They also brought college athletes, discoveries who had acting aspirations: "You can't go broke making a buck!" was the popular way to explain their pitch for a screen test.

It was a fun meeting place. They drank, swapped jokes, and relayed the latest Hollywood gossip. It was during one of those happy cocktail-hour parties in the busy spring months of 1932 that Mannix was told by gangster Eddie Nealis that Jean Harlow was oversexed and had an obsessive need for men. When Mannix passed that on to Mayer, he accepted it as verification of his earlier belief that she was a "slut."

During his long tenure as MGM studio manager, Mannix created a sort of subterranean pipeline that provided him with easy access to the intimate secrets of the studio personnel.

A telegraph office was located in the basement of MGM's front building. The little office did a healthy business. It accelerated the sending of wires for business purposes, and having it in such easy reach was a convenience for everybody working in the studio. But only a very few top executives were aware that copies of every telegram, incoming and outgoing, were delivered to Mannix at the end of each day.

After perusing the telegrams ending with "love, love, love" that Paul was receiving from Jean when she was making her personal appearances, Mannix informed Mayer about the developing relationship between the producer and the platinum blonde.

At lunch one day in the executive bungalow, Thalberg declared his objections to the practice of passing personal communications on to Mannix. Mayer had expressed alarm to Thalberg about Paul's romance with Jean, and the production head guessed at the source.

"Let's not run a police state, LB," Thalberg said. "If we do we won't have time to make pictures."

Mayer contended that the confidential information that Mannix secured was of enormous value to the studio. Organized labor was just becoming interested in film workers: union leaders were recruiting members in various departments, and telegrams concerning that activity were flying back and forth with eastern headquarters. That in itself, Mayer argued, justified secret perusals of the telegrams. He made a forceful defense, hammering at his usual theme that tactics of benefit to one benefited all. Thalberg caved in to Mayer's persuasion. A bargain was struck between them, all telegrams continued to be funneled to the Mannix office—but part of that bargain was that no roadblocks would be set in the path of romances by studio personnel. Jean continued to send her telegrams to Paul, and Mannix continued to read them even though he didn't approve of her affectionate messages.

With the information available to him, Mannix was always able to pass on ultra-exclusive material to Howard Strickling about the private activities of studio personnel that nobody was ever supposed to know.

ON AUGUST 25, 1973, I was one of a number of Howard Strickling's colleagues who joined the retired publicity man at his ranch in Chino, California, to celebrate his seventieth birthday.

I was writing my book about Mayer and Thalberg then. Howard had contributed some statistics about the profits and losses of the films the studio made. During his birthday party he walked me aside and said he had been offered a large advance from a publisher to write his memoirs. "I wish you'd work with me on it," he said, "if I decide to do it."

His memoirs could make one of the greatest exposés of Hollywood anyone could imagine. I was interested, very much so, but I had to finish my own book first. We agreed to meet again a month later on September 25.

That morning, Toni Lanier Mannix called Howard and demanded that he come at once to her home on Schuyler Road in Beverly Hills. Eddie Mannix was dead then, but that didn't stop his widow from being her usual imperious self.

Howard told her he had an appointment with me, but she said, "We're all MGM people, aren't we, we stick together, don't we, you tell Sam I want him here too, so don't give me any of your fucking excuses, just do as I tell you!"

Howard picked me up in a battered old car, a vintage Pontiac estate wagon. On our way to see Toni Mannix he said he had definitely decided to go ahead with his autobiography. "I'm still looking to you to help me write it," he said.

With a scowl that matched the black dye she applied to her hair, Toni was waiting at the ten-foot-high gate to the premises where she was living alone. The former showgirl had thrown considerable weight around MGM after she married the studio manager. "People like Toni can't accept the fact that times have changed," Howard had observed gloomily on our way to see her.

She was in a highly nervous state, her voice loud and

shrill as she began demanding what she wanted even before we walked into the house. A reporter for a nationally circulated gossip sheet had phoned her early that morning, and told her that he was writing an article about the late actor George Reeves and his relationship with the Mannixes. When he asked her for her comment, she hung up on him.

"We've got to stop it," she said. "You can do it, Howard. You must!"

"Now look, Toni," he said, "he'll love it if you make any move to stop him. He'll feature that and it will only draw more attention to the article. You do what you like but I won't get into it, and Sam shouldn't either."

She argued but couldn't shake him.

As we drove away, I said to Howard, "What was that all about?"

With his eyes glued to the road, he said, "Oh, there was an actor played Superman on television, George Reeves. He lived in that house with the Mannixes for a while and had an affair with Toni. Reeves moved out, he was about to marry New York socialite Leonore Lemmon, when he was found shot to death. The coroner ruled it suicide, but the police thought mysterious circumstances were at play. Nobody did anything about it —even when his mother claimed he had been murdered. Toni Mannix inherited his estate."

Howard hesitated, then added, "There was a hot rumor around town that Mannix had the guy killed. That's probably what that gossip sheet is going to say."

"Is that all you want to tell me about it?" I asked him.

"Well, Eddie did do it, of course."

Before I got out of his car I said, "That's quite a revelation. It brings up a point about your book. If we discuss suicides, murders, cover-ups, how many stories like that are you willing to tell?"

"I haven't thought that out yet," he said, and drove away.

• • •

Strickling and I met again in January 1974, this time with the intention of getting down to a serious discussion about his book. Howard used one of the offices that was part of the Louis B. Mayer Foundation on Wilshire Boulevard in Beverly Hills.

I sat down at a desk across from him with a notebook and a pen.

"Let me give you an example of the stuff I want to tell," Howard said. "Between 1925 and 1955, we shot two hundred thousand publicity stills in my department and not one of them shows a player with a drink in his hand."

"Are you sure that's what the publisher expects you to write?"

"If he thinks I'm going to dish out nothing but dirt, he's in for a big disappointment."

"I think he'll want facts about the stars that have never been told till now—things that only you know.

You can't just write a book about clean publicity stills. You know that, Howard."

He took a long look through the office window, staring at traffic on Wilshire Boulevard. It seemed quite obvious that he was thinking about studio secrets he had kept hidden from view since the day he showed up for work there.

"I guess it would be okay now to talk a little bit," he said. "Most of the men were hell-raisers anyway, they might even like their kids to know the kind of men they really were. We were picturing our stars like Wally Beery, Spencer Tracy, Mel Douglas, Walter Pidgeon as idols but I can't even remember all the times I was routed out of bed to calm down the call girls who wanted an extra hundred bucks more than they could get out of their ordinary customers. Or to fix things when a star cursed out the cop who pulled him in for speeding. We didn't have angels under contract, you know, Sam."

"What about the women?"

"What women?"

"Well, say, Joan Crawford."

He shook his head. "You mean those pornographic movies she did, the ones we had to buy up? No way. That, I'm never gonna tell! Listen, it was my job to make all our people adorable and I did it. I spent my whole life inventing cover-ups, hiding everything from spitting on the sidewalks to murder and I'm damned if I'm going to expose them now. I'm not doing a book that will blow away the things I worked so hard to keep secret."

Our plan to write his life story ended there and along with it went whatever revelations Howard Strickling might have told me about Paul Bern.

15

·····

Masquerade

AMONG THE PRODUCERS of Irving Thalberg's staff, Paul Bern had an intelligent uniqueness. He was fascinated by stories that expressed his own ideals and sought to provide uplifting themes that filmgoers from the lower depths could enjoy.

Many of his films led to controversy over the way he pictured life. After his death, opinions of Paul as a man received sensational attention in the press; this interest persists even to this day.

···

Wilson Mizner, an occasional screenwriter, holding court in his favorite booth in the Hollywood Brown Derby, spoke up when he was told that Paul Bern had shot himself. "He got the right man."

A New York film pundit described Bern as "sadistically impotent!" Writers in fan magazines and Sunday film supplements described Paul after his death as a sexual despoiler, psychotic deviate, a man of maniacal behavior in the bedroom. In the flood of invectives by writers who claimed to have positive knowledge of his erotic behavior, the word "impotent" seemed mild and inoffensive.

Jack Moffitt, a correspondent for the *Kansas City Star*, contributed a weekly column to *Limelight*, a Hollywood periodical. In the past, Moffitt had claimed a friendship with MGM star John Gilbert and used him as the source of the material purporting to be authentic. He offered his readers an exclusive version of Bern's behavior, through the courtesy of John Gilbert, "who shared a house with Bern and told me the director was a sexual midget."

When Gilbert's career began, in the days of silent films, the actor reigned over all other stars. And more, he was also the love idol of his time. But the great films that he made—such as *The Big Parade*— didn't have sound, and the coming of talking films destroyed his he-man image. His cultured voice simply didn't match the tough characters he portrayed.

He never forgave the men who wouldn't risk using him again in their new high-budget talking films. The chief offender, as he saw it, was Paul Bern, who rejected his desperate bid to play in *Grand Hotel*, casting instead John Barrymore in the lover's role opposite Greta Garbo.

His career slid downhill and he began to drink excessively. He died soon after. Long after the death of John

Gilbert, Moffitt continued to tarnish Paul Bern in Hollywood's history.

Moffitt wrote:

> It became a traumatic necessity for Bern to appear in public with the sexiest-looking girls in Hollywood. He'd come home infuriated by frustration. Once, after a date with Barbara La Marr, his frenzy led him to rip out the bathroom fixtures. Usually he got satisfaction by beating some woman and he found one who was sufficiently masochistic to enjoy this. She fell in love with him. Then Bern, as a supreme gesture of manhood . . . tried beating Jean and she went home to her mother. . . . The masochistic woman brought Bern's first wife (from whom he'd never been divorced) to Hollywood from the East. Knowing that his marriage to Miss Harlow had been bigamous, Bern shot himself.

• • •

A top screenwriter at MGM, Frances Marion shared honors with Anita Loos for ability and dependability. The two highly attractive fixtures on the studio's writer list were strong-minded and solidly entrenched in their positions: Anita wrote comedy, Frances wrote everything.

Anita Loos called Paul "a German psycho" in her autobiography *Kiss Hollywood Good-by.* No one disputed it.

In *Off With Their Heads!,* Frances Marion wrote that she was adapting a stage musical for Paul to do as a film.

Franz Lehár's *Gypsy Love* was the frame she hung the story on. It became, she said, a "fantastic mishmash" about a princess in love with a rebellious knight. When the knight's arrogance was too much for her she ordered him flogged in the public square.

The movie was to star the Metropolitan Opera baritone Lawrence Tibbett in his first film and of course, I had him sing defiantly when the whip curled around his body. I was a bit worried about that flogging scene, it was quite absurd, so when I took it to Paul I sat in his office and watched him read it.

He read it very intently, then put the script down. "The whip," he said, "do you see it motivated by masochism or sadism?"

"Neither," I said. "There's nothing more vapid than a singer under the lash, taking his punishment in silence. I put the whipping scene into the film so we could use Tibbett's voice, why not, it's virile and you can back him up with a full orchestra. I know it's nonsense . . ."

"Not at all," he broke in. "You're a clever woman, Frances. You assume naïveté, but it's obvious that you're a student of the psychology of sex, as I am."

"I don't know a damn thing about the psychology of sex and probably never will," I told him. "It's just a gimmick, do you want me to cut the scene out?"

"Never!" His vehemence startled me. "I'm sure it will be the high spot of the picture."

Mystified, I left the office of this soft-spoken man whose mind seemed to pursue such strange outward-bound ideas. He was extremely sophisticated, I never really approved of his marriage to Jean Harlow, she seemed so young and untutored alongside of him, but I'm afraid we'll never know what went on behind their locked doors. Jean has conscientiously refused to speak about it.

•••

After reading and rereading Frances Marion's story, I had to conclude that her denunciations of Paul were part of the artistic differences that rose up constantly between filmmakers.

But Jeanne Williams told me a real-life story about her experience with Paul . . .

Jeanne was a young blond *Ziegfeld Follies* chorus girl from Rochester, New York, who quit the show and eloped with a boy who told her he had a wealthy family in the South. That background was true, but he neglected to tell his bride he had been disowned. When they drove up to the mansion where his parents lived, having a wife from Broadway didn't improve his situation. The door was locked against them.

They headed west then, to southern California, where Jeanne hoped to break into the movies. A succession of talent agents told her that "blondes are a dime-a-dozen out here," which discouraged her bridegroom more than it did her. She dyed her hair black, assumed a Russian accent and changed her name to Sonia Karlov. Her young husband, lacking faith in such a wild escapade, disappeared with the car that had brought them to California.

The first film mogul to interview the pseudo-Russian

actress was so taken with her that he signed her to star in *The Godless Girl,* which was ready to go into production. He was the great Cecil B. DeMille, the highly acclaimed producer of spectacular biblical epics and ancient love tales. To introduce Sonia Karlov, he unceremoniously dumped Lina Basquette, whom he had slated to play the title role in that silent film.

That was 1928, when DeMille had an independent producing unit at the Pathé Studio in Culver City. Paul Bern was working there as a producer with a known talent for writing. He was asked to revise the scenario of *The Godless Girl* to accommodate the newly cast Russian actress.

"CB," as DeMille was called, was an imperious figure on the Hollywood scene. His usual attire consisted of a white Safari outfit and black leather boots; he carried a cropped whip, with which he used to beat at imaginary horses as he strode around the studio. He was a pioneer in many aspects of film production, including the invention of the legendary "yes man." To cross CB was to invite instant dismissal from his presence.

"This creature is more exciting than Basquette," said DeMille when he introduced Sonia Karlov to Paul on a rehearsal stage. "She was born to play the Godless Girl."

Sonia was wearing a leopard-skin leotard that was to serve as her sole costume in the film. She was diligently practicing how to snap the whip she had to carry, to frighten off male predators in the long-ago era DeMille planned to re-create.

When Paul spoke to her he used his rudimentary

knowledge of Russian. Sonia, who didn't understand a word he was saying, had anticipated someone might do that and was ready for it. She told him in broken phrases it was necessary for her to learn English quickly. She begged him to help her by conversing in that language.

Sonia, Paul, and DeMille went from the rehearsal hall to the studio commissary, where the Hollywood press corps was assembled to get a firsthand look at Lina Basquette's replacement. DeMille gave Sonia an eloquent introduction, predicting she would take her place among the greatest stars of the silver screen. He was in the middle of his speech when Lina Basquette threaded her way through the assemblage until she stood eyeball to eyeball with DeMille. Her voice was loud and shrill.

"This girl is no more Russian than I am! She's Jeanne Williams and she was in the *Ziegfeld Follies* with me!"

It plunged the luncheon into chaos. A furious DeMille ordered the imposter put out of his studio at once. Paul, seated beside the director on the dais, reminded him that less than an hour before he had said she was born for the role. DeMille ignored him. He depicted himself as the victim of a shabby plot from which Lina Basquette had saved him. Thereupon he reinstated her in the starring role of *The Godless Girl*.

Later that night, as Jeanne Williams related it to me, she was alone in her Hollywood apartment when her phone rang. "The man calling me was Paul Bern," she said, "and I heard in a gentle voice, 'Forgive me but I wonder if you can use a friend?' "

"I don't think I can describe how much that call meant to me," Jeanne said.

He came to her small apartment and they talked. She agreed with him that DeMille would probably make it impossible for her to find studio work. When she told him she didn't have enough money to go back east, he put two hundred dollars on the table.

"I could only think of one way to show my gratitude. I knew he was a man of the world, very sophisticated . . . so I asked him to stay with me that night.

"He shook his head and when I begged him, he ran out the door. After he died I read that he was impotent, but I knew he had had affairs with flashy women like Pola Negri and Barbara La Marr. He told me, 'My dear, if we have an affair it will change everything and take away the enjoyment I get by just helping you.'

"I always believed he said exactly what he meant to say," she concluded.

It was a story that much of Hollywood found difficult to understand. Paul had rejected going to bed with a woman he hardly knew and never romanced.

He knew the size of his penis didn't compare to that of those macho men who were working alongside him. He must have been sensitive to the taunting remarks of John Gilbert, Clark Gable, and Eddie Mannix, who openly paraded their own sexual prowess. He was out of their league in that respect.

But Paul's game was played on a different field.

Hollywood historian Seymour Stern wrote, "Paul Bern's deeds of decency affected all Hollywood. He helped legions of people, including actors, actresses, writers, ex-directors, cameramen, prop men and extras and saved them from starvation."

Adela Rogers St. Johns wrote that "Paul was the best loved man in Hollywood, a cultured mind with flashes of genius."

Herman G. Weinberg, another highly regarded historian of film-world deeds, noted in the essay "In Praise of Paul Bern" that "he was one of the gentlest and most civilized of the entire Hollywood coterie."

Irene Mayer Selznick, too, described him in her book *A Private View*, as "probably the single most beloved figure in Hollywood. He was special in many ways, the only person I ever knew who cherished people he loved as much for their frailties as for their virtues."

• • •

Paul read classic books to Jean and analyzed their meanings. She told Carey Wilson, "All I want is to sit at his feet and learn the things he knows."

He took her to previews, where his associates first saw them together, some watching with varying attitudes of concern. Jean caught the looks passing between them, Paul had to assure her that they were friendly but misguided efforts to protect him.

"They think I'm a sitting duck for actresses," he said, smiling, and urged her to laugh it off.

He took her to the final showings of the polished works after the retakes were in, the cuts were made and the music score properly inserted. Their dates averaged one a week. Afterward, he and Jean went on to late-night suppers in off-the-beaten-path bistros that provided escape from prying eyes. These were romantic trysts and they sidetracked shop talk although both knew that she was caught in a career slowdown. Paul hoped that some day he could rescue her.

He was enchanted by his charming, animated companion and her amusing comments on the types of men she encountered. Paul stood out in sharp contrast to those men, and their numerous dates were evidence that she liked him for it. She had none of the guile she conveyed on the screen, she didn't hide how she felt—and, of course, neither did he.

He steered clear of her athletic activities, he didn't go in for them, ever. She excelled at golf—a game he wanted nothing of, never joining in the studio's annual golf tournaments, as other executives did. "I'm not the athletic type," he told friends and associates.

After Paul's death and the stories that he beat Jean on their wedding night surfaced, actress Colleen Moore wrote in her autobiography *Silent Star,* "Had it been possible for a man of his nature to even try to harm her, he couldn't have hit her more than once before Jean would have floored him."

The pert bob-haired Moore was at the reception on Easton Drive, the day after the marriage. She arrived early and went into the house to talk to Jean, who, she noted, was dressed as usual in slacks. A short time later

Jean's mother came in saying, "Baby, you'd better get dressed before the other guests start arriving."

Moore writes:

Harlow never wore underclothes. She hated them, I guess if I'd had her beautiful figure—Jean was a size thirty-four—I wouldn't have wanted to bind it up with girdles and bras either. Anyway, she took off her slacks and blouse, standing there as the good Lord made her (And what a job He did!) while we helped her into her long garden dress.

Now if she'd been covered with black and blue marks or had marks covered with make-up, we would have known it. You can't fool an actress about covering make-up. Jean had no marks, no make-up. If she was anything other than her usual self, she was happier.

Marie and I were also at the reception. We saw Paul and Jean holding hands like adolescents.

WHEN JOYCE AND I were searching for the truth about Paul Bern, we sought further corroboration of what Colleen Moore remembered. William Tuttle had been head of MGM's Makeup department and Sydney Guilaroff was its hairstylist. Both of them told us they often heard talk about Jean being beaten by Paul from radio and television commentators who reported things like "he savaged her brutally."

"Jean was making tests for *Red Dust,*" said Tuttle. "She was trying on different costumes, so there'd be no way for her to hide the cuts and bruises she was supposed to have. No one I know ever saw one."

"She had to try different hairdos too," said Guilaroff. "She'd take off her dress and put on a robe while we worked on her. When I came to MGM there were men and women who remembered her well from the time she did *Red-Headed Woman,* and nobody—repeat nobody —ever saw the slightest blemish on her. She was a great favorite, in fact, there were men in the hairdressing department who thought she was the greatest. I'd say that if Paul Bern or anyone tried to beat up Jean they would have organized a posse and strung him up from the roof of Stage Six."

J. J. Cohn was in charge of MGM's overall production, guiding the making of each film through the process, for all the years that Paul was employed as a producer. It was Cohn's job to see to it that every project stayed within its budget and on schedule. He was, so to speak, a supervisor of supervisors.

"Paul was a real loner," he said, "but I knew him well, we'd hold production meetings in his office before his pictures started shooting. And he never raised his voice or lost his temper. That wasn't how it was with many of our producers, believe me. We had shouting matches you could hear for miles. No, I can't buy the idea that he mistreated Jean Harlow or, for that matter, any woman. He simply wasn't the type.

"He ran his films from his office," Cohn said. "Unlike

most producers, he rarely ever showed up on a stage or a location where his pictures were being shot. He concentrated on his scripts and left the filming of it to others. He kept his eyes on the story. If he thought he detected something missing when he looked at the rushes, he'd phone it in. I, personally, held him in high regard."

• • •

Paul engaged in sexual liaisons before his marriage to Jean. They were fast affairs involving women he felt comfortable with. They probably helped him overcome his inhibitions.

Chicago newspaper columnist and TV commentator Irv Kupcinet told us that he raised the subject of Paul's sex life while interviewing the celebrated stripper and fan dancer Sally Rand. Miss Rand enjoyed revealing her body and her sexual relationships.

On *Kup's Show* she said, "I can speak from experience. I know firsthand and can vouch for it, Paul Bern was not impotent."

• • •

"Paul is obsessed with sex," observed Thalberg.

Irving's Boys were meeting in the executive bungalow right after the preview of *Red-Headed Woman*.

Those meetings were real theater; Paul was at his best when he attended them. He was always able to visualize a full-length movie by simply hearing a verbal outline of a plot.

Thalberg was passionate about the importance of a

story and so was my assistant Kate Corbaley. She had a marvelous faculty of condensing the essentials of a book or play when she described one to the producers. We would bring them the latest and best submissions, and when she finished telling a story there would be a discussion pro and con over its screen values. If a property met with general approval and we decided to acquire it, Thalberg would make the assignment to whomever he believed best able to produce it.

Occasionally, Mrs. Corbaley would tell a story requested by a producer who saw particularly attractive features in it and, by sponsoring it that way, he had a proprietary hold on its production.

Paul asked Mrs. Corbaley to tell D. H. Lawrence's privately printed novel *Lady Chatterley's Lover*. Not only was the book banned from public sale, it was also prohibited from film production by the industry's own watchdog against sin—more officially the Association of Motion Picture Producers. That organization, which was funded by all the major companies, was presided over by a czar of movie morals, a former Indiana deacon, Will H. Hays. The Association was universally known as the Hays Office.

Chatterley was on a list of about fifty banned books and plays that the office of Will Hays circulated to the studios. All of them were judged indecent and obscene, but the more discreet word used was "unacceptable." Being listed didn't bar them absolutely, some of them did make it to the screen. As Thalberg and Paul well knew, hours were spent in story meetings like this one trying to circumvent the Hays Office edicts—an ironic twist, which could be likened to legislators scheming to outwit laws they had voted to uphold for their own good.

Mrs. Corbaley wasn't keen about *Lady Chatterley's Lover*, she was offended by its frank descriptions of an illicit love affair. But she had a high regard for Paul and after making her feelings known to him, he still wanted it told—so she agreed to tell it.

As soon as Mrs. Corbaley explained that Paul wanted to make *Lady Chatterley's Lover*, Thalberg stopped her. He knew about the book, of course, it was well publicized and invariably described as pornographic. Press previews of the still unreleased *Red-Headed Woman* were already igniting new fires of censorship.

"A film like this would really be asking for trouble," exclaimed Thalberg.

Paul made a fervent pitch for it: "If we star Jean Harlow in *Lady Chatterley's Lover*, we'll have the box-office hit of the year." He was sure that he could treat the book's steamy text subtly enough to get it past the Hays Office ban.

"I'd be crazy not to agree, of course it would be a box-office hit, especially if we starred Jean," said Thalberg. "But I'd be even crazier if I let you do it! There'll be a whole new uproar by censor boards around the country."

He looked long at Paul and then he went on.

"Are you suggesting that Jean go back and play an Englishwoman again? Wasn't that the miscasting in

Hell's Angels that you complained about? I thought you're the one who brought that up and we agreed she should do comedies from now on."

"There's a difference, now that she's being hailed as a star," said Paul. "Now we can go all out to display her sensuous qualities. She's like a tiger, she has a fire . . ."

"Hold it," interrupted Thalberg. "You know, Paul, I'm always worried about your way of portraying women on the screen."

Paul leaned across the conference table, speaking sweetly and deliberately.

"If there's any criticism of how I make films about women I'd like to hear it from them. Most of my films have dealt with women and they've yet to complain. I happen to have a wide circle of female friends."

"You have a reputation for being taken to the cleaners by every woman you meet," said Thalberg cheerfully. "Let's not continue this debate. I want Hyman and Stromberg to make the next two Harlow films, and we will not make *Lady Chatterley's Lover.*"

Paul managed to keep his emotions under control. He made a diverting reply that went like this: "My dear Irving, Hollywood is the capital of myopia. People in this town look at other people but don't see them. I have twenty-twenty vision when I look at women. I adore them and I'm fascinated by them and I do see them. If I lose a little because I love them it's a price I'm willing to pay!"

"Then, let me suggest you do something different from your usual film," said Thalberg. "It's good discipline, a way to extend your creative powers. Make a film without women. I'm not being facetious, Paul, pick up 'The Willow Walk' and see if you can lick it—and I'll give you any star that you feel is right for it, just tell me who you want and you've got him."

Paul left the meeting without another word and later he called me in the Story department and asked that the Sinclair Lewis short story be sent to him, as well as all the material about it that was in the files.

He could not object to Thalberg's assignment because the studio had bought the film rights to "The Willow Walk" at Paul's urging when he was the only producer on the lot intrigued with its possibilities.

Sinclair Lewis's 'The Willow Walk' dealt with a dapper, respected bank teller in a small town. His congenial character was the exact opposite of his dour twin brother, a strange recluse who was writing a religious treatise, a man who seldom ventured out of their isolated home. Actually, the dour twin brother didn't exist; he was invented by the teller in order to stage an embezzlement of funds from the bank where he was employed.

Perfecting every detail of his ingenious scheme, the teller commits the embezzlement and vanishes. The authorities can find no trail to follow, it was a one-man job, no clues involve the "twin brother" who goes on living in the house. Pretending he is the recluse, the embezzler plans to wait two years, when the crime should be forgotten, then go to South America with the stolen money.

But, ironically, his masquerade overwhelms him, he

takes on the recluse's personality and can no longer carry off the escape. A thief steals his hidden cache and he is left with nothing, not even the congenial personality he previously enjoyed. He tries to confess the truth but nobody believes him, they look on him as a madman. Defeated, he becomes the town derelict, trapped by his own cleverness.

• • •

Paul worked on the screenplay of "The Willow Walk" until he died. He considered the masquerade aspect of the story particularly fascinating, and with good reason. He was deeply involved in a masquerade of his own.

The film was never made.

16

·····

The Morality Clause

ALTHOUGH JEAN was a long way from being a child, Paul wasn't sure she would understand the love he once had for Dorothy.

After his death, Jean told her friend Carey Wilson that one evening, at a corner table of a small restaurant, Paul had made an effort to tell her about an earlier time in his life. Cautiously, he mentioned to her that he had an old friend who was ill and had fallen on hard times. He explained to her that this friend lived in the east and needed money and he was providing it.

Paul's reputation for generosity was well known to Jean and she took this to be another example. "He never told me his friend's name so I assumed that he was speaking of a man," Jean told Carey Wilson.

•••

Paul had told me, shortly before his death, that Dorothy had been in a coma for ten years and to her the time had passed as if it was a single night. I accepted that the way he told it and what's more, I went right on believing it.

But Joyce threw a shadow over the story I knew. She was right when she said nobody comes out of a coma after ten years and strides back into the real world. Now we were learning that "coma" was Paul's way of hiding the fact that Dorothy had a mental disease. It was known in the early twenties as dementia praecox, the merest mention of which was anathema in those days, a stigma to be avoided. Now, psychiatrists use the term schizophrenia.

By describing Dorothy in a coma, even long after she was out of the sanatorium, Paul was denying her existence as a human being to himself as well as to the film world he had moved into. He was protecting himself.

Dorothy had not been confined for ten years, as he had explained it, she stayed only one year in the Blythewood Sanitarium. After her doctors decided she was of no danger to society and able to function, they released her. She went back to the Algonquin Hotel and resumed her life at Paul's expense.

In Hollywood, Paul's secretary forwarded the monthly checks to New York and typed his letters to her.

• • •

All who remembered Dorothy Millette noticed her odd habit of dropping her lids over her eyes as she talked. It curtained off the wild light that glowed in them. That wasn't the only secret she sought to hide; her whole life was cloaked in mystery.

She was detached and reclusive by nature. Paul had concealed her place in his heart from all but his family and a few friends. He showed her off as Mrs. Bern in New York but made no move to marry her. "We laughed about it," was the way it seemed to him, but to Dorothy it may not have been a laughing matter.

Lovers and loners, they had found true companionship in each other. Once, they had shared beautiful plans for their future together, plans that crashed to earth the morning he couldn't wake her and she lost touch with reality.

• • •

The story of what happened to Paul and Dorothy was in fragments, a series of "takes," disconnected scenes that had to be spliced together to form the entire.

In his discussions of tragedy, Aristotle declared, "The entire must have a beginning, middle and end." Many filmmakers decided Aristotle's words were intended for them. French director Jean-Luc Godard revised Aristotle and brought him up to date, saying, "A story must have a beginning, middle and end but not necessarily in that order!"

• • •

One of the first to conjure up Dorothy's beginnings was Mrs. Alice Hanson. She saw the picture of Dorothy that appeared in the newspapers when the search for the "ghost wife" began, and took it to police headquarters in Los Angeles with a picture of her aunt Lena Erickson. There were striking resemblances between them.

Mrs. Hanson was sure that Mrs. Erickson, missing thirty-five years, was Dorothy's mother and she believed Dorothy was the woman's abandoned daughter. To find out if this was true, an appeal for relatives of Dorothy was circulated around the country. When no one came forward, the possibility that Mrs. Hanson had raised about Dorothy's origin faded away.

There were other avenues that might lead to Dorothy's earlier years, but most of them were closed.

The Blythewood Sanitarium in Connecticut was gone as well as all its documents. A Baptist church replaced it.

Ben Bodne, who owned the Algonquin Hotel after its celebrated manager Frank Case stepped down, made a search for his hotel's records when Dorothy resided there, but they had been lost.

Irene Harrison was reassigned to producer-director Sidney Franklin's secretarial staff in the Metro-Goldwyn-Mayer studio after Paul's death, but the slight, shy young woman soon departed without offering any word of her future plans. The little house that she lived in on Lafayette Place, Culver City, was sold to a man who bought it through real estate channels and said he never met Irene Harrison or any member of her family. All of Irene's connections with MGM had seemingly disappeared. After passing through many hands by the late 1980s, the MGM name disappeared from the studio, too.

AFTER PAUL and Dorothy returned from touring together in *Too Many Cooks* they found cheap rooms in Jersey City until East Coast movie studios began to make use of his writing and directing talents. Then, with more money in their pockets, they took up residence at the Algonquin Hotel. They were "living in sin," not the sort of status Paul wanted known to business acquaintances or his old-worldish family. She was Paul's secret, a liaison guarded closer than ever because of what he saw as odd developments in her personality.

Dorothy had joined Ben Greet's Shakespearean repertory company. The elderly British actor-manager's American group toured the East Coast, spreading the gospel of the Bard. She was part of the company that offered plain, direct Shakespeare, acting out the classics in open-air auditoriums, giving special and highly successful performances for schoolchildren. Meanwhile, Paul wrote film scripts. Their marital arrangement, unconventional for its time, went on.

But then, on the road, Dorothy began hearing voices and told her fellow actors she had become part of an inner circle of God. She returned to Paul in New York under the spell of an intense religious belief bordering on fanaticism.

She was acutely aware of her physical attractions: wanting to appear taller than she was, she wore extremely high heels, always adding lifts. She caught the attention of several artists who asked her to pose for them. One was the famous illustrator Howard Chandler Christy, who called his drawing of her "The Butterfly Girl."

But then her illness struck. It was the beginning of the ten-year stretch of time that, as Paul had explained it, passed as a single night.

During those years there were no more acting jobs for her. Paul had moved west to California and following her year in the sanatorium she stayed close to her Algonquin room. She had discarded her colorful outfits; gone were the red coat and turban that she often wore, in its place she attired herself only in dark materials. She spent nearly a decade there, a decade when the Algonquin Round Table in the dining room drew the theater's most prominent writers and producers at noon and when the hotel's central location offered one of the city's favorite meeting places every day and night. Passing unobtrusively through the lobby, Dorothy attracted no attention in the Bohemian climate of that hotel.

The few times Paul went to see her on his New York trips, he tried to talk to her—but she only heard her own voices. Unaware of the passage of time, she pictured herself as a young Shakespearean actress with a great future in biblical films. She seemed not to know there was anything wrong with her, although mentioning the Bible threw her into religious rantings. Henry Bern reported that these visits were so painful to Paul that they made him physically ill; eventually he stopped seeing her.

HENRY BERN shocked Hollywood and the world when he told reporters, "Paul was never married before he wedded the screen star Jean Harlow, but he lived with a woman once, a long time ago."

The 1930s were years of rigid adherence to righteousness. One had to be around at that time to know what an impact the man's statement had.

The Hays Office moved in then to peep intently at the way Hollywood was operating. It focused on the people who were working there and watched over every story that was considered worth filming. My assistant, Kate Corbaley, an elderly but most liberal-minded woman, reflected sarcastically during a story meeting, "If we let these bluenoses have their way, gentlemen, the only stories you'll be hearing from me will be Cinderella, Pollyanna and Little Red Riding Hood."

The Hays Office took its work very seriously, and when MGM attempted to register a title for a Norma Shearer film, Lovely as Sin, it was turned down. "The title connotates a message that is entirely unacceptable," said the written rejection from the Hays Office.

Any accusation of immorality could hang like a cloud over Hollywood. Lives could be ruined. With so much riding on the men and women playing heroes and heroines, and every prominent face and figure projected on the screen worth a fortune, studios had to protect their actors and actresses as well as themselves.

It was in this period that the Morality Clause was born: actors, producers, directors, writers and executives, everyone whose signature was on a film contract agreed to live a circumspect life. Deviation from the straight and narrow paths of clean human behavior gave a studio the right to dismiss the transgressor.

Paul Bern had such a clause in his MGM contract and so did Jean Harlow.

• • •

All story situations involving rampant sex were highly disapproved of by edict of the Hays Office. According to the code, the only acceptable punishment for transgressors at the end of such screen adventures "must end in banishment or death."

Sex was a specter that rose up vividly at a story meeting that I was presiding over late in 1931. Reflecting on the events of that day, it is obvious now that the situation that occurred there closely paralleled Paul's relationship with Dorothy Millette. But he was the only one there who knew it.

It had begun as a simple business transaction.

When talent agent Minna Wallis, a comely spinster, met thirty-year-old Clark Gable backstage in Los Angeles, he was appearing in the touring melodrama *The Last Mile.* She offered to help him seek a screen career. Minna had fine connections, her brother Hal Wallis was an important producer with Warner Brothers, which gave her better than ordinary status in Hollywood society. Making the party circuit sidestepped the strained auditions Gable would have to endure with low-echelon subordinates in casting offices. He readily agreed to be her escort.

Clark Gable was an ingratiating fellow, "more of a heavy than a hero" was the appraisal of one producer who turned him down. Minna Wallis landed a part for him in MGM's *The Easiest Way*, an ordinary role in what the studio considered an ordinary program movie.

But it exploded with excitement at its first preview. The audience in the Alexander Theatre in Glendale sat bolt upright whenever a fleeting shot of Gable appeared on the screen. He projected a tangible magic. Thalberg came out of the theater and beckoned to me.

"Start looking for stories for that fellow who plays the milkman," he said. "We have a new star!"

• • •

Three days after that preview of *The Easiest Way*, a long-term contract for Gable had been hammered out between Minna Wallis and MGM's Talent department. The routine wheels that virtually guaranteed Gable's rise to stardom could now roll and it was imperative that the public see his face as often as possible.

A new star always gave a festival air to story meetings like this. It started off on a higher than usual emotional level, animated and good-humored. Kate Corbaley and I had brought an armful of "Gable possibilities" to the office. Thalberg was joined by Paul and Al Lewin, his top literary advisers.

He was obviously fired up by his instinctive feeling

that Gable would be a superstar. He was going to cast the actor in choice roles opposite the studio's entire galaxy of great female attractions.

Addressing me, Thalberg said, "We'll want stories for him right away opposite Norma and Greta. At least one with each of them, maybe two with Joan Crawford. He should be in a couple of he-man vehicles, too. Strong action stuff. I'd like to see him do eight pictures this year so that the public is familiar with his face."

At that moment an unusually distraught Howard Strickling came into the room. He hesitated and looked around the table before he addressed Thalberg. "I have to see you about this fellow Gable. You might want to know about this before you go on with your meeting . . ."

Thalberg indicated the group at the table: "We're all friends. What's it about?"

A woman was in Strickling's office, claiming that the years she lived with Clark Gable entitled her to be his wife. Strickling read a hint of blackmail in her claim. "Her name is Rhea Langham, and she's going to be Mrs. Gable, she says, or she'll make a stink to high heaven!" At that moment, Gable was on his way to the studio with Minna Wallis.

Everyone was intrigued. Surely, Paul Bern had to be the most intrigued of all of us.

"Let's meet again tomorrow," Thalberg said. He was getting out of his chair.

Strickling urged everyone to keep the matter confidential.

When the story meeting continued next day, the Gable "situation" had been settled.

The actor didn't hesitate for a moment in deciding what he would do. He had come through years of hardships and insecurities that actors know, he had reached the very edge of stardom at last, everybody was admiring him—this was the great moment in his life, he wouldn't have been an actor if he wasn't desperate to be a star. If he didn't marry Rhea Langham then and there, she could finish him. The Hays Office would step in. The studio would be forced to invoke the morality clause in his contract, the whole industry would turn away from employing him, everything that happened to him in that one week, the opportunity, the attention he was getting, the big salary and surefire star treatment he was promised would be turned off as abruptly as one switches off an electric light. The morality clause played no favorites.

Later that day, Strickling escorted Clark Gable and Rhea Langham across the California border. When they returned she was Mrs. Clark Gable. Good clean living, as it had to be in 1931, was the winner. Romantically, Minna Wallis was the loser.

• • •

About the time Gable married Rhea Langham, Dorothy Millette's illness was flaring up again. From the Algonquin Hotel she sent new messages to Paul that she was counting on his help to launch her career in films. She told him she wanted to come to California. The very

idea that she might suddenly appear at the studio shook
him.

He wrote her back:

> *So far as work out here is concerned I think the
> present time is a horribly difficult one. Naturally,
> with the financial conditions of the country as bad
> as they are, we too have suffered. There are great
> numbers of people out of work, and it will not help
> to add to their numbers. Consequently, I don't think
> that you should come out here now.*
> *Love, regards and best wishes, always,*
>
> > *Paul*

His letter caused Dorothy to put off her proposed trip
to Hollywood and it appeared then that her renewed
ardor for an acting career had abated. It gave him a
sense of relief and he continued romancing Jean.

His studio associates were totally unaware of the
problems that Dorothy Millette was imposing on Paul. I
was close to him then, hardly a day went by that I didn't
see and talk to him, we discussed places he wanted to
visit, books he intended to read again and his observations of the romantic playboys at the studio. He enjoyed
repeating the colorful and sexy stories we'd heard from
Charlie MacArthur and Michael Arlen and Gene Markey, we had fun talking about all of those things.

Easily, the most intriguing of those conversations
dealt with the women he admired. But the woman he
once lived with in New York was never mentioned.

17

· · · · ·

Suspicions

THE BELIEF that Paul Bern committed suicide remained the official version of the tragedy. Nothing else about it was considered as the years went on. It persisted even after rumors surfaced with claims that he had been killed.

· · ·

"All of us in the German colony knew that Paul Bern was murdered!"

The speaker was Ilse Lahn, an active literary agent.

She was a dubbing supervisor at MGM when Paul died. A member of the "German Colony," Miss Lahn was part of the large international contingent working in the film industry in 1932.

Ilse was very definite that Bern had been killed and the case was hushed up. From her point of view, the MGM executives could buy whomever they wanted, for any purpose, and when they needed something they stopped at nothing. "Anything to protect the image of their little darling Jean."

"You just told us you know that Paul was murdered," I said. "Did you ever ask who did it?"

Miss Lahn treated us to a haughty stare.

"I knew better," she snapped. "If any one of us ever tried to find out who killed Paul Bern that person would have found himself on a boat back to Germany before he could say 'Gesundheit!'"

The foreign contingent looked on their MGM bosses as having given them a new way of life at "good money," which was how they described it. For all of them, it was Christmas every day for the brief time that it lasted—until the powers-that-be in their native lands woke up to the fact that dubbing English-spoken dialogue into their own tongue was lucrative, and decided it ought to be done at home. They passed laws to guarantee that, and many toilers in the Hollywood vineyards departed.

They included some Germans who might have had intimate knowledge about what happened to Paul Bern. Their information disappeared with them, though, and they left friends like Ilse Lahn with only unsubstantiated rumors.

THE MOST SERIOUS CONTROVERSY about Paul's death grew out of the magazine article by Ben Hecht in November 1960. Hecht was a novelist, journalist, playwright, scenarist, and admitted aficionado and connoisseur of murder in all forms. He writes:

> Paul Bern, remembered for having committed suicide as the impotent bridegroom of Jean Harlow, the great cinema sexpot, did no such thing. His suicide note, hinting that he was sexually impotent and had therefore "ended the comedy" was a forgery. Studio officials decided, sitting in conference around his dead body, that it was better to have Paul dead as a suicide than as the murder victim of another woman. It would be less a black eye for their biggest moviemaking heroine, La Belle Harlow. It might crimp her box office allure to have her blazoned as a wife who couldn't hold her husband. It was a delicate point of the sort that is clear only to the front office theologians of a great studio.

"The weird details of this 'suicide whitewash,'" Hecht concluded, "are in the keeping today of director Henry Hathaway, who was Paul Bern's protégé."

When Hecht's story appeared, many of the principals who were front and center in 1932 had died, prominent among them Jean Harlow and Louis B. Mayer.

William B. McKesson was district attorney and responded to "renewed interest in the once sensational case" by declaring his office would look into Hecht's accusations. Hampered by the difficulties he faced, mostly trying to locate people who could corroborate Hecht's new revelation, McKesson stated, "I actually believe there's very little probability that it was murder."

From retirement, former district attorney Buron Fitts emerged long enough to say, "I was firmly convinced it was a suicide. I am firmly convinced now."

• • •

"I was in Europe when Ben Hecht published his accusation," I told Joyce. "But I held to my theory that Paul had sacrificed himself for Jean and Dorothy."

Still, Hecht's declaration that Paul was "the murder victim of another woman" impelled us to follow up every lead we could.

Joyce spoke to a dozen people at the Los Angeles district attorney's office before she was steered to Julian Blodgett who is now a private investigator and acts as a consultant for industrial and corporate security matters.

In 1960 he was chief of the Los Angeles Bureau of Investigation under District Attorney McKesson. Because of Hecht's revelations, the D.A. assigned Blodgett to look into the case.

"I was supposed to interview people we believed had information," Blodgett told Joyce. "I remember the names: Ben Hecht . . . Henry Hathaway . . . Howard Strickling, the man we all knew as The Fixer."

McKesson was looking for new evidence, Blodgett explained.

"But neither Hecht nor Hathaway came up with any. There was little more we could do because all the D.A.'s records are in poor shape—especially the old ones. No great surprise; when Fitts left, many documents left.

"The case just fizzled out before it started," Blodgett concluded.

McKesson had no choice but to call off his investigation.

Thirteen years later, crime reporter Hank Messick embroidered on Hecht's scenario in his book *The Beauties and the Beasts*. Messick painted a lurid imaginative picture. He asserted that gangster Longie Zwillman drove Jean Harlow and Dorothy Millette to Paul's house that fateful Sunday night and Dorothy shot Paul Berns (sic) while Jean "watched in horror!" Zwillman then erased all telltale evidence, according to Messick, dropped Jean off at her mother's home, and drove Dorothy to San Francisco.

Messick's account of happenings on Easton Drive failed to even raise the eyebrows of Los Angeles authorities. Or, for that matter, ours.

• • •

We would have dropped the whole Hecht story, too, if it hadn't been for an entirely unexpected development.

Hecht's revelation had collapsed after Henry Hathaway told an investigator at that time, "I certainly don't deny that Ben and I discussed the Bern case, but no one ever told us anything beyond what was speculated. There was only speculation then—and now. I wasn't there and I would never have had any access to information. I'm in no position to add anything. I'd like to forget it."

But Hathaway contradicted that earlier statement

when he told a different story in a remote location far from where the Bern tragedy had occurred. His disclosure was relayed to us by Roddy McDowall, still on the crest of a lasting Hollywood career. Our friendship began in 1943 when I produced the movie *Lassie Come-Home* with Roddy starring as young Joe Carraclough, and we remained friends as the young actor's career carried him from child star into a long succession of important roles.

Roddy told Joyce and me, "Some years back I was on location in Durango, Mexico, with *Five Card Stud*, a film that Henry Hathaway was directing. We were sitting around one night, and he startled me when he suddenly said, 'I nearly went to prison once. The district attorney was looking into the truth of an article that Ben Hecht wrote about Paul Bern being murdered. Hecht had mentioned me as his source.'"

Roddy, the consummate actor, became Hathaway as he continued telling us about it: "They suspected I was withholding information that I knew, an investigator in the district attorney's office actually threatened me. He said, 'If you are withholding evidence we can put you in jail.'

"Sure, I knew more about it, but it wasn't really hard evidence. It was only hearsay, but I knew it was accurate. Anyway, I didn't want to add any more scandal to Paul's death, there had been enough already."

Hathaway told Roddy, "I knew some things about Dorothy Millette from Paul. He talked to me about her every once in a while."

Late in 1931, Paul had received a letter from Frank Case, the manager of the Algonquin Hotel. He showed it to Hathaway, and the director told Roddy, "It went something like this:

Dear Mr. Bern,
I'm concerned, the lady who's on the top floor is acting very strange. Her room is filled with movie magazines,. she sits there all day reading them and has an obsession about going to Hollywood and you will star her in a biblical epic. She hardly ever goes outdoors. I think you should look into it.

"Hathaway was planning to go to New York at that time, and after he read the letter, Paul told him, 'I can't make it to New York right now. Can you do me a favor and check into this?' "

Hathaway agreed to go and see Dorothy but then his trip was called off.

"I felt terrible that I had to let Paul down," was what Roddy recalled Hathaway saying. "I never talked about that woman to anyone for almost thirty years. When I finally told Ben Hecht, he wrote that magazine piece and suddenly it was in all the papers.

"You see, Roddy, I can't prove it, but the letter and conversations I had with Paul convinced me that this woman, Dorothy Millette, was insane. I'm sure that she was the person at Paul's house the night he died."

Roddy sat back, observing our reaction to his story.

"Did you know," we asked Roddy, "that immediately

after Paul's body was found, there was a widespread rumor that Jean Harlow was involved in the death of her husband?"

"Tsk, tsk, tsk," was Roddy's reaction as he shook his head. "Come on, Sam, we actors understand one another. In spite of all her gloss and brassiness and exhibitionism Jean was a frightened little bird, scared to death of Louis B. Mayer. She did as she was told, followed orders to the letter. I think she was a very tragic figure. No, Jean could not be a killer, it's preposterous! However, I can tell you that Hathaway never believed Paul Bern was a suicide, and he knew the man well. Hathaway was convinced that it was a murder and he thought that woman Dorothy did it."

18

·····

Valley of Retakes

WHEN WORLD WAR II was raging many of MGM's stars, including Clark Gable, Robert Taylor and James Stewart, were serving in the armed forces. To keep the studio ranks filled during their absence, Louis B. Mayer kept up an endless search for other acting talents.

MGM comic Red Skelton put a group of young people into a show at Fort Ord in northern California in 1943. He asked that MGM cover their talent, and I drove there with Ida Koverman, who worked in Louis B. Mayer's office.

I compiled notes about what happened around me in those days, memoranda for myself, a collection of references about the actions of people who I thought I might write about in a future time. The time had come to remember Ida Koverman, for she was the one who had first revealed the suspicions about Jean Harlow—and, more important, the ways of a former Los Angeles district attorney.

Mrs. Koverman was an interesting woman, a widow, tall, thin, her tortoiseshell spectacles giving her a schoolteacher appearance. She had a hard face and a soft heart. We drove together on California's Route 101 for a full day.

In 1928 Mrs. Koverman had turned down Herbert Hoover's invitation to join his staff when he became President of the United States. Instead, she took Mayer's offer to assist him in the political field. It made good sense: if she had gone with Hoover she would have been out of work in 1932.

Here she was, still at MGM in 1943. Although Mayer's political ambitions had faded away, Ida Koverman was still by his side. With a strong love of arts and artists —she was a fine pianist herself—she was one of many studio employees who always kept a watchful lookout for potential stars. She brought her discoveries to Mayer's attention in a nonstop parade.

During our long drive north along the California coast to Fort Ord, I brought up the way Paul Bern's death affected me. It was a loss that I considered one of those irreparable events that invade all of us at times.

"The Paul Bern tragedy was hell on the boss, too," Ida told me. "It happened in the middle of the 1932 presidential campaign. Mr. Mayer had his hands full, working to get Hoover reelected and, what with the market crash and depression—to say nothing of Franklin D. Roosevelt's charisma—well, Hoover was my old boss, but let's face it, he wasn't exactly a barrel of fun when they put a microphone in front of him. He was well read, he knew books and could quote from the classics, yes . . . he was very accomplished in many ways, but he was also a colossal bore. Anyone but Mr. Mayer would have thrown in the towel and conceded the election to Roosevelt. But not LB, he wouldn't give up, he was out making speeches for Hoover all over the state. Then, in the midst of it the Bern thing happened and he had to protect Jean Harlow. As keen as he was about politics, the studio and its people came first."

Mrs. Koverman and I rode on in silence while I tried to analyze what she told me. "Protect Jean from what? A fear that her ties to Paul Bern could destroy her career? Did anyone *seriously* believe that Jean had killed Paul?"

Ida said, "Los Angeles district attorney Buron Fitts did! Imagine what a startling development that would have been!"

She knew that Fitts loved to see his name in the headlines, any incident involving a movie star guaranteed that he would look into it, and everything concerning Jean was sure to get him great personal publicity.

"Fitts had the studio over a barrel," according to Mrs. Koverman. The mere suggestion of a murder indictment could destroy Jean's film career.

From what Mrs. Koverman said, Mayer had an unusually busy day, Tuesday, September 6, 1932. Unlike the manic power that he displayed at noon when confronting his executives about Paul's "impotence," he was composed and completely in charge when he called a group into his office that afternoon. Ida Koverman was there, along with Howard Strickling and the studio's police chief Whitey Hendry. Mayer had also summoned Marino Bello and MGM attorneys Mendel Silberberg and Ralph Blum.

"I'm going to let Hendry make the first move," Mayer said.

Before coming to MGM, Whitey Hendry was police chief of Culver City, the hometown of the studio. He had all the requisite connections for dealing with the district attorney's office and knew the proper way to offer a bribe without appearing to do so.

Hendry dialed the phone on Mayer's desk, the one that bypassed the studio switchboard operators.

Blaney Matthews was the chief of the Bureau of Criminal Investigations for District Attorney Fitts. He came on the wire immediately. Their introductory pleasantries were brief. Hendry said, "First of all, Blaney, a matter of some public interest has arisen of which you must be aware."

Matthews knew, of course, and Hendry got down to business quickly, just a short interchange but a jargon the two men understood and instantly interpreted.

"Blaney," said Hendry, "I want to promise you there will be full and complete cooperation on the part of the MGM studio in any investigation into those recent matters of concern . . ."

There was a short conversation, it signified the two men fully understood the purpose of the call, a hint that the studio was willing to reward the D.A. for alleviating the problems that Paul Bern's death was causing them.

Hendry said, "I knew I could count on you." He made a circle with the thumb and middle finger. The knowledgeable, like Ida Koverman, knew that bribery of Buron Fitts had been agreed upon, beginning when the offer of "full and complete cooperation" was accepted.

"Okay," Hendry concluded on the phone, "we'll keep in touch." Then he hung up.

Mayer, pleased, said he'd follow up with District Attorney Fitts. "Buron's never a problem," he told his visitors as he showed them to the door. He turned to Bello and said, "You, Bello, you tell Jean I don't want her to say a word to anybody! Let her play the bereaved widow. That's it, nothing more!"

Before we reached Fort Ord, I asked Mrs. Koverman if that was the end of the Buron Fitts incident. "Oh," she said, "Fitts dropped the investigation after Mayer spoke to him. But, Fitts was a sly one. He put his hand out from time to time. Through the years, he did very well for himself."

In 1932 Los Angeles's maverick District Attorney Buron Fitts was a thirty-seven-year-old Texan who had ridden roughshod over any bodies standing in his political path.

His artful behavior in legal fields didn't come from his professors at the University of Southern California

Law School, but from a legendary tutor in the private sector. Fitts had worked his way through college as clerk to Earl "Harry" Rogers, the sharpest, wiliest attorney who ever practised before local bars—those that dispensed justice and those that dispensed whiskey.

Fitts shared his admiration of Harry Rogers with the lawyer's daughter Adela, who wrote about him as constantly as she wrote about Jean Harlow and other film stars. Adela Rogers St. Johns's novel *A Free Soul* was produced by Paul Bern; it's semiautobiographical plot provided Norma Shearer with a notable characterization and won the Academy Award for Lionel Barrymore as Shearer's dissolute lawyer-father.

Another of Roger's admirers was Alfred A. Cohn, the Hollywood screenwriter who had awakened me early Labor Day morning to tell me of Paul Bern's death. He coauthored *Take the Witness!*, a biographical study of Rogers, and hugely enjoyed the way the lawyer clowned through a number of cases, mixing merriment with enough shrewdness to win the verdicts he needed.

Both Cohn and Buron Fitts were present for one of those ingenious courtroom antics, when Rogers swallowed a vial of toxic liquid. The potion was resting unguarded on a table near the jury. It had been introduced as an exhibit by an attorney for an irate farmer who claimed that Rogers's client poisoned his dog.

Drinking it, Rogers convinced everybody in the courtroom that the noxious fluid couldn't have caused the canine's demise and he won an immediate dismissal of the case.

Clerk Buron Fitts then helped Rogers across the street to his law office where a stomach pump was ready and an antidote administered in the nick of time.

In an interview, Fitts stated that his service with Harry Rogers taught him that there was no risk too great in pursuing one's goals in life; he cited the case of the swallowed poison as a perfect example of winning through cunning, courage and daring.

Back in 1917, when he was twenty-two, Fitts had joined the U.S. Army, enlisting the day that America entered the ongoing war in Europe. He served as an infantry lieutenant. He was wounded in the knee during action in France's Argonne forest: a bullet crippled him severely and left him with a limp the rest of his life.

Returning to Los Angeles after the war, he worked actively in veteran affairs. This carried him into the realm of politics and, once there, he moved up speedily. He was appointed a deputy district attorney by then district attorney Asa Keyes, who soon promoted him to chief deputy district attorney. Fitts marched onward and upward to lieutenant governor of California and occupied that office for two years.

He was elected Los Angeles district attorney in 1928. When he won that post, he immediately indicted and successfully prosecuted his predecessor Asa Keyes, the man who had helped him to importance in the community. Fitts's prosecution of Keyes earned him the reputation for toughness that he obviously wanted. It set his price high and he took advantage of it. Louis B. Mayer and his contemporaries in the film world knew that favors could be bought from Fitts, and they continued to do business with him throughout his twelve years in office.

• • •

The information we were acquiring about Paul Bern and Jean Harlow came at us from many sources. Much of it didn't seem to lead anywhere and offered little promise of supplying the answers we needed. In my experience, when a story for a film defied a workable solution, the thing to do was to shelve it, swallow the pain, and move on. That's how it was in the film world.

However, Joyce Vanderveen came from a different background. She grew up in the dance world and was trained to live with the discipline and determination of that demanding life. I had gained a persistent collaborator who was resolute about following through until the truth was revealed.

Joyce had ties to many governmental representatives in Los Angeles that were formed when she was an active community leader in her San Fernando Valley area. She always retained her city hall connections; most of the political representatives she had worked with were still downtown.

One morning Joyce located a friend in District Attorney Ira Reiner's office. He was familiar with the day in 1932 when Fitts shelved the investigation of Jean Harlow's role in the Paul Bern case. He had heard the story from an old man who used to work for Fitts. Joyce went to see her friend.

She reported back to me: "The old man is dead but my friend says that what Ida Koverman told you about the bribery of Buron Fitts was correct. He says it was common knowledge at the D.A.'s office. All that the studio people had to do was contact Blaney Matthews—he was the one to call, and if MGM hadn't taken care of Fitts, the case against Jean Harlow would have gone to the grand jury.

"I asked him if there are any records that we can see but he says that the files are in terrible shape. Whatever is there is still confidential and hard to get your hands on. Very hush-hush."

Joyce's friend wasn't sure he could come up with anything. However, he gave her a list of the people who were at the Bello house when Jean was questioned late Tuesday, the day after Paul's death. The list named a larger cast of characters there than previously known. Chief of Detectives Taylor and Inspector of Detectives Davidson had joined Detective Lieutenants Condaffer and Ryan that day.

But they weren't alone with the film star.

Also present were Howard Strickling, Marino Bello, and attorney Mendel Silberberg, who since that afternoon had become the legal representative not only of MGM, but of Jean, Mama Jean, and Marino Bello. Dr. Harold Bernard stood by, concerned with Jean's health.

Louis B. Mayer was there. His presence must have cast an ominous shadow over the gathering. Jean Harlow sobbed, "I can't understand why this terrible thing had to happen!"

That was all she had to say.

•••

A month passed without hearing from Joyce's friend, so she called. He was no longer there. To our dismay, his replacement had just taken over. She hurried downtown and returned with a promise from the new man that he would do all he could to find any documents relating to the case.

"I think the only reason he will do it is because I'm a woman," Joyce said. "He made a pass at me . . ." She smiled at the recollection. "I still dance very well, you know."

The new man was insistent that we keep his name out of any writing about the case. It was remarkable: here was a story that happened five decades ago and still there were men who wanted to keep their activities secret.

"On top of it," Joyce told me, "this new man talks in a whisper."

"That's like Benny Thau at MGM," I said. "He talked in a whisper, too. Let's call your new man Benny."

Everything about the real Benny Thau was virtually indescribable. His executive title was nondescript, he was listed as MGM's talent coordinator in the studio phone book, but even he couldn't explain what it meant. He wasn't very tall or very short, his complexion was a kind of off-pale, like a color that Nature hadn't yet got around to perfecting. He didn't cut or comb his hair in any unusual way or wear distinctive clothes. He was of the type who gave the impression when he stood right before you that he wasn't there. Wherever he was, he melted into the woodwork.

Benny Thau's reluctance to speak above a whisper inspired gagman Hoppy Hopkins to say, "When Benny opens his mouth, dust flies out!" But Benny was also a respected member of Mayer's Men, with a talent for getting things done.

• • •

Ida Koverman had given us a clue that Buron Fitts put out his hand from time to time and that gave us reason to believe the Paul Bern case did not die after Fitts was bribed to drop the investigation.

With the help of our Benny we learned that in fact, early in 1933, foreman William Widenham of the Los Angeles County grand jury, together with assistant secretary O. G. Lawton, wanted to know why Buron Fitts had not moved forward with a thorough investigation into such a controversial case. They ordered a new inquiry.

Joyce said, "Sam, this is most unusual. Instead of the D.A. going to the grand jury, the grand jury went to the D.A."

Of course, they didn't know that MGM had stymied the earlier investigation. The grand jury ordered Fitts to go back into the Bern case and see if the original finding of the coroner's jury that Paul was a suicide should be overturned.

Joyce asked Benny, "Is it possible to find a transcript of that investigation of February 1933?"

"No way," he said. "Those hearings are not public record. They are secret proceedings. What's more, anything to do with the grand jury, dated before 1946, is gone."

In spite of that gloomy statement a sealed envelope arrived from Benny two weeks later. Inside was a document marked CONFIDENTIAL.

What it said almost put an end to our investigation.

Meeting Held Tuesday, February 28, 1933

RESOLUTION

"Some time ago, information concerning the death of Paul Bern was handed to Foreman Wm. W. Widenham of the Los Angeles County Grand Jury, that called for an investigation. Foreman Widenham consulted with Mr. O. G. Lawton, Assistant Secretary of the Grand Jury, and, after a conference, both decided to submit the evidence to this office with a request for assistance in determining the truth or untruthfulness of such evidence.

•

Therefore, since last Monday, almost without cessation, this office has cooperated with Foreman Wm. W. Widenham and Mr. O. G. Lawton in a re-examination of persons having possession of facts concerning the death of Paul Bern last September, to the end that it be determined whether or not there was sufficient evidence to formally present the matter to the entire Grand Jury. We have not only examined every witness available at the time of the inquest before the Coroner's Jury, but many others as well. No substantial facts have been developed which would overturn the verdict of the Coroner's Jury, to wit, that Paul Bern took his own life.

•

The suicide note found at the time of the discovery of the body was submitted to Clark Sellers, a handwriting expert of unquestioned integrity and ability. His opinion was unequivocally that the note was in the handwriting of Paul Bern.

•

No motive for the taking of Paul Bern's life has been developed; no question raised as to the ownership of the gun with which his life was taken; no question has arisen but that the death actually took place where the body was found, as evidenced by the bullet hole in the wall of the closet; no denial has been forthcoming from any witness but that, prior to taking his life, he discussed the methods of suicide, indicating that, at the moment, there was in his mind a thought of suicide.

•

The movements of every person in close relationship to Mr. Bern are accurately accounted for, with ample corroboration.

•

We are definitely of the opinion at this time that Paul Bern died as a suicide.

•

After a thorough and exhaustive examination, we are of the opinion that the facts as disclosed do not warrant the expenditure of public moneys for further proceedings in this case.

The only person who signed the document, however, was District Attorney Buron Fitts. The record shows that Wm. W. Widenham, foreman of the 1932–33 grand jury, and assistant secretary O. G. Lawton refused to sign it.

The "resolution" provided us with a strange conclusion to an inquiry we had not seen.

19
· · · · ·
Dangerous Game

BURON FITTS was no angel. Everybody knew that and it was certainly Dr. John P. Buckley's opinion. He had become W. W. Widenham's successor as the Los Angeles grand jury foreman. The City of Angels had a large share of sinners and plenty of iniquities, and all were possible for Buckley to concentrate on—but to him, the most important of all was to see if he could nail Buron Fitts for any misdeeds committed while in office.

He wanted to study the records of all Fitts's questionable activities. There were so many that it took months before Dr. Buckley finally decided to concentrate on three cases. One of them involved possible financial wrongdoing in the Bern investigation.

The first was popularly described as the "Girl Mart" case. It was a mixture of rape, prostitution, and murder, and the featured principals were theater owner Alexander Pantages and his wife. Fitts prosecuted them and both were convicted but later exonerated. Fitts and his secretary, who was also his sister, Mrs. Bertha Gregory, were indicted for perjury in the case. Both were tried; the jury, however, couldn't agree on their guilt and the charges against them were dropped.

The second case Buckley looked into involved the suspicious way Fitts tossed out a charge of statutory rape that had been filed against wealthy real estate developer John P. Mills. The Buckley grand jury discovered that Mills was involved in an illegal sale of a citrus grove, one from which Fitts and his sister personally benefited. Fitts was hauled before the grand jury on that case, but he escaped an indictment by a split vote.

Buckley now had only one chance left to indict Fitts —the misuse of the district attorney's expenditures at the time he was investigating the Bern case.

But in the end they could not find sufficient evidence to prosecute him and their efforts came to nothing. District Attorney Fitts sailed along in office, and our investigation of Fitts seemed to have come to nothing, too.

•••

It would have remained that way if Joyce had not found an unusual article about Buckley's grand jury proceedings, which appeared in the *San Francisco Chronicle* on November 11, 1934.

In February 1933, when Fitts had been ordered by Widenham to look again into Paul's death, he had apparently been reimbursed $302 for a suite in the Los Angeles Ambassador Hotel to question Jean Harlow. According to the newspaper account, Fitts told Buckley's grand jury, when pressed about the results of his get-together with Jean, "She merely repeated her earlier statements that she was at the home of her mother at the time Mr. Bern died and that she and her husband had been on excellent terms."

Jean also told him she had never heard the name Dorothy Millette and did not know of the woman's existence until after her husband's death.

Asked by Buckley why he needed hotel rooms on the occasion, Fitts said, "Miss Harlow was very upset about the grand jury investigation and I didn't want to embarrass her."

Dr. Buckley thought $302 a lot of money for that touch of solicitude. The article further stated that he ordered the Bern file turned over to auditors, along with instructions to find out if the taxpayers had been stuck with other expenses of a frivolous nature.

That article told us that the auditor of the Los Angeles County grand jury had been handed inside information and testimony concerning the Paul Bern case. He would know things that would excite anybody curious about what happened the last night of the producer's life. He knew the questions that were asked and how various men and women answered.

Those were the very things we wanted to know.

• • •

There was a whisper on the other end of the line: "I found some of the stuff you were looking for."

It was unmistakably Benny's voice.

"The Paul Bern case?" Joyce asked.

"The one you asked for, yeah," he said. "The auditor's file."

"Can we see it?"

"It's in no condition for copying. If you want to see it you have to come down here . . ."

The file that was shown us carried the name of C. E. Momory, assistant auditor. Inside, we found frayed, tattered, and often illegible documents. Now, after more than fifty years had passed, some of the pages lay before us in dust.

MGM had been willing to pay Fitts handsomely to keep quiet, so he had wrapped the whole case in a mantle of silence and, backed up by the coroner's jury, he expected it to stay that way. But because of the simple sum of $302 this file was still in existence.

What the district attorney spent was all that mattered to the auditor. His audit at an end, the records went into the files where they slumbered unobserved, slowly disintegrating.

Our interest was quite the opposite to the auditor's.

For instance, here was fresh information from gardener Clifton E. Davis and the Carmichaels. When these statements were taken, six months after Paul's death, the household staff was no longer influenced by the power of MGM.

Davis, the man who told Thalberg and me what happened on Labor Day, 1932, informed Fitts and Widenham in 1933 that Marino Bello had telephoned him early on the day after Bern's body was found and said, "You are talking too much. Move your wife and children over to the garage and keep your damned mouth shut."

"Didn't Mr. Bello like Mr. Bern?" Davis was asked.

"No, and Mr. Bern did not like Bello."

Davis told how he had become suspicious on the night of the tragedy when a "big limousine" drove up.

"I saw a woman in the car, but I didn't know who she was."

"The next morning," Davis said, "I went about my usual duties looking around the swimming pool and getting things in shape. A broken glass was at the swimming pool by Mr. Bern's favorite chair. It looked as though he had cut his hand with just a few drops bleeding there."

"Was it a blood smear?"

"No," Davis replied. "I picked up the broken glass and washed the bloodstains."

"Have you any suspicions as to how the blood got there?" Davis was asked.

"Yes, I think that if he was murdered that is where the blood came from."

"You don't think Mr. Bern committed suicide?"

"No, I think it was murder. I thought so from the very beginning."

Davis also made a flat accusation that houseman John Carmichael lied at the coroner's inquest.

"Do you know in what respect Carmichael lied?"

"Yes. He told them they didn't have a fuss the evening before Mr. Bern's death. He said they got along fine that Sunday. But he had told me they did have a fight, a big fight, Mr. Bern didn't raise his voice much but Carmichael told me he sure did that time."

"Do you know why he raised his voice?"

"Yes, it was because of their house. Mrs. Bern didn't want to live in the canyon, she didn't make any secret of that. Mr. Bern gave her the deed, but he wouldn't let her sell it. She said she'd use the money to build another one somewhere else. I heard her say one time that if he didn't want her to sell it, he should let her exchange it for her mother's place."

"Did Mr. Carmichael know about this?"

"I don't understand why he said he never heard anything about turning the place over to Mrs. Bern's mother, when he had. We all had.

"And he said they were hugging and kissing all the time and Mr. Bern was talking of committing suicide, when really they didn't do any hugging and kissing that day and Mr. Bern never did say anything about committing suicide."

Finally, Davis was asked about the widely accepted suicide note.

"The note was written in a book and the book was open," Davis testified. "I saw it long before Mr. Bern died."

•••

A half-decayed and yellowed sheet of paper recorded the testimony of handwriting expert Clark Sellers. He was the best-known handwriting expert of his time and his verification of the handwriting pleased Fitts, who pointed out to the press that the "suicide note" was indeed authentic. Sellers gave as his opinion "unequivocably the note is in the handwriting of Paul Bern."

• • •

Harold "Slickum" Garrison testified that he worked regularly for Paul Bern as chauffeur and ran errands. He started to describe the odd jobs he did for other studio executives but that was considered irrelevant.

"Yes sir, I seen it all and I done it all."

The witness was asked if he knew about disagreements between Mr. and Mrs. Bern.

One night, he recalled, he came to the house to pick up Mr. Bern and drive him to a preview. "The minute I got there he walked to the car without telling her goodbye."

Then, driving home after the preview, Mr. Bern told Slickum that before picking him up in the morning, he was to stop at the Beverly Hills Hotel and get a dozen roses. Slickum stated that Mr. Bern had lost his temper that night and felt very badly about it.

"He was apologetic?"

"Yes sir, that's the word."

"Do you know what they were fighting about?"

"They was always fighting about the house."

"About when did this happen, Mr. Garrison?"

"It was about almost exactly a month after the wedding."

Next morning Slickum brought the flowers to the house.

"I saw Mr. Bern put them on the desk and I seen him write in his pretty book. He was always writing things."

• • •

Paul's secretary Irene Harrison told what she knew of the courtship between Jean and Paul.

"Jean bombarded my boss with letters at the time she was out of town. He was flattered by them, he kept reading them over and sometimes he came out and told me about them. They had a lot to do with her personal appearances but she was also writing about her feelings for him. She sent him telegrams too."

Miss Harrison explained that the correspondence was mostly on Miss Harlow's side, and after her return to Hollywood and the production of *Red-Headed Woman*, their friendship developed into something more intimate.

"By intimate I do not mean the use of the word as meant in Hollywood. I could see that she was pressing for marriage and he had fallen in love with her. I think he was very happy at the idea."

• • •

Winifred Carmichael told how on Sunday night she saw a woman arriving in a limousine at sundown just as she was leaving for the Bello home.

"I had made a devil's food cake and knowing that Miss Harlow loves that kind, before I left I put a piece with a note 'from your staunch admirer' in the bedroom.

"Well, Miss Harlow never came home that night. But

the cake was gone and the note was all crumpled up beside it. And Mr. Bern never ate a piece of cake in his life."

When Winifred came back from the Bello home Sunday night she retired to the servants' quarters. Mr. Bern was arguing with somebody at the pool and she heard him say, "Get out of my life." They went on talking, however, Mrs. Carmichael asserted. Then she added, "I'm not the type that eavesdrops on things that are none of my business." She and her husband went to bed. At times they thought a radio was playing loudly.

Later, she knew it couldn't be a radio "because I never heard a radio make sounds like that before. I was awakened by an unearthly scream."

Startled, she listened. The quiet that followed seemed suspicious to Winifred who decided to get up and investigate. She found a yellow bathing suit beside the pool, still wet. As she went to pick it up Winifred saw the mysterious woman flee into the darkness, losing a shoe as she ran. It had a high heel and an additional lift in it.

"Why did you keep those things secret?" asked jury foreman Widenham.

"I wasn't asked those things before and I didn't tell them."

Widenham showed her a picture of Dorothy Millette.

Winifred said, "This is the woman that I saw. I'm sure of it."

20

. . . . .

The Butterfly Girl

BY 1932 it would have been obvious to anyone but Dorothy that she had lost her place in Paul's life. The letters he wrote her were brief and businesslike, typed by his secretary. His monthly checks totaling $350 were routed to her through his brother. By then, Henry Bern had become the chief contact between Paul and Dorothy; he had developed a personal affection for her and he showed it. But Henry wasn't who Dorothy wanted.

Then, tired of waiting for Paul, she told hotel manager Frank Case she had to go to Los Angeles. When Case conveyed that to Paul in California, the producer asked Henry Hathaway to try and talk her out of it. But Hathaway didn't go to New York that time and it wasn't likely he could have succeeded anyway because Dorothy was adamant. She was determined to go west and all Henry Bern could do was get her to make San Francisco her destination. It was a city she once lived in and knew.

At this point, Paul wrote her and suggested she

choose between the Clift and the Plaza Hotel. She decided on the Plaza. Henry bought her ticket to San Francisco and took her to the train.

Dorothy arrived in San Francisco May 4, and remained isolated and alone. Her room in the Plaza Hotel became like the one at the Algonquin, a place to wait for Paul. He never came. However, she was now fully aware of his romance with Jean. Dorothy littered her room with newspapers and magazines as they reported Paul and Jean's courtship.

Miss Lucy Hole, who worked as a cashier at the Plaza, recalled, "Her shoulders rather drooped at times and she often seemed to be turning some problem over in her mind. She took her meals, always alone, in our grill, sitting quietly in the corner. I have been in there several times while she was also there. She would merely bow, how sad, and I noticed that she had but a few words with the waitresses. She was a recluse."

• • •

Today there are few San Franciscans who know that a Plaza Hotel was ever there. In its place the huge structure of a Hyatt Hotel towers over Union Square.

• • •

Zilfa Estcourt was a feature writer on the staff of the *San Francisco Chronicle* and also wrote a daily column "Right off the Chest." A long-established writer in the Bay City, she turned out to be a journalist who knew

Dorothy before she ever met Paul Bern. "She had an air of timid reserve," wrote Miss Estcourt after Dorothy's existence was first revealed to the world.

"A butterfly girl crushed on the wheel of life," Miss Estcourt recalled in her melodramatic style. She remembered Dorothy as a "fragile blond orphan who, in moments of confidence, gave little glimpses of herself as a child and as a woman. She hinted sometimes that she didn't know her origin." Dorothy told Zilfa that she had been reared in a home of wealth and educated in a fashionable school.

But Dorothy was given to flights of fancy. What she told Zilfa was based on her dreams. The reality was that her name at birth was Dorothy Roddy and she was the ward of a Board of Children's Guardians in Indianapolis. Rather incredibly, no one who knew the young Dorothy ever reported at any time that she had living family ties. She seemed to be entirely devoid of blood relatives.

Gifted and intelligent, the young Dorothy became stalled in a stenographic job, working for a coal company in Indianapolis, a dead end allowing her no opportunities to further the acting career that had become her all-consuming ambition. Even those men and women who knew her slightly could see she was disturbed when life in the theater continued to elude her grasp.

Zilfa Estcourt wrote that Dorothy met and married an ambitious newspaperman in Indianapolis after a short romance. Although Miss Estcourt preferred not to reveal the name of Dorothy's husband, she knew that they moved to the state of Washington, where he edited a small-town newspaper.

He spent his leisure hours writing a play he was sure would give Dorothy the acting chance she hoped for. It was never completed and, maddened by housewife labors so far from Broadway, her hopes of making her dream come true fading, she struck out for New York on her own. It was a show of fierce determination, uncharacteristic of the woman Paul Bern would soon meet, but as time passed she was growing more unpredictable.

She divorced her husband after two years and he never reappeared in her life. But when she applied at the American Academy of Dramatic Arts, she registered as Mrs. L. Melett before settling on the stage name of Dorothy Millette.

• • •

On Saturday, July 2, word flashed around the world that MGM producer Paul Bern had married Jean Harlow. He was, of course, aware that Dorothy had been waiting for him for two months at the Plaza in San Francisco. He told me about her just before Labor Day, as though she had just arrived. The producer was playing a dangerous game.

• • •

Eyebrows would be raised after Paul's death, when it was discovered that Jean made a visit to San Francisco in mid-August, less than six weeks after her wedding.

The bride was at the Mark Hopkins Hotel with her

mother and stepfather. Paul was not with her. After his death, reporters speculated about that trip. To them it all seemed very suspicious.

But Jean had simply planned the sort of let's-get-away-from-it-all that movie stars indulged in between pictures. When she suggested a vacation, Paul agreed to take time off and go along. They could relax in Santa Barbara, he said, or maybe Coronado, down south near the Mexican border. However, Jean wanted to do some shopping in San Francisco and he backed out. A great many scripts had piled up in his office, he told her.

To be in San Francisco in company with Jean and in hailing distance of Dorothy was obviously not the way he wished to go.

One hour after Jean checked into the Mark Hopkins Hotel, producer Hunt Stromberg called her back to Los Angeles. *Red Dust* was ready for the camera. It was a change of plans that happened often in the volatile movie business, but to the press Jean's short visit to the Bay Area and swift departure seemed a curious event. The two women in Paul's life didn't meet but newspaper clippings about Jean's visit that were later found in Dorothy's room showed that she had to know the star was there.

Dorothy stayed in her room in the Plaza until the start of the Labor Day holiday. One of the hotel's cleaning maids, Lena Meredith, told a detective she had looked in during the weekend and found the room unoccupied. The bed had not been slept in.

TUESDAY MORNING Dorothy was seen back in the Plaza lobby buying the San Francisco papers, all carrying front page stories that Jean Harlow's husband had committed suicide. There was no mention of Dorothy, no identification of her, nothing about a "mysterious woman" who spent hours at Paul's home, not even a report that a woman's shoe and bathing suit had been found.

She went out and bought new shoes costing $10.50, paying an extra fifty cents for heel lifts to be put in them. Then she went back to her room and stayed there alone until later that day when she made her decision. She was going to travel light, and in the course of time she might need to earn her own living, so she prudently packed an old instruction book on shorthand and stenography.

She left a packet of letters from Paul behind in the room.

At four o'clock on Tuesday afternoon she checked out of the hotel, paying in cash the $25.89 bill that she owed there. She said she would be back and asked the clerk at the desk to keep her room locked until she returned; he agreed and gave her a receipt for the trunk and grip she left with him. (If the clerk's action seems surprisingly generous now, it was not uncommon in 1932, when the depression had emptied half the hotel rooms around the country.) A taxi took her to the pier, where she bought a round-trip ticket on the *Delta King,* the overnight ferry to Sacramento. Only Dorothy knew if the return stub of her ticket meant that she really did intend to come back to San Francisco.

• • •

Nothing at all was known about her relationship with Paul Bern until Wednesday when Henry Bern tied them together. Then a real chase began. She was traced to the Sacramento ferry, but by then the *Delta King* that had carried her away from San Francisco was already at its destination and all its passengers were gone.

The San Francisco police went back to the Plaza but there the manager explained that he considered himself custodian of the missing woman's property and adamantly refused to open up her room.

Three more days passed with no sign of Dorothy. At midnight, Saturday, officially recognizing that Dorothy was missing, Superior Court Judge Conlan issued a search warrant from his sickbed to police inspector Allen McGinn. He did so on McGinn's presentation that Miss Millette's disappearance indicated she had been kidnapped or murdered. When Judge Conlan granted access to her hotel room, he wrote "Foul Play" on the warrant.

After presentation of the warrant, the hotel management turned over to the police a neatly ribboned package of letters from Paul, explaining that a maid had found them when she cleaned the room. The trunk that

Dorothy had left behind contained Parisian perfumes and costly finery, much of it purchased from exclusive Fifth Avenue shops in New York. Tossed in with her exquisite lingerie were six pairs of dress shoes, all of them, of course, with lifts to make her appear taller. They found no clues in the room as to Dorothy's whereabouts.

At this point the maid who had cleaned Dorothy's room in the Plaza revealed more to the press than she had previously disclosed. Lena Meredith declared that, while at first determined not to be drawn into the case, she had realized that she might be helpful in clearing up the mystery of Miss Millette's disappearance.

"I just have to tell what went on in that room," the maid said. "She kept the door locked and all she did was read movie magazines. The room was full of them and I always saw her staring at articles about *Red-Headed Woman*. She had one of the magazines propped up and opened to 'The Life of Beautiful Jean Harlow,' and others that showed pictures of the wedding. After she checked out I went into the room. There was a bunch of letters tied up that she left on the desk. I turned them in to the office downstairs."

The letters were all from Paul. They contained hints of rejection, similar to the one that advised her not to come to Hollywood. Dorothy had wrapped them in a desk blotter and tied them with a ribbon. A single word in heavy black ink stood out on the blotter. When held to a mirror the word read JUSTIFICATION.

A WEEK HAD PASSED after Paul's body was found and Dorothy was still missing.

MGM's studio executives made no attempt to get Jean back to work. They shut down the production of *Red Dust* as a gesture of respect for her feelings.

Any Clark Gable film at that time was a great attraction, and the company's Sales department in New York began applying pressure on Thalberg to deliver *Red Dust* on the scheduled release date. They were more interested in box-office returns than in the sentiments about Jean that the studio was displaying. Reluctantly, Thalberg decided to replace Jean.

In order to use some of the shots in which Jean had already appeared, the casting office delivered a number of young blond actresses for consideration as her substitute. Producer Stromberg and director Victor Fleming auditioned them all.

Before any decision was reached, Thalberg got a telephone call from Jean Harlow: "This hanging around the house is driving me crazy," she told him. "I've got to get busy—and forget."

He sent a studio limousine to bring her to his office and then escorted her to the stage.

The crew was setting up lights. Gable was rehearsing a test scene with a pretty blond actress in a squalid hut that represented his living quarters in a rubber plantation in the tropics. Director Vic Fleming and cameraman Hal Rosson were seated in camp chairs, watching the new girl. Suddenly, without any warning, Jean stepped out of the surrounding dark. She tapped the girl on the shoulder and said sympathetically, "I'm sorry, honey, but the part's taken."

Jean's return touched off a celebration. The soundstage lit up with friends made happy by the sight of her. At the request of the hurriedly summoned Howard Strickling, she went back to the stage door and posed for a photographer with Gable holding it open for her.

Jean wasted no time getting back to work, Rosson's camera was rolling within an hour. In the movie plot, Gable had just lost the love of Mary Astor, who portrayed a society girl unwilling to live with him in the tropics. He sat at a table in melancholy contemplation, a bottle of whiskey in front of him.

Playing a flip character throughout the film, Jean sauntered into the scene, wearing a flowing white kimono. Tossed aside by Gable while Mary Astor was there, she had played a hand in breaking up his romance. Now, she had the first lines in the scene.

"Well, if it ain't ol' massa Fred, back after all these years. Is the burial private or didn't you bring the body with you?" She picked up the whiskey bottle. "Thanks, old man, don't mind if I do. Well, now tell me everything you've been doing."

"Where'd you get that kimono?" Gable asked.

"Don't change the subject. What are you trying to do, get drunk?"

"Not a bad idea."

"Mind if I get a little drunk with you, Fred?"

Gable pulled her closer to him. "Come here."

Jean reacted. "Well, it's about time. Hallelujah, brother!"

"You're not a bad kid, Lilly. We belong here." He paused. "You know something, it's a dirty rotten country—"

Jean broke in: "And we're dirty rotten people!"

"Yeah, real lovable characters just made for each other."

Director Victor Fleming took a close shot of Jean and then quit for the day. The star's haggard looks made her close-ups unusable.

• • •

A very different kind of action was going on in the Sacramento area. The studio's searchers wanted to find Dorothy and find her first. They wanted to prevent her from compromising their evidence of Paul Bern's suicide, which was so carefully in place.

Her existence had tumbled the conspirators off their cloud of euphoria, it wasn't their beautiful blond star they had saved that holiday morning, the killer was this elusive creature who had lurked unseen in the wings, a new and scary threat to derail the plot.

And, if she could prove she was truly Paul's wife, then Jean had participated in a bigamous and scandalous marriage. Their frantic search for her ranged up and down California. Among the clues Dorothy left on the *Delta King* were diaries and fine clothes. Also thirty-eight dollars and a rubber bathing-suit bag that contained a pretty orange bathing cap with a white rosette, but no bathing suit.

That missing bathing suit led virtually everyone who was looking for her to believe that Dorothy had perpetrated a hoax. It appeared to them that she jumped off the *Delta King*, swam to the shore and disappeared into the surrounding countryside.

Nevertheless, a week was spent dredging the Sacramento River at what was considered the logical spot to look for her. They found the body of a man, about fifty, wearing a blue suit, a light shirt and a black tie. He had a stateroom key from the *Delta King* in his pocket, which was a coincidence that could have tied him to Dorothy . . . until they realized that his body had been in the river more than a month.

Efforts to determine who he was were set aside when a Japanese fisherman called the police from Walnut Grove early on the morning of Wednesday, September 14, and reported he had seen the body of a woman in the water at Georgiana Slough.

Sheriff Don Cox of Sacramento sent deputy Charles J. Ogle there while the woman, badly decomposed, still lay in the river. Coroner Garlick called the manager of San Francisco's Plaza Hotel to meet him at Georgiana Slough.

The body was brought on land after all of them had arrived. Garlick was convinced that the remains were those of Dorothy Millette and said so. If indeed it was she, there had been no pretense, no hoax, no phony escape.

• • •

"As soon as the body was found, those MGM people rode into Sacramento like a thundering herd," said Sheriff Cox.

They brought their lawyers and the private police force who had searched for her around the clock. Even before her body was found, Sheriff Cox noted, the studio contingent set wheels in motion to keep the press from learning what they could. "They came to kill the story," he said, "and luck was on their side."

That "luck" was because September was the month when the annual California State Fair in Sacramento had everybody's attention, and there was elaborate preparation going on for Franklin D. Roosevelt coming to town to persuade voters to elect him president. "For a small town like Sacramento those were big events," Cox said. "They took the attention away from Dorothy Millette and I got pushed aside."

Fifty years later Sheriff Cox was still suspicious.

"After she was identified they did the same thing in Sacramento as they did in Los Angeles when Paul Bern was found dead. A quick autopsy, the coroner's jury had no choice but to declare her a suicide. I felt Dorothy Millette could have been murdered but none of the important questions were ever asked. Why was she coming to Sacramento of all places? Did she want to start a new life as a stenographer or get lost in the crowd going to the fair? Was she meeting someone? Her diaries and letters disappeared and must have been destroyed, they were never seen again. And what happened to her bathing suit? If she wanted to drown herself, why do it in the Sacramento River? Plenty of water in San Francisco, you know. I was prevented from doing my job. Those film folks were all over the place, they took over the whole government, for Pete's sake. It's too late now, we'll never know, did she fall, did she jump, or was she pushed!"

21
·····
Flight

WE FOLLOWED the trail of Dorothy's last voyage aboard the now retired *Delta King*. The Sacramento River is neither wide nor deep, and when the boat was still in service the river was being constantly dredged to keep it open to big ships. Its once verdant edges have now been replaced by banks of stone by order of the U.S. Army Corps of Engineers. But the little towns bordering the river are in decline and we had a feeling of melancholy for times gone by.

"It must have been charming to see the *Delta King* make its run upriver at night, its lights shining on fruit trees along the shore," mused Joyce. The *Delta King* is tied up now in Sacramento, an imposing tourist attraction. A twin vessel, the *Delta Queen*, cruises the Mississippi.

Bill Pettite was familiar with all that happened in Sacramento when the events surrounding the search for Dorothy Millette was at its height. He has spent his life in a variety of functions from judge to newspaperman and is now a political consultant who knows all the ins and outs of Sacramento. With that background he joined us as our guide as we picked up Dorothy's trail after she boarded the *Delta King*.

We stopped for lunch in Rio Vista, a small town on the river. Bill Pettite opened the door to Foster's Bighorn, a restaurant close to where Dorothy's body was found.

We followed seemingly endless walls crammed with animal heads, trophies of many hunts. A table was waiting under the dead gaze of what were once magnificent African animals—a bull elephant's head virtually covers one entire wall. Animal lover Joyce promptly lost her appetite.

The restaurant décor was brought to the old West by Bill Foster, a great white hunter who met Ernest Hemingway in Nairobi, where they chased lions with a club. "I met Hemingway in New York at the 21 Club," I recalled. "The lions were literary, he was one of them, and a lot of women were chasing him."

"I can do without the jokes," said Joyce. She cast her dark eyes upward, straight into an equally impressive pair of limpid dark eyes staring down from the head of a defunct moose. She shuddered and walked out.

• • •

We passed the town of Locke, a decaying community that housed the Chinese who toiled in the surrounding pear orchards. Not too far away lived the Japanese and it was one of them who found the body of Dorothy Millette in Georgiana Slough, an arm of the Sacramento River.

We stood on the bridge at Walnut Grove which opened that night so long ago when bells on the *Delta King* signaled its approach, making its way to the state capital. In the distance we could see Georgiana Slough trailing off to the left. We went down to the riverbank where Dorothy's body had been found floating facedown.

MGM had been keeping a close watch on everything going on, but now they no longer feared that she would destroy the scenario they had so carefully contrived. The element of surprise that could have exploded the Bern case into a national scandal had been averted.

The coroner for the County of Sacramento, forty-five-year-old James R. Garlick, scheduled an inquest into Dorothy Millette's death. The home-grown politician came from a Mormon family that had trekked west in 1849, in a wagon train, across the plains and mountains.

Jim Garlick was a devout joiner. The list of lodges and associations that he belonged to ranged from Elks and Odd Fellows to such orders as the Eastern Star, the White Shrine of Jerusalem, and the Sacramento Parlor of the Native Sons of the Golden West. They gave him great political clout in the burgeoning state capital, where he had been elected to the city's board of education when he was only twenty-one.

The day that Jim Garlick was to present his findings on the body of Dorothy Millette, she lay in his own mortuary and funeral parlor next to his home. He was to be in charge of her burial, he held embalmer's license number 31—one of the earliest issued by the state of California.

• • •

San Francisco's Plaza Hotel manager Edward J. Sullivan, who saw the body of Dorothy Millette at Georgiana Slough, as well as in Garlick's office, was unable to attend the inquest. He told Garlick he had to go to his mother who was ill in Santa Barbara and he sent the coroner this letter:

My dear Garlick:
Following my examination of the remains of the woman in your office and her effects I have tonight checked with members of the staff of my hotel as I informed members of your office I would, and several points on which I was in some doubt at the time of my visit, the result, considering garments and a number of other points, is that I am convinced that the woman in question is the one I registered at the Hotel Plaza last May as Dorothy Millette of New York City.

Dorothy's identification created quite a stir among the politicos in the state capital because her sobriquet in Hollywood as the "ghost wife" of the man married to Jean Harlow gave her celebrity status. Coroner Garlick went ahead and scheduled the inquest for September 21, and—as it was so quaintly titled for Paul—the inquest "upon the remains of Dorothy Millette" was also called an "inquisition."

A jury of eight men was assembled to determine what had happened to her. A local attorney, Alfred Sheets, was engaged by MGM and he sat in and observed.

• • •

The first witness was general passenger agent for the River Lines, L. I. McKim, who was in his office in Sacramento on September 7.

"Here is the whole layout of the *Delta King*," he said. "The steward came to me as soon as the boat got here in the morning and he said he thought we had somebody go overboard, as the watchman had found two pieces of clothing on the deck. I asked him if he knew what room it was and he said 'No.' There was no way of finding out at that time because everyone was asleep, so when they made a check of the boat they found this room 304 with this other clothing and a bag left in there. We went down and went through her clothing and then I called for the register and the register noted 'D. Millette' in room 304. Now, she didn't sign that register. They just come to us and purchase a room to Sacramento and the clerk asks the name and that is all there is to it. Yes, just the same as on a Pullman car. We just issue them a ticket, they don't sign the register. She was assigned room 304."

"What became of the clothing after that?"

"We had the clothing brought up here in my office

and it was turned over to the police department. Every bit of it, yes, and I have their receipt."

"Where did she get on the boat?"

"At our pier, pier number three, in San Francisco. She purchased one round-trip ticket to Sacramento and return. I found the stub of the room ticket and the return portion of her round-trip ticket tucked in her purse when we examined it."

Coroner Garlick then declared, "I will state there is a couple of Filipino boys that work on the boat, and it is pretty hard to get them to leave the boat, they would have to tie the boat up here to get them off, so we took a statement from them which we have here."

A. P. Cantor worked and lived on the vessel. He recalled that a lady in room 304 rang the bell for him about five minutes to six on the evening of September 6, just before the boat left the pier in San Francisco.

"She asked for Bromo Seltzer and we didn't have any," Cantor stated. "She was acting worried and nervous and everything like that. She said she had a headache."

"What kind of looking woman was she?" he was asked.

"Long face, just like I see in the papers."

"What color hair?"

"She had her hat on when I saw her."

"You never seen her or talked to her any more than the conversation you just admitted here?"

"No sir."

"Did you think anything was wrong with the lady or anything at the time?"

"She walked around the room. What I thought, I thought she was nervous and worried. She was worrying, yes. She didn't look me right square in the face."

"She hid her face, did she, when she was talking to you?"

"Yes."

• • •

Lorenzo O'Hero was a waiter and he also lived on the *Delta King*. He served dinner to Dorothy at about eight o'clock when she came into the vessel's salon . . .

"What attracted your attention to this woman particularly?"

"Well, she was sitting down at the table and I waited on her and I ask her, 'What kind of soup you going to have?' and she says 'I don't think any soup, I want a fruit cocktail,' and then after that I ask her 'What kind of soup you going to have, Madam?' She don't look at me, she says 'I don't want any soup and give me spaghetti and ice cream, that is all I want.'

"And after she ate the ice cream and I ask her 'Madam, I am sorry you don't eat very much,' I said 'I will have to charge you seventy-five cents just the same.' She said 'That is all right,' and I say 'All right.' "

"Will you describe this woman that you waited on?"

"Well, she is about forty or forty-five years of age and round face."

• • •

Henry L. Garrick was a lumberman on his way home to Walnut Grove, waiting on the deck of the *Delta King*. He was going to disembark when the vessel stopped at Rio Vista.

Coroner Garlick asked him, "Did you notice anybody particularly on that boat nervous or anything?"

"Well, I noticed what I considered a very beautiful woman, and she had pretty hair and pretty eyes, and she seemed to be quite nervous and she kept walking around. She walked clear around the boat. She didn't seem to notice anyone, she seemed to have her eyes away off in the distance. I got off at Rio Vista. I think the boat got in there at one-thirty."

"Did you notice particularly the color of her hair, Mr. Garrick?"

"Why, she was a blonde."

"She was probably the only one walking around on the outside of the deck, was she, at that time?"

"No. There were several men who were walking around, and there were three women who were walking around, and then there was one woman that danced until about one o'clock. She walked around on the deck with a couple of men, but this woman seemed to be all alone that I noticed and I didn't know who she was. I spoke of it when one of the boys met me at Rio Vista with the car, took me home. I spoke about it, saying the woman seemed to be quite nervous to me."

• • •

Charles J. Ogle, the next witness, identified himself as a criminal deputy in the sheriff's office in Sacramento.

"The watchman who made his rounds on the boat discovered this clothing and wraps and shoes on the deck at a time that would possibly put the boat between Painterville Bridge, which it passed at 2:55 A.M. and Freeport Bridge, which it passed about 4:30 A.M. We made a search of that territory for three or four days. We notified the fishermen all up and down the river and everybody that was on the bridges. Then, on the 14th, a Japanese boy told of the finding of the body in Georgiana Slough. I went down where this body was below Walnut Grove and a couple of coroner's men and we went down and got the body out of the river. The little jacket, as I would call it, that goes with the dress apparently fit the dress that this woman had that we found in the river. I think that is about all I can tell you about it."

• • •

The coroner summed up the proceedings and said, "There being no other evidence in this case, gentlemen of the jury, you will pick one of your members as a foreman in this matter and bring in your verdict."

Thereupon foreman J. J. Kearney declared that "38-year-old Dorothy Millette came to her death on the 7th of September, 1932, by asphyxiation by drowning."

Jim Garlick approved the verdict, switched from coroner to undertaker and turned his attentions to her burial.

22
· · · · ·
Reunion

THE INCREDIBLE SUDDENNESS with which Paul died provoked a feeling of loneliness in me and at least three others who felt close to him, who mourned for him, and missed him. These feelings pervaded the sad reunion—it could be called a wake—we held in his office one evening while there was still excitement at the studio about Paul's life and death. Carey Wilson and I, Al Lewin and Willis Goldbeck, the writer who was close to Paul and escorted Jean to his funeral, gravitated to his office late that day, as we used to do when he was alive.

The small building that housed so many MGM executives was emptying out, the jumping spirit of the day was over, we settled glumly into the room. Lewin and Wilson sat down on the floor; almost unconsciously we were taking the places we used to occupy when he was there, when we reflected on filmmaking, exchanged news of the studio, told the latest jokes. Paul's chair behind his desk, of course, remained empty.

• • •

Under the steady prodding of Joyce Vanderveen I began to find memories of the times and events of 1932 I had long left buried and forgotten. Yes indeed, the four of us had recalled incidents worth exchanging after our friend's death. But at that time they didn't change my theory of suicide, they simply added force to the fact that Paul had much to live for.

In the brief moments I had spent with Henry Bern, when Dorothy was still being sought, he spoke of her ambition to be a screen star. He mentioned that this had grown to a frantic desire. Her need grew out of the life and training she had put into acting thus far. Paul's importance at MGM made it seem to her that he could easily give her what she wanted.

Dorothy was unaware of the years that had passed, as Paul had also said, and she was oblivious of advancing age and time. Henry told me he had reported on this to Paul after Dorothy had described what she wanted from him.

Recalling those moments, at this time when Paul was dead and Dorothy still missing, created so much emotion in Henry that he could not continue. He concluded his recollection in tears.

As the others in Paul's office that evening had never heard of Dorothy's existence until Henry had revealed it worldwide, my story about her yearnings for stardom closed out the meeting. We all thought that when Dorothy appeared she would supply the curtain lines still missing, provide the fade-outs still lacking in so many of the incidents connected with the death of our friend.

Ever since May, Dorothy had wanted Paul to come see her in San Francisco. When Labor Day grew near and he had not appeared, she let him know that she was coming to see him.

Four days before the holiday, he was involved with the details of the new life insurance policy that he was taking out for Jean Harlow's benefit. He had carefully planned it to provide security for his young wife; it would also deliver funds to take care of the mortgage on the house that he had given her.

His long-delayed confrontation with Dorothy was inevitable. Stress over how he was to handle her unpredictable actions mounted in him, anxiety took over. If Dorothy had any desire to torment him, she succeeded. Knowing Dorothy's volatile unpredictability he had no way to be sure exactly when she might arrive.

To offset his fears that Dorothy would show up at his home while Jean was there, he had to get his wife out of the house.

Theater owners helped him overcome that dilemma when they clamored for *Red Dust*. To speed up the film's release, the studio asked Jean to work through the Labor Day holiday weekend. Consequently, she went to the studio Saturday morning and shot scenes for *Red Dust* all day with Clark Gable. That evening "the King" headed for a desert hideaway for two days and nights of fun with Marino Bello and friends.

Mama Jean asked Baby Jean to spend Saturday night

with her "to keep her company," a suggestion that surely met with Paul's approval.

When Dorothy had not shown up by late Saturday afternoon, Paul had Slickum drive him to the Ambassador Hotel, doing the favor he had promised Bernie Hyman. Then, passing up an invitation to a party at the residence of actor Fredric March, he went back to his own house. With no sign of Dorothy, his agony continued. He was visibly unnerved, enough that Slickum noticed it and wondered about it. But the hours went on and there was no sign of Dorothy that Saturday night.

Leaving her mother's home Sunday morning, Jean went straight to the studio and shot scenes that did not require her costar Clark Gable.

There was to be dinner at her mother's house that evening, prepared for them by Winifred Carmichael. Paul indicated to Jean he would come over and join her there. Then, to his shocked surprise, Jean came home after finishing work that afternoon and said that she wanted him to drive to Mama Jean's with her.

In the frantic moments that followed, Paul sought desperately to get her to leave. He knew he could upset Jean by mentioning his dislike for her mother's home, which contrasted sharply with her dislike for the house that he had built on Easton Drive. A furious argument followed—the servants heard him shouting, "Your mother's house is terrible!"

Jean was stunned by his anger. She screamed back, "I'd rather live down there than in this godforsaken canyon!" She turned defiantly and left him to go to her mother. John Carmichael, who heard them argue, drove her. Davis remained behind to bring Winifred Carmichael, who was still fixing dinner in the kitchen of the servants' quarters.

Mrs. Bello later reported that when Jean arrived for dinner that evening, she phoned Paul, demanding that he join her. He told her that he had a headache and refused. He told Jean to stay overnight again with Mama Jean, and their quarrel remained unresolved.

Paul faced the culmination of his affair with Dorothy, which spanned twenty years. He sat out in the balmy California night, waiting. The time Dorothy had said she might appear had arrived so he prepared for it. This was to be the climactic moment, it would need delicate handling. There would only be the two of them, a simple scene, no magic of the kind they knew when they met, no orchestra in the pit, no audience—just two former lovers meeting after a long separation.

He took a bottle of champagne and two crystal goblets out to the swimming pool, a nice touch. He lit the lanterns along the walkway up the hill, they provided dim lighting, a few highlights and many shadows, the way a good designer would illuminate an impending drama. The stage was set, the curtain was up, but one of the principals had yet to make her entrance.

Alone by the pool early that September evening, Paul sat in the growing shadows, reflecting on how to deal with the woman he was waiting to see. He had achieved his position in Hollywood without her, and perhaps tact and diplomacy, maybe reason too, would prevail and convince her it was best to continue the arrangement that had governed their lives in the years since they separated.

There was a serious problem to contend with, one he would have to handle like a director ad-libbing a scene in a movie without a script. What if she insisted she was entitled to share the life he was enjoying? What if she believed she was Mrs. Bern? What if she wanted everything Jean had?

The late summer temperature remained high, the air was hot and humid. He put on his bathing trunks and after a dip in the pool, opened the champagne and drank almost half the bottle.

A car brought Dorothy up the hill and she dismissed the driver. She started up the path to his house as he came down to meet her. They embraced. It was all very civilized.

He guided her to the swimming pool where he had her champagne glass filled and ready. She had brought a small bag with a few personal belongings and set it down close to her. Their reunion lifted off to a congenial start and would progress through the night hours with highs and lows, punctuated by Dorothy's sudden changes of mood.

Paul wanted her to agree that the ways they had been living was their solution and should continue. "I heard loud voices," Slavko Vorkapich had said. "A man and a woman laughing and shouting, sometimes the shouting was angry and ugly."

She wanted to be a film star and she wanted recognition as Mrs. Paul Bern. She did, indeed, want all the things that Jean had, she felt she was entitled to them and demanded them. She was still in love with him and couldn't believe that he no longer felt the way she did. As the night wore on, they both became more frustrated and furious, he was emotionally drained, close to a breaking point. So was she.

According to records in the MGM Transportation department, noted alongside the charge for ninety-six dollars, Paul called and ordered a car at 1:04 A.M. to come to his house, the driver to stand by to take a passenger to San Francisco. The cost was to be charged to his personal account.

• • •

The Carmichaels had returned from the Bello home, retiring to their own quarters down the hill. Meanwhile Dorothy's arguments grew louder, so much so that at times she became incoherent. Terrified that the servants would call Jean and tell her what was going on, Paul tried to quiet her down. The harder he tried, the less effect he had. It was then that he told Dorothy to leave: "Get out of my life!" Winifred Carmichael heard him shout.

But Dorothy continued to argue. Trying to make peace with her again, Paul endeavored to get her back to reason on a conversational plane. She careened between violent outbursts and lapses into silence. It was in those less explosive moments that Paul had every reason to believe she would accept their situation as he wished she would.

When Lymie, MGM's popular cockney driver, brought his car up the hill it was almost two o'clock in the morning. Paul went to talk to him and asked him to wait for his passenger. He said she would be ready shortly.

But when he returned to Dorothy, she wasn't ready to leave, her determination to stay had hardened even more. Paul tried a different form of persuasion. It was a sweltering night and he suggested they take a swim. She agreed and went into the house to the bedroom, carrying her bag in order to change into her bathing suit. It was then that she found a piece of devil's food cake and ate it, crumpling the note that Winifred left for Jean.

She came back to Paul, wearing her bright yellow bathing suit and time passed while both of them cooled off in the pool. The mood had changed, and it must have appeared to Paul that he had achieved his aims. The car was still waiting and after they climbed out of the water, he reminded her that it was time for her to go.

Dorothy listened, smiling at him. Thinking that all his problems were resolved, he turned and picked up his champagne glass to offer her. But she ignored that and he froze as she slowly removed her bathing suit and stood before him naked.

He stepped back and gasped, "For God's sake! Don't!"

Frustrated, he smashed the glass against his chair,

cutting his hand as he did so. His blood began dripping on the stone floor. He stifled the cut on his right hand, pressing his left hand hard against it. Then he went into the house, stopped at the sink and washed off the blood. He moved into the dressing-room closet, stripped off his wet trunks and prepared to don one of the robes hanging there.

As usual his two guns were on a table in the bedroom. Suddenly Dorothy was behind him, pressing her nude body against his. She was holding one of the guns at his temple. When she pulled the trigger the sound was muffled in the confines of the closet.

She backed into the bedroom and threw the gun across the floor with a scream later described by Winifred Carmichael as "unearthly." The lights came on in the servants' quarters.

Dorothy was frantically putting her clothes on; she grabbed her bag and ran out of the house. Then she suddenly stopped running and hid in the garden when Mrs. Carmichael came out to investigate what she had heard and was coming close to her.

Winifred Carmichael picked up the yellow bathing suit just as Dorothy bolted across the lawn, losing one of her shoes. The fleeing woman kicked off the other one, grabbed it up and ran barefoot toward the street. Winifred tried to catch up with her but couldn't. The stout woman stopped and watched her—and waited six months before revealing what she had seen.

In that awful moment when Dorothy fired the gun she had ended the love saga that dominated her life. She had killed the one person in the world she had depended on.

METRO-GOLDWYN-MAYER'S Transportation head Lou Kolb impressed on his drivers the meaning of confidentiality. Some of them, like the English-born Lymie were veteran studio drivers, permanently on the payroll. Some were local residents with their own cars available for hire. But it didn't matter where they came from, the world they traveled in was filled with sex and secrets, all had strict instructions to keep their eyes on the road, their ears shut and their tongues tied. Lymie was the man who drove Dorothy north on Route 101 for nearly eight hours. He returned leisurely after that holiday weekend, and in time he submitted the ninety-six-dollar charge that would show up in Paul's probate and be paid for by the Bern estate.

Kolb was curious about Lymie's late-night woman passenger.

"She didn't want to talk," Lymie insisted. "You know the kind."

Kolb reminded him that on such a long drive they must have stopped along the way for refreshments. "You mean to tell me she never said anything to you?"

"Cripes, man, she just kept telling me to go faster."

Kolb, the man who always told his drivers it was their duty to keep secret what went on in their car, wanted to hear more. But Lymie said all he was going to say.

23

· · · · ·

"Make It Pretty!"

SHE WAS TO GET a quick burial, but with only thirty-eight dollars in Dorothy's purse there wasn't enough to pay for it. Jim Garlick, in his role as undertaker, declared, "Unless some relative or friend takes charge of the body, we can only arrange to put her in a pauper's grave in Potter's Field."

He telegraphed Henry Bern but didn't receive an answer. Henry's silence was significant. He was never to be heard from again in connection with the nagging matters that were lingering on regarding Paul and Dorothy. Many loose ends still had to be tied together but no one was coming forward to do the job.

Then, to Garlick's relief, attorney Mendel Silberberg called from Hollywood to tell him he was sending $250, the gift of a donor, he reported, who preferred to be anonymous.

"My client wants Dorothy Millette buried in the best cemetery in Sacramento," he said. Garlick used the money to pay for Dorothy's funeral and reserve a place for her in the rich soil of East Lawn Memorial Park.

• • •

County Public Administrator Herman Koch stepped in. It was his function to settle estates without a will, to find possible heirs. Dorothy had certainly appeared to be all alone in the world, and anyone familiar with the way she had lived her last years would surely confirm that. Herman Koch saw a way to make use of her desolation.

Koch was an ambitious fellow, he didn't get many cases tied to Hollywood and unlike Sheriff Cox, he welcomed the intervention of MGM's people and thought they would contribute to the costs of the case that loomed ahead of him. It presented a glorious opportunity to the man who told intimates that Dorothy Millette's estate might make him so well known it would be the springboard he needed to rise from his county position to state treasurer.

Although Dorothy died destitute, newspapers around the country reported she was Paul's designated heir in an old will he had written many years ago. In that will, he left his entire estate to "my wife Dorothy."

Koch had no doubt that the movie producer was a rich man, it could mean lots of money. If all went well it would be a real bonanza, because once he proved that Dorothy had no heirs, her share of the Bern estate would automatically go to the treasury of the state of California. It was a coup, a real feather in the cap of Herman Koch.

Administrator Koch hurried to Dorothy's funeral services. Five curiosity-seeking women and three newspapermen were all that were grouped around the casket. Coroner Garlick also had enough money on hand to buy two funeral wreaths. Another, composed of gardenias and gladioluses, bore a card: "From a mother." No one knew who she was. Reverend J. J. Evans of the First Christian Church of Sacramento preached a sermon, saying, "No one living should judge those who have passed on."

Determined to keep track of Paul's estate and to safeguard Dorothy's interests, Herman Koch sent his attorney, Chester F. Gannon, to Los Angeles, where he was allowed to monitor Paul Bern's probate proceedings. And attorney Henry Uttal, in New York, advised Gannon he had documents in his files, signed back on August 30, 1920, naming Dorothy as Paul's only beneficiary.

In Hollywood, Irene Harrison was unable to produce the new will that Paul had supposedly written. There was no sign of it in Paul's Bank of America safe-deposit box when it was opened in the presence of state of California inheritance-tax collector Theodore L. Pettit. The emptiness brought consternation to Jean Harlow's advisers. Where was the will that would show that Paul had left everything to Jean Harlow?

"I'll search my memory and make efforts to locate it," the embarrassed Irene promised Jean.

It appeared that Paul's possessions were to be caught in a tug-of-war between Jean Harlow and the state of

California, which was acting on behalf of the deceased Dorothy Millette.

Then, while the search for his last will went on, there was a new development, as strange as it was unexpected. Herman Koch was contacted by two women wanting the legacy that they claimed was legitimately due them. Sisters of Dorothy Millette had materialized, belatedly identifying themselves as her only close relatives. They informed Koch that they were positive that Paul and Dorothy were legally married and were never divorced.

Mrs. John A. Hartranft of Findlay, Ohio, the former Mary Elizabeth Roddy, claimed that a wedding license existed, signed by Dorothy and Paul. Dorothy's other sister, Viona Hessler, of Longview, Washington, concurred. If they could show proof of a legal marriage, then the courts would have to rule that Paul's marriage to Jean Harlow was invalid and the star would have no rights whatsoever to Paul's estate.

The sudden appearance of the sisters shocked and surprised everyone with any connection to Paul's estate. They had never shown themselves when the police broadcast their appeals for information about the dead producer's "phantom wife." They had steered clear of Dorothy during her illness, never visited her during her years in the Algonquin, never revealed their relationship to Dorothy when the hysteria over Paul's death was at its height.

But the sisters succeeded in proving their legitimate kinship to Dorothy. They shared Herman Koch's belief that Paul was a rich man and they saw a good chance of raking in his money for themselves. To gain that objective, they took advantage of the services of attorney Chester Gannon, who agreed to represent their interests.

Attorney Gannon, like his friend Garlick, led a colorful life, loving sports and photography, passionate about the theater, enthusiastically studying the history of the Civil War and making constant visits to the battlefields of that conflict. He leaned toward aggressive acts, was an excellent boxer and, during monthly stag smokers at his Sacramento Athletic Club, challenged any and all comers to meet him in the ring. He fought for Dorothy's sisters, confident that he would win the decision and knock out Jean's claims to Paul's estate.

A building in Sacramento was the cozy conclave for these men looking into the matter of Dorothy Millette's death. It housed the offices of Gannon and coroner-undertaker Garlick, the two old friends could exchange observations by simply knocking on the other's door. Before retreating back to Hollywood, though, MGM's contingent kept their hold on attorney Alfred Sheets; he would continue keeping an eye on everyone for them. It was a judicious decision for he, too, had his office in the building.

The sisters' hopes of collecting Paul's riches depended on displaying the wedding certificate they said was signed by Paul and Dorothy. All they had to do was find it.

The complications that loomed up over Paul's wishes faded away when a triumphant Irene Harrison located his last will in her own safe-deposit box. It took precedence over the will he had made out years before in favor of Dorothy.

He left everything to Jean.

JEAN NEVER DIVULGED what Louis B. Mayer told her after Paul's death was discovered. She knew that the note was not intended as a suicide farewell and that Paul was not impotent. She also knew that a woman had come to see Paul, although at that time she didn't know how involved he had been with Dorothy Millette. She certainly knew that Louis B. Mayer took actions intended to protect her. He believed that what was done would remain secret forever.

They had reached an understanding. In maintaining strict silence, as he wished her to do, "the slut," as he once called her, had become a member of his family, he had saved her career, she would have a job for life, she was indeed one of his beloved "children."

Jean never lost the influence of Paul Bern. She would always personify the image of gloriously sexy Lil Andrews that he perceived for her in *Red-Headed Woman.* It was the part she played best; she was so natural in it that audiences assumed she was that character, not just in her movies.

Katharine Brush, who created Lil, and therefore contributed toward creating Jean, too, described them as interchangeable.

Lil, she wrote, was "a Gilded Babe, the kind the boys always hailed as 'Hello, Gorgeous!,' ultra-modern, sweet with perfume, proud of her flawless figure and exquisite legs, able to use men to get what she wanted and move on.

"I can give myself credit only for the fact that if I'd written the book expressly for Harlow, it couldn't have fitted her better, or she it."

After *Red-Headed Woman*, MGM let Jean play Lil Andrews, the all-American sex symbol, all the rest of her career. The character names changed but the girl was the same: she was a facsimile of Lil through her greatest successes, *Red Dust*, *Libeled Lady*, *The Girl from Missouri*, *Suzy*, *Personal Property*, *China Seas*, *Dinner at Eight*, *Bombshell*, and *Saratoga*, which was halfway through production when she died. Unlike the situation with *Red Dust* when Paul Bern died, *Saratoga* resumed with a look-alike for Jean filling in the missing scenes. The movie was shown starring Jean Harlow and once more and for the last time, her costar was Clark Gable.

• • •

Long after we knew the tragic circumstances concerning the deaths of Paul, Dorothy and Jean, a development emerged that showed us how deeply Jean had been touched by Paul.

It arose when coroner Garlick became concerned that he didn't have the money to pay for a tombstone for Dorothy. He informed Koch that her grave was unmarked, so the public administrator scheduled an auction sale of Dorothy's personal effects, believing the funds to be raised would be sufficient to take care of the matter. Two suitcases of clothing were sold amid the clatter of an auctioneer's hammer in a crowded room at 1220 K Street. There were more sightseers than bidders, the amount raised was a woeful $105, far less than the undertaker needed for a stone in keeping with the elegant surroundings of East Lawn Cemetery. Dorothy continued to lie in an unmarked grave.

• • •

Undertaker Jim Garlick was startled.

Jean Harlow was phoning from Hollywood and wanted to talk to him. But first he had to settle his nerves. Finally he took the call.

Jean came on like an old friend. She told him she had heard about the auction and knew that it didn't raise enough money for a tombstone over Dorothy's grave.

"Y'know, Miss Harlow, I got money from an MGM attorney, and I gave Miss Millette a beautiful funeral—"

Jean broke in. "Mr. Silberberg was acting for me. I sent that money."

"I appreciate that, Miss Harlow."

"And I appreciate what you've done, but how much do you need to mark the grave?"

Garlick estimated $350 would do it.

"You got it," Jean said. "May I tell you the way I'd like it to read?"

"First, there's something you ought to know," Garlick said. "Her birth certificate has come in. She was older than we thought she was. She was forty-six years old."

There was a pause, as Garlick recalled. Then Jean told him what she wanted to do. She wanted to give Paul's name to the woman she never knew.

"Make it pretty," she told him.

Epilogue

JOYCE AND I planned working through Labor Day.

We were eager to write the end, and the holiday would be a good time to fade out. Suddenly it didn't seem so inviting.

"I'm taking today off," I said to Joyce when I called her, and added, "Labor Day always gets me down. End of summer blues, I guess."

Then I hung up fast. This was the anniversary of the day when Paul Bern was found dead.

I chose the streets of Beverly Hills to walk off the memories. The area has a splendor of its own, as if it wants to distance itself from Hollywood and other rowdy neighbors.

I barely noticed the Beverly Hills house where Marie and I had lived. It cost us $22,000, complete with tennis court, in the Great Depression; but its value since that time, like every home around it, had soared into the stratosphere. Paul's estate, with its swimming pool, would likely command a hundred times more than he spent to build it.

• • •

Metro-Goldwyn-Mayer was in the news. My mind was occupied by the slow death of the lion, the long-cherished trademark of the old studio. It had been newsworthy from the day Mayer and Thalberg breathed life into it. It came into existence with them in 1924 and lived more than sixty-five years.

The studio was where timeless figures were born, men like Ben-Hur, Fletcher Christian, Andy Hardy, women like Mrs. Miniver, the Red-Headed Woman and the Divorcée—and timeless places, where one heard a Broadway Melody, saw a Big Parade, met in St. Louis or spent a Night at the Opera.

The company had faded fast by this Labor Day. Entrepreneur Kirk Kerkorian, the one-time aviator who controlled it, tried to fly it with a cast of inadequate filmmakers from A to Y, Aubrey to Yablans, until all the magic was gone. Then he sold the studio in one direction, its library of films in another, offered the leftovers to buyers so far offshore they might not clearly focus on the tattered remnants.

F. Scott Fitzgerald, who had wanted so desperately to be a success at that studio, wrote, "Show me a hero and I'll write you a tragedy." The Metro-Goldwyn-Mayer lion that personified ten thousand heroes born inside the studio walls was the last tragedy.

• • •

I called Joyce from a pay phone in the Beverly Hills post office.

"Your tour is over?" she asked.

"I still have to collect some mail. It's been sitting here in my P. O. box nearly a week. I may find something fascinating, like a love letter from Garbo."

"One never knows. Good luck."

The Beverly Hills post office building is an impressive landmark, running the length of a city block, high-ceilinged, gunmetal-colored marble floor, cream-colored walls rimmed with faded murals depicting the U.S. mail from Pony Express days to the flimsy craft that flew the airmail in 1932 when the building opened for business.

On this holiday evening, the lighting fixtures were dimmed, the cavernous interior darkened, quiet and funereal. A very stout, gray-haired woman in black rags, crouched in a corner, was making Beverly Hills her home. Her belongings were lumped beside her on the floor. The truly poor in the citadel of the truly rich.

A stocky man, rather gray-faced, was looking me over while pushing some letters through a slot. Then he said, "Hey, I know you! Jesse White says you're doing a book about Jean Harlow and that bird she was married to. Am I right, pal?"

I nodded cautiously.

"She sure was a sexy dish," the man said, and reached over to shake hands. "Louie Quinn, we met at the Friars' Club only you forgot. Yeah, I'll betcha I know something about that case you don't know. Whitey Hendry, he's the one who told me. Yeah, Whitey told me, 'I made that guy's murder look like a suicide! I put the gun in his hand!' "

"Are you sure of that?"

"Come on, would I make up a thing like that?"

"Tell me more," I said.

Quinn began gathering his thoughts. "Lemme get it straight first. Whitey and me, we were having a beer one night in the Trap, you know, that little bar over by MGM. Okay, it was more than one beer."

He was grinning, as if the memories rolling around in his mind were exceedingly pleasant. I waited, recalling then that we had met through Jesse White, popular for his television commercials as the lonesome repairman of washing machines. White had introduced Quinn as a talented gagman and fellow comic. Both of them were immensely friendly and genial, with personalities given to furtive smiles typical of the characters who ply the precarious trade of fun and joy.

Suddenly, Quinn began to talk.

"Whitey was retired. Oh man, how he loved those great days they had at the studio. It was the high spot of his life. He missed them.

"Listen, I got stories of my own and I'm a good story-teller, just ask Jesse or Miltie Berle . . . I guess we all like to talk about ourselves. But that night Whitey felt like talking and I never got a word in."

"What did he say about Paul Bern?"

"It was a murder. Man, you better believe it! Whitey

was at the house where it happened that morning, he was there with his boss, you know, Mayer, and that publicity fellow who was always following him around . . .

"Whitey said to me, 'Hell, I knew the guy was murdered soon as I saw him. He was lying in the closet and the gun was on the floor halfway across the room. Whoever killed him threw it there, it didn't walk there.

"The publicity guy said he could see the headlines already. It scared the bejesus out of him.

"Oh my God, we can't have a murder,' Mayer said.

"That's when Whitey spoke up, you know, he was a real pro. 'If you want, I'll make it look like a suicide' was what he told them.

"Mayer went for it big. He had faith in Whitey. 'Go ahead, Hendry, do what you have to do' was what he said.

"Mayer thought Bern should look like he had been standing in front of the mirror when he did it, he thought that looked better than all the way in the closet. So Whitey moved the body to where his boss wanted it —it wasn't far from the mirror anyway, so that was no big deal for Whitey—he was such a pro that even the guy's blood on the floor wound up in the right place. Then he wiped the fingerprints off the gun with oil, that's how he did it. He put the gun in the guy's hand and fixed it underneath his body.

"Whitey wanted more time, he didn't want the cops to show up too soon. He called one of his pals, a writer who had a ticker tape that carried police reports. Whitey told the guy that Bern was dead and he asked him to call immediately if any news about it came over his tape.

"Whitey said he could see that Mayer and the publicity guy were real worried about what was going on but they still wanted it that way. They left after they picked up papers and things in the bedroom. Thalberg had arrived, he was outside at the pool and through the window Whitey could see him keep a couple of studio guys who had shown up from coming into the house. It was a good thing, they could have loused up the whole shebang."

Quinn stopped. He was studying my reaction. "You know about this?"

"Some of it," I said.

Quinn was winding down. "Everybody thinks it was suicide. They think that's what happened that time. But it didn't. Whitey said his boss was shaking with fear they'd be found out and y'know something, they never got over it. But Whitey was proud as hell over the job that he did. It was like he wished they'd given him an Academy Award."

Quinn started to leave. "Gotta go. Could be I'll remember something else, so gimme a ring sometime."

He hurried away.

I stood there, remembering that morning when I raced to Bern's house.

Funny how all the tangled threads in the Bern case have come untangled after so many years. Whitey revealed Paul's death to Al Cohn to guard against the word getting out before they were ready. But Al, knowing how friendly I was with Paul, went ahead and called me. That's why I heard about it so early that morning and why I startled Irving Thalberg when I showed up. I thought no one else was there, but Whitey was inside the house. He saw me talking to Irving. Vorkapich was the other person he saw. But Vorkapich and I had no idea a conspiracy was going on.

Only four men knew there was a cover-up, a great way to keep it quiet. Mayer, Strickling, and Hendry handled the job, and Thalberg went along. Inventing new details in tragedy was an everyday routine when one made fifty films a year.

The cover-up was successful, but as time went on they obviously felt pangs of conscience about it. Howard Strickling tried to tell what they had done but couldn't. He had lived a lifetime of guarding secrets, he was unable to bring himself to reveal the whole story. Mayer and Thalberg never talked.

• • •

Exactly nine days after meeting Louie Quinn, I called Jesse White for his friend's phone number. I wanted to tell him that our book was finished and we would quote what he had told me.

"You'll need a connection to Heaven, pal," said Jesse. "Louie died two days ago!"

Postscript

MARINO BELLO retired from the Hollywood scene after he led a treasure hunt to the Cocos Islands. He was joined in that search by Beverly Hills socialite Contessa Dorothy Di Frasso. Film star Cary Grant invested in the expedition. No treasure was found. Bellow was divorced by Mama Jean in 1934 and married again soon afterward. His wife, Violette, survived him briefly after he died August 15, 1953. He is also buried in Forest Lawn, but some distance away from Baby and Mama Jean. There were no services.

HENRY BERN, a center of attraction on his arrival in Hollywood, dropped out of sight after departing in silence. He never spoke publicly of his brother or Dorothy Millette again. A Henry Bern residing in New Rochelle is not related to Paul Bern's family.

In 1940 Los Angeles DISTRICT ATTORNEY BURON FITTS lost the election to John Dockweiler, a member of a prominent family, who revealed MGM as the chief contributor of funds to Fitts's campaign. From a jail cell where he was being held on a murder charge, mobster Bugsy Siegel had contributed $30,000 to the Dockweiler campaign. True to his promise to clean up the District Attorney's Office, Dockweiler fired Blaney Matthews and the entire Bureau of Investigation. At that time, a key witness in the Bugsy Siegel case, who was being held by authorities in a New York hotel, allegedly committed suicide by jumping out of a high window. His body landed so far from the building that it was generally believed that he was pushed. Dockweiler immediately released Bugsy Siegel for lack of evidence. Fitts retired to the mountain community of Three Rivers in Tulare County, California. He was found there the morning of March 29, 1973, dead of a bullet wound from a .38-caliber revolver. He was seventy-eight years old and wearing pyjamas. The county coroner lists his death as a suicide.

Just over a year after Paul Bern's death, on September 18, 1933, JEAN HARLOW married her third husband, Hal Rosson. He was fifteen years older than Jean and the highly regarded cinematographer on most of her MGM films. It was a short-lived marriage. Jean announced plans to divorce him May 7, 1934, but Rosson fell ill of polio at that time and she deferred her divorce action until he recovered in 1935. Rosson continued his career and won many honors as a cinematographer until retiring to Palm Beach, Florida, where he died in September

1988 at the age of ninety-three. Jean Harlow was romantically involved with film star William Powell when she died. She is buried in a private mausoleum at Los Angeles's Forest Lawn Memorial Park. Her grave is marked only "Our Baby." Her mother died June 11, 1958, and is buried beside her.

IDA KOVERMAN died November 24, 1954, of a heart attack. Louis B. Mayer attended her funeral, as did Chief Justice Earl Warren of the United States Supreme Court, Governor Goodwin Knight of California and FBI Chief J. Edgar Hoover. Ex-President Herbert Hoover, on a government mission in Germany, cabled his condolences. There were no pallbearers. The ushers were all members of the Musicians Union.

EDDIE MANNIX continued as MGM studio manager until his death in 1974. Toni Mannix outlived him by ten years.

BLANEY MATTHEWS lent the full force of his power as chief of the Bureau of Criminal Investigations under Buron Fitts when he helped eliminate a drunk-driving rap against Warner Brothers' famed dance director Busby Berkeley. Later, fired from his county job, he was rewarded by Warner Brothers and made chief of police at its studio, a position corresponding to that of his friend Whitey Hendry at MGM. He died in 1962.

Louis B. Mayer was ousted from his command of MGM in 1951 and died October 29, 1957. At his funeral, singing star Jeanette MacDonald sang "Ah, Sweet Mystery of Life." Since then, MGM has passed through several hands, its many parts torn from the whole and dispersed. The films produced in Mayer's time were purchased for one billion dollars by Ted Turner of Atlanta, Georgia, and will likely live on for generations to come.

Howard Strickling never wrote the story of his life. He bequeathed a few personal scrapbooks and MGM studio statistics to the Motion Picture Academy Library and the reading room of the Motion Picture Country Home. His official MGM obituary quotes him as stating, "Someday I am certain someone will do the real story of Jean Harlow, which will be quite different from that written in recent books."

Bibliography

Barondess, Barbara. *One Life Is Not Enough*. New York: Hippocrene, 1986.

Brush, Katharine. *This Is on Me*. New York: Farrar & Rinehart, 1939.

Granlund, Nils T. *Blondes, Brunettes, and Bullets*. New York: David McKay Co., 1957.

Kotsilibas-Davis, James, and Loy, Myrna. *Being and Becoming*. New York: Alfred A. Knopf, 1987.

Loos, Anita. *Kiss Hollywood Good-by*. New York: Viking Press, 1974.

Marion, Frances. *Off With Their Heads!*. New York: Macmillan, 1972.

Messick, Hank. *The Beauties and the Beasts*. New York: David McKay Co., 1973.

Moore, Colleen. *Silent Star*. Garden City, N.Y.: Doubleday, 1968.

Selznick, Irene Mayer. *A Private View*. New York: Alfred A. Knopf, 1983.

Shulman, Irving. *Harlow*. New York: Bernard Geis Associates, 1964.

Tully, Jim. *A Dozen and One.* Hollywood, Calif.: Murray and Gee, 1943.

Yezierska, Anzia. *Red Ribbon on a White Horse.* New York: Charles Scribner's Sons, 1950.

Index

Aristotle, 211
Arlen, Michael, 220
Arnaz, Desi, 87–88
Astor, Mary, 261
Ayres, Lew, 97

Baer, Max, 57, 133–134
Ball, Lucille, 87–88
Barondess, Barbara, 72–73
Barrymore, John, 110, 192
Barrymore, Lionel, 234
Basquette, Lina, 196, 197
Beery, Wallace, 77, 189
Bellamy, Ralph, 97
Bello, Jean Carpenter (mother of Jean Harlow), 18, 19, 30, 33, 39, 40, 54, 70, 80, 81, 104, 106, 107, 109–110, 112, 132, 137–138, 156, 277–279, 303
Bello, Marino (stepfather of Jean Harlow), 30–31, 32–33, 37–38, 39, 40, 48, 52, 54, 61, 64, 109–110, 112, 132–142, 145–146, 148–150, 232, 233, 237, 246–247, 250, 251, 277, 281, 301
Bello, Violette, 301
Berkeley, Busby, 303
Berle, Milton, 297
Bern, Henry (brother of Paul Bern), 37, 60–62, 64, 70–71, 74, 85, 92, 103, 148, 165, 214–215, 252–253, 258, 276, 285, 301
Bern, Paul (Paul Levy)
  acting training of, 102–104
  audit of Buron Fitts and, 244–251
  in biography, *Harlow*, 89–90, 99
  coroner's inquest for, 61, 63–64, 147–170, 239–242
  courtship of Jean Harlow,

25–26, 114–116, 181,
184, 185, 199–200, 250
death of, 1–7, 40–42, 91–
101, 120, 221–228, 230–
233
as a director, 105, 108, 213
Dorothy Millette and, 58–
66, 70–71, 81, 92–93, 98,
99–100, 102, 104–105,
107, 124, 170, 176, 209–
216, 219–220, 224–225,
226–228, 245, 252–260,
262–291, 301
early years of, 102–104
Entertainment Tonight
segment on 94–100
family history of, 85, 102
Free Soul and, 234
funeral of, 64–66, 126–127
home of, 2–4, 19–20, 38,
117–122, 248, 249.
Hungry Hearts and, 11
impotence and, 46, 48–49,
51–53, 56, 57, 60–62, 73,
94, 97–99, 123, 169,
175–176, 191–192, 203
kindness of, 45–46, 197–
200, 209
Lady Chatterley's Lover
and, 204–206
last days of, 71–73
marriage to Jean Harlow,
37–39, 69, 93, 97, 136–
137, 194–195, 199–201,
255, 259

in *Photoplay* article, 17–18,
85
probate procedure for, 123–
125, 144–146, 287–288
as producer, 11–13, 23–37,
44, 111–112, 114, 116,
139, 191, 203–208, 217
as a production supervisor
at Pathé Studio, 110,
126, 196–198
Red-Headed Woman and,
23–37, 116, 139, 203,
205, 250, 290–291
relationship to the Marxes,
6–8, 10–13, 14, 16, 38,
58–59
suicide note of, 41–42, 100,
167, 175–180, 223, 241,
248–249
talking films and, 10–13,
14, 111–112, 192
wardrobe of, 8, 10
"Willow Walk" and, 207–
208
as a writer, 107–108, 213
Bernard, Harold, 237
Bernson, A. S., 123
Blaine, Louis, 95
Blodgett, Julian, 224–225
Blum, Ralph, 61, 232
Bodne, Ben, 212
Booth, Edwin, 102
Boyer, Charles, 35–36
Bradley, David, 127
Brown, Johnny Mack, 57

Brush, Katharine, 21–23, 290–291
Buck, Pearl, 77
Buckley, John P., 243–245

Cantor, A. P., 271–272
Capra, Frank, 25
Carmichael, John Herman, 3, 40–41, 118, 150–155, 160–161, 170, 246, 247–248, 279, 281
Carmichael, Winifred, 40, 118, 155, 246, 250–251, 278–279, 281, 283
Carpenter, Harlean. *See* Jean Harlow
Carpenter, Jean (mother of Jean Harlow), 106, 109–110. *See also* Bello, Jean Carpenter
Carpenter, Montclair (father of Jean Harlow), 104, 106
Case, Frank, 227, 252
Chaplin, Charlie, 44, 50, 113
Christy, Howard Chandler, 214
Clarken, George C., 62
Cody, Lew, 111
Cohn, Alfred A., 1, 167, 234, 299–300
Cohn, Harry, 82, 143
Cohn, J. J., 202–203
Condaffer, F., 168, 237
Conlan, Judge, 258
Conway, Jack, 33

Corbaley, Kate, 204–205, 215, 217
Coulter, Dorothy, 147–148
Cox, Don, 263–264, 286
Craven, Frank, 105
Crawford, Joan, 24, 45–46, 67, 111, 189, 218
Cromwell, John, 105
Crosby, Bing, 31
Cudahy, Michael, 46
Cunningham, Ann, 129–130

Datig, Fred, 114–115
Davis, Clifton Earl, 2–5, 41, 118, 152, 160–161, 246–248, 279
DeMille, Cecil B., 46, 110, 196–198
De Sano, Marcel, 23, 26–28, 33, 35, 45
Di Frasso, Dorothy, 301
Dockweiler, John, 301–302
Dorn, Dean, 125, 126–127
Douglas, Mel, 189
Dressler, Marie, 24, 43
Duchess of Windsor, 177
Duncan, Mary, 11

Edington, H. E., 107–108
Erickson, Lena, 212
Estcourt, Zilfa, 253–255
Evans, J. J., 287

Fineman, B. P., 125
Fitts, Buron, 224, 232–247, 248–249, 301, 303

Fitzgerald, F. Scott, 22–24, 26–28, 130–131, 295
Fleming, Victor, 260–262
Flynn, Errol, 177
Forrest, Sally, 121
Foster, Bill, 267
Frank, Milo, 121
Franklin, Sidney, 212

Gable, Clark, 7, 67, 77, 135, 145–146, 198, 216–219, 229, 260–262, 277, 278, 291
Gannon, Chester F., 287, 289
Garbo, Greta, 67, 77, 111–112, 114, 192, 218
Garlick, James R., 263, 268–274, 285–289, 291–293
Garrick, Henry L., 273
Garrison, Harold Allen (Slickum), 37, 161–165, 249–250, 278
Gibbons, Cedric, 45, 49, 51, 60
Gibson, Wynne, 31
Gilbert, John, 50, 192–193, 198
Godard, Jean-Luc, 211
Goldbeck, Willis, 140, 275
Goldwyn, Samuel, 10, 50, 79–80, 82
Goudal, Jetta, 108–109, 126, 127–128
Goulding, Edmund, 111
Grant, Cary, 177, 301

Greenwood, Martin, 159–160
Greet, Ben, 213
Gregory, Bertha, 244
Grieve, Harold, 125–126, 127–128
Griffith, Corinne, 111
Guilaroff, Sydney, 201–202

Hale, Ron, 118–121
Hanson, Alice, 211–212
Hardy, Oliver, 113
Harlow, Jean (Harlean Carpenter)
    biography of, 89–90, 99
    birth of, 104
    China Seas and, 77, 291
    contract with MGM and, 33–35, 68–69, 228
    coroner's inquest for Paul Bern and, 64, 148, 165
    death of, 80, 98–99, 303
    death of Paul Bern and, 2, 3–4, 40–42, 52–56, 64–70, 80–81, 98–99, 175–180, 228–238, 244–245
    early relationship with Paul Bern, 25–26, 114–116, 181, 184–185, 199–200, 250
    education of, 105–107, 109
    Entertainment Tonight segment on, 94–100
    estate of Paul Bern and, 123–124
    Hell's Angels and, 25, 35,

96–97, 113, 115–116,
205–206
Howard Hughes and, 25,
35, 69, 113, 116
marriage to Charles F.
McGrew II, 109–110,
112, 113
marriage to Hal Rosson,
302–303
marriage to Paul Bern, 37–
39, 57, 61, 63, 69, 93,
97, 136–137, 194–195,
199–201, 255, 259
Platinum Blonde and, 25,
113
Red-Headed Woman and,
25–26, 28–30, 32–37,
116, 139, 202, 203, 250,
259, 290–291
Red Dust and, 6–7, 55, 67,
202, 256, 260–262, 277,
291
relationship with Marxes,
6–7, 18–19, 38
relationship with mother,
18, 19, 30, 33, 39, 40,
54, 70, 80, 81, 104, 106,
107, 109–110, 112, 132,
137–138, 277–279
stepfather of. *See* Bello,
Marino
writes *Today Is Tonight*,
140–142
Harlow, Sam "Skipp"
(grandfather of Jean
Harlow), 109

Harrison, Irene, 18, 33, 139,
212, 250, 287, 289–290
Hartranft, Mrs. John A., 288–
289
Hathaway, Henry, 89, 140,
223–228, 252
Hayes, Helen, 77
Hays, Will H., 204–205
Hearst, William Randolph, 44
Hecht, Ben, 89, 222–227
Hemingway, Ernest, 267
Hendry, Whitey, 5, 161, 170,
183, 232–233, 297–300,
303
Hessler, Viona, 288
Higham, Charles, 176–177
Hill, George, 130
Hirsh, Henrietta, 102
Hoffman, Ancil, 133–134
Hole, Lucy, 253
Hoover, Herbert, 57, 76, 230–
231, 303
Hoover, J. Edgar, 303
Hopkins, Bob "Hoppy," 239
Hubbard, Lucien, 77–78, 79
Hughes, Howard, 25, 35, 69,
116
Hume, Cyril, 17
Hyman, Bernard, 43, 49, 54,
71–73, 206, 278

Ince, Thomas H., 44
Ingersoll, Ralph, 47
Ingram, Rex, 140, 172–174

Jacobson, Laurie, 97–99
Jehlinger, Charles, 104–105

Jones, Edward Brant, 61, 73, 123
Jordan, Wayne, 168–169
Joy, Leatrice, 108–109

Karlov, Sonia (Jeanne Williams), 195–197
Kearney, J. J., 274
Keaton, Buster, 43
Kennedy, John F., 88
Kennicott, Robert Helm, 64, 123, 165
Kerkorian, Kirk, 295
Keyes, Asa, 235–236
Kirkland, Muriel, 32
Knight, Goodwin, 303
Knopf, Edwin, 78
Koch, Herman, 286–289, 291–292
Kolb, Lou, 284
Koverman, Ida, 229–233, 237, 239, 303
Kupcinet, Irv, 203

Laemmle, Carl, 14, 20
Lahn, Ilse, 221
Lake, Harriette, 32. See Sothern, Ann
La Marr, Barbara, 45, 193, 198
Landau, Arthur, 31, 89, 139
Langham, Rhea, 218–219
Lanier, Toni (Mannix), 183, 186–187, 303
Lansdowne, Judy, 141

Lansky, Meyer, 137
Larrimore, Francine, 24
Laughton, Charles, 77
Laurel, Stanley, 113
Lawford, Peter, 88
Lawrence, D. H., 204
Lawton, O. G., 239–242
Lee, Dixie, 31
Lehar, Franz, 194
Lemmon, Leonore, 187
Levy, Julius, 102
Levy, Paul. See Bern, Paul
Lewin, Albert, 38, 44, 46, 49, 51, 52, 54, 60, 115–116, 139–140, 217, 275
Lewis, Sinclair, 207
Lloyd, Harold, 20
Loew, Marcus, 173
Loos, Anita, 27–29, 32, 33, 55–56, 90, 193
Loy, Myrna, 111
Lubitsch, Ernst, 108, 113
Lymie (chauffeur), 282, 284

MacArthur, Charlie, 220
MacDonald, Jeanette, 304
Mackaill, Dorothy, 31
Magnin, Edgar, 64
Mahin, John Lee, 55–56, 134
Mannix, Bernice, 181–182
Mannix, Eddie, 43, 49–54, 135–138, 142, 181–188, 198, 303
Mannix, Toni Lanier, 183, 186–187, 303

Manson, Charles, 121

March, Fredric, 163, 278

Marcus, Friederike Bern, 37, 65–66, 85, 103

Marion, Frances, 130, 133, 193–195

Markey, Gene, 114, 220

Marx, Marie, 1–2, 6–7, 10–11, 13, 15, 18, 79, 86, 87, 91, 95, 115, 201, 294

Marx Brothers, 77

Matthews, Blaney, 232, 237, 302, 303

Mayer, Irene, 106–107. *See also* Selznick, Irene Mayer

Mayer, Louis B., 5, 8, 26, 43, 45, 48–54, 56, 57, 61, 65–69, 73, 76–80, 82–84, 88, 91, 94, 98, 106, 124, 133–138, 142–145, 148, 161, 170, 173–175, 177–181, 184–186, 223, 228–233, 235–237, 290, 295, 298–299, 303, 304

McClanahan, Rue, 96–99

McDowall, Roddy, 84, 226–227

McGinn, Allen, 258

McGrew, Charles F. II, 109–110, 112, 113

McKesson, William B., 223, 224–225

McKim, L. I., 270–271

Mellett, Mrs. L., 104, 255. *See also* Millette, Dorothy

Meredith, Lena, 256, 259

Merkel, Una, 29–30

Merman, Ethel, 32

Messick, Hank, 225

Millette, Dorothy, 58–63, 65, 70–71, 73, 74, 81, 92–94, 98, 99–100, 102, 104–105, 107, 124, 148, 170, 176, 209–216, 219–220, 224, 225, 226–228, 245, 251–260, 262–274, 276–293, 301

Mills, John P., 244

Minter, Mary Miles, 131

Mizner, Wilson, 191

Moffitt, Jack, 192–193

Momory, C. E., 246

Moore, Colleen, 200–201

Moran, Polly, 43

Muhl, Eddie, 86

Nagel, Conrad, 65

Nance, Frank A., 61, 64, 148–170

Nealis, Eddie, 138, 183

Negri, Pola, 108–109, 198

Nissen, Greta, 113

Nolan, Mary, 182. *See* Wilson, Imogene

Normand, Mabel, 131

Novarro, Ramon, 172

Ogle, Charles J., 263, 274
O'Hero, Lorenzo, 272
O'Neill, Eugene, 111
Orsatti, Frank, 124–125, 142–146, 183
Orsatti, Victor, 145

Pantages, Alexander, 243
Parsons, Louella, 73
Perry, Margaret, 32
Pettit, Theodore L., 287
Pettite, Bill, 267
Pidgeon, Walter, 189
Powell, William, 111, 303
Pratt, Jim, 86
Pringle, Aileen, 111

Quinn, Louie, 296–300

Rand, Sally, 203
Rapf, Harry, 43, 45–46, 48, 52, 83
Reeves, George, 187
Reiner, Ira, 236
Robinson, Edward G., 91
Roddy, Dorothy, 254. See also Millette, Dorothy
Roddy, Mary Elizabeth, 288
Rogers, Earl "Harry," 234–235
Roland, Gilbert, 132
Rooney, Mickey, 84
Roosevelt, Franklin D., 75–76, 230, 231, 264
Rosenberg, Aaron, 86

Rosson, Hal, 29, 33, 261, 302–303

Sachs, Charles, 179–180
St. Johns, Adela Rogers, 81, 90, 199, 234
Sargent, Franklin Haven, 103
Schary, Dore, 84, 88
Schenck, Joe, 143
Sebring, Jay, 121
Sellers, Clark, 241, 248–249
Selznick, David Oliver, 76, 78, 136, 152, 156
Selznick, Irene Mayer, 76, 106–107, 199
Selznick, Lewis J., 135–136
Selznick, Myron, 135–136, 139, 142
Shannon, Peggy, 31–32
Shearer, Douglas, 129
Shearer, Norma, 24, 26, 38, 67, 69–70, 77, 129, 215, 218, 234
Sheets, Alfred, 270, 289
Shulman, Irving, 89–90, 99
Siegel, Bugsy, 302
Silberberg, Mendel, 63–64, 175, 232, 237, 285–286, 292
Skelton, Red, 229
Skolsky, Sidney, 73
Slickum. See Garrison, Harold Allen
Sothern, Ann, 32
Stern, Seymour, 198–199
Stewart, James, 229

Strickling, Howard, 36–37, 43, 48–52, 54, 56, 62, 71, 83, 90, 126–127, 170–178, 185–190, 218, 219, 224, 232, 237, 261, 304

Stromberg, Hunt, 43–44, 46, 144, 206, 256, 260

Sullivan, Edward J., 269

Sweetser, Kate Dickinson, 106

Tate, Sharon, 121

Taylor, Elizabeth, 84

Taylor, Robert, 91, 229

Taylor, William Desmond, 131

Thalberg, Irving Grant, 3–5, 9, 11–14, 16, 17, 21, 23–28, 31–36, 37–38, 43–51, 53–56, 60, 64, 66–68, 69–73, 76, 77, 79, 82–85, 91, 101, 110–111, 114, 119, 136, 152–153, 156–159, 162, 166, 170, 173, 184, 185, 191, 203–207, 217–218, 246, 260, 295, 300

Thau, Benny, 18, 238–239

Thomas, Bob, 97

Tibbett, Lawrence, 194

Tracy, Spencer, 189

Tully, Jim, 18, 85

Turner, Ted, 304

Tuttle, William, 201–202

Twelvetrees, Helen, 31–32

Uttal, Henry, 62–63, 287

Valentino, Rudolph, 172

Vanderveen, Joyce, 86, 95–97, 99–101, 117, 122, 124–125, 127–128, 144–145, 147–148, 151, 152, 168, 178–179, 180, 210, 224, 226, 236–238, 244, 246, 266, 267, 276, 294, 296

Vidor, King, 130–131

Vogel, Joseph M., 88

Vorkapich, Slavko, 4–5, 60, 280, 300

Wallis, Hal, 216

Wallis, Minna, 216–219

Warga, Wayne, 94

Warren, Earl, 303

Webb, Frank R., 168–169

Weinberg, Herman G., 199

Weingarten, Larry, 43, 45–46

Weissmuller, Johnny, 57

Wertheimer, Al, 181–182

Westman, Nydia, 31–32

White, Jesse, 296, 297, 300

Whitehead, Joseph, 166–167, 175

Widenham, William W., 239–244, 246–247, 251

Williams, Blanche, 165

Williams, Hope, 24

Williams, Jeanne, 46, 195–198

Wilson, Al, 6

Wilson, Carey, 140, 141, 199, 209, 275
Wilson, Imogene, 182–183
Winchell, Walter, 73
Wodehouse, P. G., 17
Woolf, Edgar Allen, 18

Yezierska, Anzia, 11
Young, Loretta, 113

Ziegfeld, Flo, 144
Zwillman, Abner "Longie," 137, 138, 225

ABOUT THE AUTHORS

SAMUEL MARX grew up on Manhattan Island ambitious to be a writer. Leaving Columbia University for a job at Universal Pictures, he met Irving Thalberg, a young secretary in the next office. When Thalberg rose to head of MGM production, Marx went to California and became his story editor. Later, he produced films and television for MGM, Columbia, Desilu and Universal. Finally settling on his desire to write, his first book was *Mayer and Thalberg: The Make-Believe Saints*, followed by *Queen of the Ritz, Rodgers and Hart* (with Jan Clayton), *The Gaudy Spree* and now, *Deady Illusions* with Joyce Vanderveen.

JOYCE VANDERVEEN knows the entertainment world from many angles. Born and educated in Holland, she became one of Europe's leading ballerinas and danced in the major capitals of the world with the famous Grand Ballet du Marquis de Cuevas. As an actress in Hollywood she has performed in many motion picture and television productions. Miss Vanderveen has authored magazine and newspaper articles. Her interest in the mystery surrounding the lives of Jean Harlow and Paul Bern has led to this, her first book.